Moral Knowledge

The Problems of Philosophy
Their Past and Present

General editor: Ted Honderich
Grote Professor of the Philosophy of
Mind and Logic
University College London

Other books in the series:

PRIVATE OWNERSHIP
James O. Grunebaum
RELIGIOUS BELIEF AND THE WILL
Louis P. Pojman
MIND–BODY IDENTITY THEORIES
Cynthia Macdonald
PRACTICAL REASONING
Robert Audi
PERSONAL IDENTITY
Harold W. Noonan
IF P, THEN Q: Conditionals and the Foundations of Reasoning
David H. Sanford
THE INFINITE
A. W. Moore
THE WEAKNESS OF THE WILL
Justin Gosling
THOUGHT AND LANGUAGE
J. M. Moravcsik
HUMAN CONSCIOUSNESS
Alastair Hannay
EXPLAINING EXPLANATION
David-Hillel Ruben
SCEPTICISM
Christopher Hookway
THE NATURE OF ART
A. L. Cothey

Now available in paperback:

RATIONALITY
Harold I. Brown
THE RATIONAL FOUNDATIONS OF ETHICS
T. L. S. Sprigge
MORAL KNOWLEDGE
Alan Goldman

Moral
Knowledge

Alan H. Goldman

London and New York

First published in 1988

First published in paperback in 1990
by Routledge
11 New Fetter Lane, London EC4P 4EE

Simultaneously published in the USA and Canada
by Routledge
a division of Routledge, Chapman and Hall, Inc.
29 West 35th Street, New York, NY 10001

Printed in Great Britain by T J Press (Padstow) Ltd, Padstow, Cornwall

British Library Cataloguing in Publication Data
Goldman, Alan H.
Moral knowledge.—(The problems of philosophy).
1. Morals
I. Title   II. Series
170

Library of Congress Cataloging in Publication Data
Goldman, Alan H.
Moral knowledge/Alan H. Goldman.
p.   cm.—(Problems of philosophy)
Bibliography: p.
Includes index:.
1. Ethics.   2. Hobbes, Thomas, 1588·1679—Ethics.
3. Hume, David, 1711-1776—Ethics.   4. Kant, Immanuel,
1724-1804—Ethics.   5. Realism.   6. Emotivism.
7. Truth—Coherence theory.   I. Title.
II. Series: Problems of philosophy (Routledge (Firm))
BJ1031.G65   1990
170—dc20 90-35734

ISBN 0-415-05518-0

For Joan, again

Contents

Contents

Acknowledgments

I am grateful to Ted Honderich for providing the incentive to write this book. Much of it was written during two Orovitz summer grants from the University of Miami, for which I am also grateful.

Parts of chapter 2 appeared in *The Journal of Philosophy*, and parts of chapter 5 appeared in the *American Philosophical Quarterly*. I thank those journals for permissions to include those materials.

Introduction

This study will address the question whether there is moral knowledge. An affirmative answer will demand an account of the nature of such knowledge. How is it similar to and different from ordinary knowledge of the physical properties of objects? How does it compare to theoretical knowledge in science, or to mathematical knowledge? Often such other subject areas are simply assumed as models for moral knowledge, and the latter is affirmed or denied on the grounds of such assumptions. We shall seek the appropriate model by first canvassing some plausible alternatives.

Which model a particular philosopher assumes will depend on his view of the right and the good, and of the nature of moral truth. Hence I shall approach the topic of moral knowledge by looking first at some of the most plausible accounts of the good and the right by major figures in the history of philosophy. I shall draw the implications of their views for the question of moral knowledge and also assess the plausibility of the accounts themselves in so far as they bear on that question. We shall see whether coherent accounts of moral properties emerge from the prominent historical attempts at analysis, and then in the second half of the study determine whether criteria for moral knowledge can be satisfied in light of our conclusions regarding the existence and nature of these properties. Different criteria for knowledge and truth will affect the need for appeal to moral properties in the account of moral knowledge.

This first chapter will provide some preliminary analyses and draw some initial distinctions to guide the later inquiry.

1

Moral Knowledge

A. Knowledge

In approaching the question of moral knowledge, we must first strive for clarity as to the nature of knowledge generally. A general analysis should be capable of accommodating different sorts of knowledge, such as perceptual, theoretical, mathematical, and so on. Philosophers disagree at present about the correct analysis of knowledge. Since Edmund Gettier attacked the traditional account,[1] there has been no consensus as to what knowing something amounts to. That account, perhaps dating back to Plato, held that a subject S knows some proposition p if, and only if, S believes p, p is true, and S is justified in believing p. Gettier showed that if S correctly infers a true belief from a false but justified belief, then he will have a justifieid true belief that fails to qualify as knowledge. Imagine my inferring that there is a building in a certain field from my justified but false belief that there is a barn there. There was a barn there that I knew about yesterday. Unbeknown to me, the barn burned down last night and was just replaced by a prefabricated house. Then I have a justified true belief, but I do not know that there is a building in the field.

The extensive post-Gettier literature on the analysis of knowledge pursued three main paths. The first was to beef up the justification condition by requiring that one's justification for a belief must not be defeated when true propositions are added to the corpus of one's beliefs.[2] In the barn example, if the proposition that the barn burned down is added to my beliefs, then I am no longer justified in believing that there is a building there. If the defeasibility account requires that I add only that single true proposition, then it correctly implies that I lack knowledge in this case. There remains a problem, however. If I also add the proposition about the house being placed in the field, then I am once again justified in believing that there is a building there. The account then becomes too weak in allowing me to have knowledge when I do not. One possibility is to correct only my false beliefs in considering whether justification is defeated. But this would make my knowledge in the example dependent on whether I have any false beliefs about there being other buildings in the field. I may or may not have such beliefs, but the acceptability of my knowledge claim does not seem to depend on whether I do or

2

not. Defeasibility accounts have not been successful in handling this sort of problem.[3]

Another main tactic has been to require that the source of a subject's belief be reliable if she is to have knowledge.[4] Inferring from false beliefs is not a reliable way to acquire new beliefs, even if the false beliefs are justified. Thus reliability accounts rule out Gettier cases, as they should. But, again, there remain problems in more complex contexts. The main one concerns the generality of the source whose reliability we are to consider in evaluating knowledge claims. Suppose that I am reliable in identifying barns by looking at them from a certain distance, that is, when I form beliefs about the presence of barns in such circumstances they are mostly true. But suppose also that I am not reliable in similar conditions in identifying buildings; I cannot from that distance tell buildings of many sorts from structures of other kinds. It seems that, despite this general unreliability, I can, on a given occasion, in such conditions, know that there is a building in a field by knowing that there is a barn in the field. This suggests that we should construe the source of my belief narrowly when evaluating my claim to knowledge. In fact the relevant source must be narrowed to include whatever may be relevant to its reliability in the circumstances in question. Suppose, for example, that I am good at identifying red barns but not green ones, and yet can pick out *this* green barn because of its peculiar shape. Then once more I can know that there is a building in the field from that source. In such cases, however, as the relevant circumstances approach uniqueness, it becomes clear that the crucial factor is not the general reliability of the source of my belief, but rather whether my belief is connected in the right way to the fact to which it refers in the very circumstances in question.

This last point brings us to the third major strand in recent attempts to provide an account of the nature of knowledge. Here one notes first that in Gettier cases the subject's belief is unconnected to the fact that makes it true; it is only accidentally true, and this nullifies its claim to be knowledge. Thus a proper analysis of knowledge should specify the required kind of connection between belief and truth. The first attempt to do so was the causal theory of knowledge, according to which the fact believed must be among the causes of the belief's being held.[5] This theory is clearly too strong, however, since it is highly doubtful that knowledge of mathematics or logic rests on such causal connections. It is also too weak, in that a subject may be causally connected in a suitable way to the object of his belief and yet lack knowledge of it. Suppose that I am looking at a barn in a field and believe on that ground that there is a barn in the field. Suppose also that in those circumstances I could not distinguish a barn from other structures abundantly found in the vicinity. Then I lack knowledge despite the causal connection provided by vision.[6]

A more recent attempt to specify a broader and stronger sort of connection between the belief and the truth conditions for knowledge is Nozick's counterfactual account.[7] Here S is held to know that p if, and only if, he truly believes p and the following counterfactual conditions obtain: (a) if p were not true, then S would not believe it; (b) if p were true (given other alterations in the circumstances), then S would continue to believe it. These conditions might handle the examples so far considered, but once again they prove to be both too strong (in ruling out acceptable knowledge claims) and too weak (in allowing false claims). The following example shows that the analysis is too strong. I know that unsupported objects fall even if the (closest) possible world in which this is false is so drastically different from our world as to affect beliefs, including this one, in totally unpredictable ways. That the counterfactual analysis is too weak can be seen from a possible situation in which some philosopher tricks me into holding a Gettier belief (in order to disprove Nozick's analysis). Imagine in our original example that this philosopher burns down the barn and substitutes the house so that I will truly believe that there is a building in the field. If the belief were not true, he would not have caused me to have it. Let us also suppose that he compulsively performs such tricks in all sorts of circumstances, so that condition b is satisfied as well. Then both counterfactual conditions are met, and yet I lack knowledge. We still feel that my belief is not connected in the proper way to the fact that makes it true.

In other works I have defended an account that accepts this third approach to the analysis of knowledge, that seeks once more to specify the connection between a belief and the fact that makes it true which is required if the belief is to qualify as knowledge.[8] The proper account must weaken the counterfactual connection between belief and truth, but also must add a further constraint in order to accommodate cases such as the intentional Gettier trick. The analysis that I find plausible requires not that the truth of a belief be counterfactually connected to its being held, but only that its truth (or the fact that makes it true) significantly raise the probability of the belief's being held. For empirical knowledge, the probability of the belief, given the fact to which it refers, must be higher than the antecedent probability of the belief. When this relation obtains, the fact to which the belief refers helps to explain the belief's being held. The explanation normally will be causal in the case of empirical knowledge, but need not be in other areas.

Knowledge is belief that is best explained by reference to its truth. This analysis handles the sorts of cases we have considered. If, for example, I cannot distinguish barns from many other structures in the vicinity, then my seeing a barn might not significantly have raised the probability of my belief that there is a barn in the field. It will not have done so if it was very likely that I would have seen one of these other structures and would have believed it to be a barn. Then an equally good explanation for my belief would be that I saw some such structure (barn or otherwise) in the field and believe all such structures to be barns when I see them. The explanationist account thus implies that I lack knowledge here, as it should. It accommodates equally well the case mentioned above that defeats the counterfactual account. The best explanation for my belief that unsupported objects fall refers to the fact that they do (and to my perceptual experiences of such events), even if there is no telling what I would believe (if, indeed, I would exist and have beliefs) in a world in which the laws of physics (laws that govern also how human brains operate) are very different.

For many cases we must allow not only direct explanatory connections, but also chains of explanation. Consider an example of knowledge of the past. If I know that it rained last night because I see that the pavement is wet this morning, then what explains my belief is itself explained by the fact to which the belief refers. (The rain explains the wet pavement, which helps to explain my belief.) In other cases, for example, knowledge of the future, what explains my belief might also explain the fact to which it refers. (Dark clouds might explain both the impending rain and my belief that it will rain.) When we allow such chains, it turns out that we must add an additional constraint. Each link in the chain (each probabilistic connection) must make the next link more probable. This constraint disallows knowledge claims in cases like the intentional Gettier trick. There my believing on the basis of the evidence presented is not made more probable (explained) by the evidence's being connected (via the trickster) with the fact that makes my belief true. Contrast that case with an ordinary case of perceptual knowledge. When I have visual knowledge, my believing that there is a certain object before me on the basis of my visual experience is made more probable by the connection between such experience and its objects. Our visual systems have evolved so as to secure such connections and hence make visual knowledge possible.

We need not concern ourselves further with such complications here. I shall assume this explanationist account of the nature of knowledge in addressing the issue of moral knowledge.

B. *Moral Knowledge*

A subject *S* has moral knowledge if, for example, the truth of her belief that some action is right or that some person or object is good helps to explain her holding that belief. Alternatively, the fact that some action is right or that some object or person is good must help to explain a subject's belief that it is so if the subject's belief is to count as knowledge. Once more we must allow for explanatory chains. Thus, for example, the fact that a person is a good person might help to explain why he performs a certain action, and *S*'s perception or knowledge of that action might help to explain why she believes that he is a good person. Then she will know that he is a good person.

The truth of a person's moral beliefs must enter the best explanations for their being held if the person is to have moral knowledge. This claim is neutral between realist and nonrealist, subjectivist and objectivist moral metaphysics. As yet I have said nothing of the nature of moral truth or moral facts, if indeed there is any. If there is moral knowledge, according to the explanationist account of knowledge, then there must be moral facts, in some sense of 'facts', or at least moral truth. An understanding of the nature of moral knowledge demands an analysis of the facts or criterion of truth involved. This in turn will determine the type of explanation relevant to the evaluation of claims to knowledge in ethics. Not all explanation is causal, although we normally conceive of causal explanation as the paradigm. Presumably the truth of many mathematical propositions is among the reasons why mathematicians believe them, but such explanations do not appeal to causal relations between mathematical propositions or facts and beliefs. As in ethics, an understanding of mathematical knowledge would demand an account of these explanations, which would in turn require an analysis of mathematical truth and mathematical facts.

Thus semantics and ontology must go hand in hand with epistemology (and with some understanding of normative ethics) if we are to gain a grasp on moral knowledge. Although not all explanation is causal, certainly empirical knowledge, where the relation between fact believed and belief most often is causal, has been traditionally a model for conceiving of moral knowledge. Those who have believed in moral knowledge have also believed in moral facts as states of affairs quite similar to empirically ascertainable facts. Such states of affairs consist in objects having properties, and having them independently of whether we know or believe they have them. The contrapositive is also true. Most philosophers who do not believe in moral facts or properties of this sort have seemed also to doubt that there is genuine moral knowledge. (I shall argue eventually that they have been wrong.)

Most non-skeptics regarding ethics, I have just claimed, have been moral realists. We may define realism semantically as well as metaphysically. In fact, in the case of physical realism, for example, it may be easier to capture in semantic terms what is intuitively meant by saying that objects have physical properties independently of our beliefs and other subjective states. What we mean is that the truth of an assertion that an object has a physical property is logically independent from the truth of statements about sets of beliefs and other subjective states. In Dummett's terms, truth is verification transcendent.[9] It is always possible that an empirical proposition be false, whatever the evidence (in the form of sensory states and coherence with beliefs) for its truth. Returning to more intuitive terms, the truth of propositions interpreted realistically consists in correspondence to (non-epistemic) fact, not in coherence with other propositions believed.[10] This at least defines a necessary condition for physical realism. For the typical realist's thesis to be true, there must also be some objects with such independent properties: some existentially quantified propositions in the domain must be true.

Moral realism may be defined similarly, except that here it is necessary first to distinguish beliefs from other subjective states, and then to distinguish agents from recipients of actions and evaluators. Moral properties are real in the relevant sense if, and only if, the truth of their ascriptions is not dependent on coherence with evaluators' sets of moral beliefs. Realism (and anti-realism) must be distinguished from objectivism (and subjectivism) in ethics. According to objectivism, the truth of moral judgments is independent from the existence of all subjective states, not merely from other moral beliefs. Values must exist in objects themselves, apart from how they affect sentient subjects.

The objectivist position appeals to some environmentalists, in that it posits values in the environment quite apart from our appreciation of them. The destruction of such values may be wrong, they hold, even if we prefer it. Despite this possibly attractive implication of the position, and whether or not there exist some values of this sort, the fact that the truth of most statements about the rightness or wrongness of actions seems to depend so obviously on how the actions affect other subjects, and the fact that statements about goodness seem to be so relative to the desires and preferences of agents who pursue it, render full blown objectivism a non-starter in moral metaphysics. Indeed, we shall see that the most plausible analyses of both rightness and goodness refer to subjective states such as desires and preferences and to properties such as rationality.

Realists may want to allow also that beliefs of both agents and recipients of actions can affect their rightness and wrongness. In regard to recipients, beliefs can affect expectations, which in turn can affect the moral status of actions toward those whose expectations have been altered. In regard to agents, if one does what she believes to be wrong, this may itself tend to make the action wrong; and if one does what she believes to be right, this may have an exonerating effect on actions otherwise wrong. More broadly, if one is committed to a certain set of values embodied in some social role such as that of parent or professional, and one believes that this role (construed according to these values) is morally acceptable or admirable, then one might be justified in acting differently than those with other sets of values and moral beliefs. The moral realist may want to allow this sort of relativism, may want to grant that beliefs of agents as well as recipients can affect the moral status of their actions, while holding that these factors help to determine real properties of rightness and goodness.

What the realist must deny is that the truth of judgments about rightness or goodness depends on the beliefs of those judging (in their roles as evaluators). Such truth must be determined by the presence of the properties being ascribed, not by coherence between the evaluators' judgments and their other moral beliefs. Construing moral realism in this way, as the claim that moral properties are independent from evaluators' beliefs about them, renders the position similar to realism about psychological states and, more specifically, to realism about beliefs themselves. In the latter case we certainly cannot demand independence of the states from beliefs of the subjects of these states, but as realists we can still require that the truth of judgments about these states be independent from ascribers' beliefs about them. The similarity between realism about moral properties and realism about psychological states is welcome if, as argued above, rightness seems to depend on the psychological springs and effects of actions.

Despite the immediate implausibility of objectivism in ethics, realism, the existence of moral properties independent from evaluators' beliefs about them, has been much more widely endorsed or assumed in the history of ethical thought. It has often been assumed that moral knowledge is possible and that, in describing it, we can use empirical knowledge as a model. As in the case of empirical knowledge, according to this view we will have true moral beliefs when our ascriptions of moral properties accord with their independent presence. And we will have moral knowledge when the possession of these properties (rightness and goodness) by actions or policies, and by objects or persons, helps to explain our ascriptions of them or our moral beliefs. The great problem in filling out this picture lies in providing a description of the properties of goodness and rightness.

One source of this problem is the phenomenon of widespread apparent disagreement in moral judgments both across and within moral communities and cultures. The realist's account of moral properties must explain why there appears to be such great difficulty in apprehending or detecting their presence. This apparent difficulty seems to require an account of moral properties more akin to that of theoretical properties than to that of observational properties. If we could intuit moral properties in objects and actions as we can see certain physical properties, then widespread disagreement would be inexplicable. On the other hand, if moral properties are complex, made up of clusters of other properties that may be present to differing degrees, or if we must infer the presence of moral properties in explaining certain events or experiences, much as we infer to unobservable physical properties, then we could better understand and explain the extent of disagreement among moral judgments. (Other objections, nevertheless, face such accounts, as we shall see.)

Another way to accommodate seemingly interminable ethical disputes is to embrace relativism. According to this view, the truth of moral judgments is relative to the subjects who assert them, or to their moral communities. What is good or right is not so absolutely, only good or right for John or Mary or for the groups with which they identify. And what is good or right for John may not be so for Mary. Acknowledging such relativity of moral judgments to individuals or communities is compatible with the realist view as I have defined it, as long as the truth of the judgments is not relative (in terms of coherence) to the moral beliefs of evaluators. Relativity to other subjective states, I have held, is acceptable to the realist. It remains to be seen, however, whether realism can accommodate interminable disagreement by providing coherent relativist accounts of moral properties. We shall return to this question several times in the ensuing chapters.

The most direct way to model moral knowledge on empirical knowledge is to show that moral properties can be reduced to empirical (psychological or physical) or 'natural' properties. Were this reduction to succeed, it would remain questionable whether moral properties so reduced help to explain beliefs about them (or other phenomena, that in turn explain such beliefs). One's view of this matter, and hence one's view of the depth or genuineness of moral knowledge, will depend on the type of reduction envisaged. I shall have more to say on varieties of reduction or identity theories below. First, we must consider briefly the objection to all such proposals raised by G. E. Moore in his well-known 'open question' argument.[11]

Moore pointed out that, in attempting to define 'good' in terms of natural properties, whichever properties we propose, it will remain sensible to ask whether an object having those properties is good. If, for example, we attempt to equate being good with being desired, it will still make sense to ask of any object that is desired whether it is really good. Hence no such definition can succeed. If our concept of the property good were identical to our concept of some other property or set of properties, then, in response to the correct definition, Moore's question could not make sense to us. But, he maintains, it always does. He did not doubt, however, that goodness was a genuine property. He therefore held that it was a 'simple' (undefinable), 'unnatural' property. If goodness is a moral property, then this analysis implies that moral knowledge is both like and unlike empirical knowledge, and utterly mysterious.

Successors to Moore such as A. J. Ayer accepted his argument against reductions of moral properties, but not the positive conclusion that he drew from it.[12] For Ayer and other positivists the implication was rather that there are no moral properties at all, hence no moral knowledge either. Embedded in this reaction to Moore are three major errors (and other minor ones). First, philosophers nowadays recognize that successful reductions need not be definitional. This lesson came from the philosophy of science and philosophy of mind.[13] Water may be H_2O even if many or all people do not include a concept of the latter in their concept of the former. Second, even if water can be defined (in some sense) as H_2O, the open question argument applied to the concept of water will strike anyone unaware of this (correct) definition as plausible. Similarly, it may be that definitions more complex than those explicitly considered by Moore are correct although not universally conceived to be so. If, for example, we define good as rationally desirable rather than simply as desired, it is not clear that the open question argument will work, or that it should. Third, even if there are no moral properties, this does not rule out the possibility of moral knowledge, although it does require a moral epistemology quite different from that which takes empirical knowledge as its model.

One key to the nature of moral knowledge, then, lies in the

answer to the question whether there are real moral properties, and if so, of what sort. Empirical knowledge might well be a suitable model for knowledge of real moral properties. If there are no such properties, then some other model is more appropriate for describing moral knowledge (if it exists), perhaps mathematical or, better yet I shall argue, legal knowledge, knowledge of propositions of law (despite certain disanalogies). In the absence of real properties to which moral judgments could correspond, such judgments might still be true by cohering within broader maximally coherent sets. In other areas, perhaps mathematics for example, and more assuredly law, a proposition is true if and only if it coheres with others. A proposition of law (of the form 'It is the law that . . .') is true if and only if it coheres better with the settled body of law than its negation (not if it corresponds to some property, being legal, independent of other propositions of law). Perhaps moral judgments are true or false in a similar way. To defend such a view, one would have to show, first, that there are no real moral properties to which judgments could correspond and, second, that there is a good reason to think of coherence here as determining truth, as opposed to say, justification,.

If there are real moral properties, they may be distinct from, or reducible to, physical and/or psychological properties. Different sorts of reductions, I noted, are compatible with the premises of Moore's open question argument. But, when certain intuitive further premises are added, some naturalist interpretations of moral properties become less plausible than others. The latter interpretations would form the most promising basis for a successful account of moral knowledge along the lines most often assumed to be natural, taking empirical knowledge as a model.

C. Some Distinctions Among Questions and Answers

I have pointed out that questions concerning the existence and nature of moral knowledge fall in the boundary areas between normative ethics, epistemology, and (moral) metaphysics and semantics (concerning the nature of moral truth). Moore and some of his successors rather saw the fundamental question of philosophical ethics as one concerning the meanings of moral terms, and derivatively, the illocutionary status of moral judgments (are they statements of fact, expressions of attitudes, or commands?). Even if we accept a distinction between questions of meaning and questions of beliefs or facts, I do not take the matter of the exact meanings of moral terms to be of fundamental philosophical importance. We saw above that moral properties might reduce to physical and/or psychological properties even if not definable in terms of them. Similarly, our concepts of moral properties might reflect our realist assumptions whether or not those assumptions are true. We might intend or take ourselves to refer to non-relational moral properties in objects themselves, but we might be entirely mistaken in assuming that we succeed in doing so.[14] For the purpose of this study, the important questions concern the existence and nature of moral properties and the type of moral knowledge possible, given answers to those ontological questions. None of these matters primarily concern our moral concepts or linguistic intentions. Of course, our moral concepts set limits to what can be recognized as a moral judgment. But the precise boundaries of our concepts or linguistic intentions cannot determine moral truth.

The question regarding the status of moral judgments may seem to relate closely to our inquiry into the nature of moral truth. But the problem with the way that meta-ethicists earlier in the century typically posed the question lay in the assumption that the different functions possible for moral judgments are mutually exclusive. In actuality, the judgment that a certain action is right can state a fact, express an attitude, and recommend the action to others, *if* certain attitudes normally attach to certain kinds of facts. Furthermore, if moral judgments essentially express attitudes, this does not imply moral relativism of any interesting kind.[15] As the case of Hume illustrates, if moral judgments express some universal attitude such as sympathy for others, then their truth values need not vary with speakers or communities (at least in identical relevant circumstances). On the other hand, it is not sufficient for a non-relativist account that moral judgments express some universal attitude. Persons, all of whom are sympathetic to others, may yet interminably disagree as to right actions or policies when conflicts of interest occur. Some might think that rightness correlates with maximal collective utility; others might express their sympathy in support for the protection of individual rights incompatible with maximal collective utility. Once more a relativist account of rightness might best accommodate such apparently unsettleable dispute.

Moral judgments appear to express attitudes and guide actions, and they purport to state facts as well. Their action guiding character may not be uniform, however. When I assert to another person that an action is right, I normally intend this expressed evaluation to guide her conduct. But the same judgment, expressed internally, may not reflect the same intention, or have the same motivational effect on me, especially if the course of action opposes my self-interest or that of those I care about. Whether the judgment that this action is right guides my action, or even tends to do so, will depend on my moral character and prior social conditioning. When it comes to judgments of goodness or about the value of various states of affairs, the motivational, action guiding aspect, may be more universal. But this may be, as I shall argue later, because accounts of goodness can accommodate more easily relativity to the speaker than can accounts of rightness.

If moral judgments are to serve these diverse functions, as they purport to do, then once more the crucial questions concern the nature of the properties to which they purportedly refer. Are these properties non-relational or relational? If the latter, are the attitudes expressed by the judgments parts of these relations? If so, are there philosophically important differences between emotivist and realist moral views? If the attitudes expressed in moral judgments are included within the relational properties with which rightness and goodness are identified, are these attitudes universal or restricted to particular subjects or communities? If the latter, is the relativism implied compatible with moral realism? Are coherent relativist accounts along these lines available for analyses of both goodness and rightness? Is the normativity of moral judgments, their evaluative functions, somehow localizable in the attitudes they express? And how does this affect proposed reductions of moral to 'natural' properties?

Such questions in moral ontology must be answered before we can find an appropriate model in terms of which to conceive the possibility of moral knowledge. For the answers we can best look to the most plausible reductions of moral properties proposed in the ethical systems of the great moral thinkers of the past. We shall look to Hobbes, Hume, and Kant. Before embarking on that historical investigation, I shall offer a few more preliminary remarks on reductionist analyses. As mentioned above, different types of (non-definitional) reductions of particular properties or states of affairs to others are possible, all surviving Moore's open question argument, at least if that argument is considered in itself, without augmentation. Once more the map of conceivable positions on the relations of supposed moral properties or states to psychological and physical properties or states can be derived from the philosophy of mind.[16] There we find a well-developed taxonomy of positions on the relation of the mental to the physical.

At one extreme is dualism. The dualist holds that mental states cannot be reduced to physical states, because there are (first order) mental properties that cannot be located in the physical realm at all. The colors of mental images, for example, are not to be found in the brain. At the other extreme is type identity theory. Here types of mental states are held to be identical to independently identifiable types of states of the brain or nervous system. Thus, according to this theory, a pain of a particular sort would be identified with a particular kind of configuration of neural states. More popular nowadays are token identity theories. Here particular mental states are identified with particular states of the nervous system, but the categories or types into which these states are sorted differ. This may be because mental states are type identified by their second order, relational, functional, or explanatory properties. For example, pains of various types may be whichever particular (neural) states typically follow certain stimuli, and prompt, together with other types of mental states, certain responses. Or beliefs and desires of various kinds may be whatever particular (brain) states fit in certain ways into explanations for behavior that ascribe practical rationality to agents.[17] The physical states of the nervous system that play these functional or explanatory roles may not be independently classifiable into similar sets in ordinary physical terms.

Finally, there is eliminative materialism.[18] According to this view, the reporting and explanatory functions currently served by mental state discourse could in principle be taken over by discourse couched exclusively in physical terms. If this could be done without loss of function, then we would lack reason for believing in mental states or properties as distinct in any sense from physical states and properties. Ultimately, appeal to mental states would not explain anything. The truth of beliefs about mental states would not help to explain these beliefs; such explanations would rather appeal to the use of archaic theories by their subjects. In that case, we could predict that after a time such beliefs would no longer arise.

We need not concern ourselves directly with the plausibility of these positions in the philosophy of mind. It suffices to note that structurally similar positions are available to the moral ontologist. Here we may use Moore's argument, properly pruned and augmented, to distinguish initially the appeals of the possible reductionist and non-reductionist views. Moore took his open question argument to establish moral dualism, the irreducibility of the moral to the non-moral. But this position is less plausible in ethics than in philosophy of mind. First, while we sometimes have the feeling of reporting directly on the presence of moral properties, that feeling is much stronger and harder to dispel when we report on the properties of our occurrent mental states. Second, the epistemological problem for moral dualism seems more serious. For many philosophers, knowledge of occurrent mental states such as thoughts, pains, and images, mental states apparently distinct from states of the brain, has seemed not only unproblematic, but paradigmatic of our most immediately justified beliefs. By contrast with intuition of the properties of certain mental states, moral intuition strikes us as highly suspect, making disagreement in ethics unintelligible and moral knowledge mysterious.

Thus we must prune Moore's argument of its conclusion (and so of the premises that equate reduction with definition and that simply posit the existence of moral properties). We may augment it in a way that turns it into an inductive argument against certain kinds of reduction. Here we ask why the open question argument should seem plausible to us as a weapon against all candidates if moral properties can be type identified with ordinary physical or psychologial properties. If the latter were observable, then only ignorance could explain our failure to make the correct identifications. But ignorance does not seem to underlie all moral disputes. If moral properties were theoretical and inaccessible, then it would be difficult to see how their presence would be capable of guiding action. Yet judgments that ascribe such properties also serve an action guiding function.

Supervene →depend?

In light of this revised interpretation of Moore's argument, something akin to the token identity theory seems more plausible as a way to describe the relation between moral and non-moral properties, if the former are real. Ethicists agree that moral properties at least supervene on non-moral (much as philosophers of mind agree that the mental supervenes on the physical). This means that there cannot be a difference in the value or rightness of objects or events without some difference in their non-moral properties. One way to explain supervenience is in terms of identity. If moral properties are identical (reducible) to certain non-moral properties, then the former will certainly supervene on the latter. But identification of moral properties with independently identifiable kinds of ordinary physical or psychological properties seems to run foul of Moore's revised argument. So something akin to a token identity theory, where particular instantiations or moral properties are identified with particular instantiations of physical properties (as they relate to psychological properties), seems most promising for the moral realist.

It seems plausible that, if there are moral properties, they are typed according to their normative or evaluative aspects. That would explain why we could not type identify moral with non-moral properties. If, as suggested earlier, we locate the normative force of moral judgments in the psychological states or attitudes they express, then the best prospect for the moral realist is to interpret moral properties in terms of objects or events being such as to elicit (rational) desire or approval, or being such as to be (rationally) willed. We can then identify particular instantiations of moral properties with the instantiations of physical properties that make their objects such as to elicit these responses. But even if we could determine the entire extensions of such properties at a given time, we could not identify them as types with moral properties, since changes in the physical properties could be offset by changes in subjective responses. This would create a different extensional equivalence, showing that the prior one did not really support identification of the types of physical with moral properties.

Although not concerned with these fine distinctions between kinds of reductionist theories, the historical accounts of moral properties to be examined all take the form I have endorsed as most plausible. Before turning to the first of these, I offer a final preliminary word on the place of reason, and reasons, in such accounts. One ontologically neutral way to analyze judgments regarding the right and the good is in terms of reason and (practical) rationality. Saying that an action is right is saying that one morally ought to do it (or at least that it is not the case that one ought not to do it). Saying that one ought to do it is saying that one has (the best moral) reasons to do it, or that one would be (maximally) rational (from a moral point of view) in doing it or in willing to do it. Similarly, an object or state of affairs is good if, and only if, one ought to desire or approve of it, that is, one has (the most) reason to desire or approve of it and therefore would be rational to do so.

These analyses preserve ontological neutrality until we specify what it is to have moral reasons or to be practically rational (perhaps only from the moral point of view) in acting, willing, desiring, or approving. We must also decide whether moral reasons equate with, or override, others and whether being morally rational can be equated with being rational *tout court*. Other question ensue. Are such reasons relative to subjects or non-relative? Are they independent from beliefs about them and from other moral beliefs? If so, then there is no guarantee that a person who rationally deliberates will discover the best reasons he has and act on the basis of them. If not, then we cannot use empirical knowledge as a model for moral knowledge, but rather require some other paradigm (assuming a realist view of the physical world as the object of empirical knowledge).

We are driven back to the same ontological and epistemological questions that arose earlier. It is time to take a closer look at some plausible answers. We may begin with Hobbes's accounts of the good and the right, which I believe to be both realist and subjectivist.

CHAPTER I

Hobbes: Subjective Realism and Prudential Rationality

The fitness of ordinary empirical knowledge as a model for moral knowledge depends on the possiblity of naturalist reductions of moral properties along the lines suggested in the introduction. The first plausible attempt at such reductions was made by Hobbes. In this chapter I shall describe Hobbes's implicit position on the properties of goodness and rightness, draw the implications of these analyses for the question of moral knowledge, and comment on the acceptablility of the proposed reductions.

A. Goodness

In a famous passage in *Leviathan*, Hobbes writes:

> But whatsoever is the object of any man's appetite or desire, that is it which he for his part calleth *good:* and the object of his hate and aversion *evil;* and of his contempt, *vile* and *inconsiderable.* For these words of good, evil, and contemptible, are ever used with the relation to the person that useth them: there being nothing simply and absolutely so; nor any common rule of good and evil, to be taken from the nature of the objects themselves; but from the person of the man, where there is no commonwealth; or, in a commonwealth, from the person that representeth it; or from an arbitrator or judge, whom men disagreeing shall by consent set up, and make his sentence the rule thereof. (I, 6, 48–9)[1]

This passage is a good place to begin (but not end) an exposition of Hobbes's views on the nature of the good. At first glance the passage might suggest that Hobbes was (in contemporary terms)

19

an emotivist. It might seem that, according to the view expressed, when I say '*X* is good', I mean simply that I desire *X*; or, more true to the spirit of emotivism, by uttering these words I simply express my desire for *X*. Certainly Hobbes is explicit that values are subjective, relative to evaluators, and not to be found in objects themselves apart from their effects on evaluating subjects. In other places Hobbes notes that there are no universal (first-order) desires, no uniformity or fixed structure to desires for objects in the lives of individuals over time, and no natural coherence among the desires and values of different persons. This may seem to combine an extreme relativism with the emotivism previously suggested and the subjectivism that Hobbes clearly intends to endorse.

But although Hobbes is a subjectivist, and a relativist of sorts, his considered view is not that of an extreme relativist nor of an emotivist. There are clues to a different view in the very passage cited. First, he says that men *call* good what they happen to desire. This leaves room for a different notion of real goodness, although this notion will have to remain relativist, given what Hobbes says in the remainder of the passage. Second, he suggests that conflicts arising from different values should be settled by appeal to a judge or arbitrator, who will determine what is really good for the group of individuals. The latter might be interpreted as what they should rationally desire, so as to avoid the conflicts that might otherwise ensue. He says later that judging value solely by private measure or appetite is a sin within a commonwealth, suggesting once more that the individual is not to have the final word on goodness (II, 30, 252).

The interpretation of the good as the object of *rational* desire is coherent with Hobbes's overall moral theory and psychology. According to him all actions of an individual aim at some good for her, but individuals can nevertheless act irrationally (I, 6, 54). Hobbes explicitly contrasts good and evil consquences that may occur as distant effects of one's present actions from *apparently* good or evil consequences that one envisages in deliberating (I, 6, 55). One can therefore be mistaken as to the best means to realize one's desires, be overwhelmed by passion for the short-term benefit as opposed to the greater long-term good, or mistake the true object of one's desire. In the first of these cases, one will be mistaken in desiring false means to the satisfaction of one's other desires; in the second, in desiring more what one should desire less; and in the third, in desiring what one should not. In all these cases, recognized by Hobbes, the implication is that an individual might desire what is not truly good for him, the latter coinciding with his rational desire.

This account of goodness or value also coheres nicely, as we shall see, with what Hobbes has to say about rightness or obligation. The right for him coincides with rational prudence and opposes certain natural passions and their immediate fulfilment. If one acts rightly in pursuing true value, then this suggests again that the good is the object of rational desire, and not simply the object of any desire that individuals might momentarily possess. If individuals are rational in pursuing what is (truly) good, then we cannot equate the good with the objects of all desires, since such pursuit would lead to irrational and irresolvable conflict, the greatest social evil for Hobbes.

Goodness as what is rationally desired qualifies as a real property in the sense previously defined, in that, as noted, individuals can err in their beliefs about it. The property nevertheless remains relational and subjective. Hobbes adds further coherence or unity to our conception of the good by specifying certain universal values of special importance to morality or rational prudence. In his view there is unbounded diversity among particular first-order desires for objects, but at the same time there are certain second-order desires, those relating to first-order desires, that all agents rationally must have. Pleasure is not among them, as many later moral philosphers thought. For Hobbes pleasure is not the object of desire, but rather its appearance, or the appearance of its fulfilment, or of the vital motion expressed as desire (I, 6, 49). It is an epiphenomenon, not a motivating force. Universal objects of rational desire rather include self-preservation, power, happiness, and peace.

The fundamental desire is for self-preservation. According to Hobbes one naturally fears death itself, but also, and more pertinent to our present point, the loss of a necessary condition for satisfying one's other desires (loss of power). Power is defined straightforwardly as the means to the future satisfaction of other desires (I, 10, 72). Happiness or felicity is the continual satisfaction of desires over time (I, 6, 55; I, 11, 80). Peace and the means to peace are universally good as necessary for the achievement of happiness or 'comfortable living' (I, 15, 123–4). Thus all universal rational desires (desires that rationality requires agents to have) are second-order. They are either necessary as means to the satisfaction of first-order desires, or represent a process of such satisfaction.

I have not yet said what it is for a desire to be rational or rationally required. To my knowledge Hobbes is not explicit about this. One possible analysis is that a desire is rational if its object would be desired for the agent by a perfectly benevolent and omniscient observer. Another is that a desire is rational if it would be supported by informed second-order desires of the agent, reflecting what he would prefer to desire given knowledge of the objects in question. A analysis akin to the latter that is more in the spirit of what Hobbes has to say about prudence, and one that avoids appeal to an ideal being, holds desires to be rational if they fit the most coherent, fullest set of informed first- and second-order desires of the agent (strength of desires would also need to be taken account of in specifying this set). Desires are coherent if mutually realizable, and more so if the satisfaction of some makes more probable or easier the satisfaction of others. They will be irrational if based on ignorance of the true nature of their objects, or if their satisfaction would block the realization of other stronger or more numerous desires. The most coherent set for any agent will include those second-order desires that she is rationally required to have. An agent is rationally required to have those desires whose fulfilment is necessary for the satisfaction of other desires within coherent sets.

We may note the implications of this account of the property of goodness for the possibility of knowledge of values. As pointed out, the property remains relational and subjective when we add the property of rationality as a component. But this occasionally counterfactual component renders the property of which it is a part clearly real in the sense defined, in that our beliefs about what is rationally desired do not determine what is truly rationally desired. Nevertheless, if we can unpack rationality here as suggested above, in terms of coherence among informed first- and second-order desires, then the full property of goodness, while complex, is reducible to physical and psychological properties. A particular object's being good (for a particular agent) consists in its being such as to prompt rational desire (from that agent).

This is the sort of property of which we can have fallible knowledge. We will be motivated to aim at such knowledge, but we will not acquire it automatically, either by introspection or by observation of the objects of our desires. Even if we are automatically aware of our desires when we reflect on them (something that psychoanalysts deny), we will not, by that process, automatically become aware that these desires are rational, that is, informed and coherent in the sense defined. Nevertheless, when we do attain beliefs about what we should rationally desire, these beliefs may qualify as knowledge under the explanatory criterion briefly defended in the previous chapter. If we have carefully reflected on the relevant full set of our desires and on the characteristics of their objects, then the best explanations for why we believe these objects good, that is, objects of rational desire or worthy of being desired, may include appeal to the fact that they are good. Furthermore, the fact that certain objects are, or would be, rationally desired by particular agents, may explain aspects of the agents' behavior (which may in turn explain beliefs about their behavior and the objects toward which it is directed).

Such explanations will be especially pertinent when agents discover irrationality in their previous desires and adjust their behavior accordingly. Consider first an everyday adaptation of a Hobbesian example. A child who is punished for violating cooperative agreements after having made them may come to realize that such behavior is not truly good (for him). He will then become inclined to pursue more genuine benefits or goods. There are many other everyday cases in which we appeal to genuine, as opposed to apparent or short-range, values or disvalues to explain behavior and attitudes as well as judgments about behavior and attitudes. Suppose, for example, that Susan has for years smoked cigarettes, unaware of their connection with lung cancer. If her discovery of this connection leads her to break the habit, then we can say that she acted as she did because she realized that smoking was bad for her (not simply bad for her health, but bad *tout court*, given her stronger desire to be healthy and to live to satisfy her other desires). Or consider nineteen-year-old John, who had always desired the life of a professional tennis player, and had deluded himself into thinking that he had talent and had simply lacked luck in tournaments. In his second year in college he reached a moment of truth, which could be described as the

23

realization that pursuit of a tennis career was not good (for him), and perhaps that pursuit of a career in law was better, given his real talent for analysis and debate. The latter would cohere better with his other first- and second-order desires, desires for material success, self-respect, exercise of his real talents, and so on. This realization of what was more likely to be of true value could explain John's change of heart and subsequent change of behavior, and this in turn could alter others' perceptions of his behavior and beliefs about what is good for him.

Thus the Hobbesian account of goodness or (non-moral) value as interpreted here provides a promising reduction of the property that suggests an account of knowledge of values as a kind of empirical knowledge. The reduction allows for relativity and diversity in values, which are subjective but real, while also positing certain things of universal value, such as life, power, peace and happiness. Relativity and diversity here can be incorporated into a coherent and knowable property, since what is good for each agent will be what is rationally desired by him, what it is rational for him to desire given his other desires.

It remains to be seen whether Hobbes can provide an account of morality, rightness, or obligation along similar lines and with similar implications for the possibility of moral knowledge. For him, as we shall see, morality lies in the pursuit of universal values, so that a similar account should indeed follow. But here, as we shall also see in the end, diversity may prove to be a more intractable stumbling block, since now we will have to be concerned not only with desires of different individuals, but more directly with conflicts among their desires and interests. The question now becomes whether there are universally rational solutions to such conflicts, whether rationality requires particular solutions, as Hobbes claims.

B.   Morality, Prudence, and the State of Nature

Hobbes states in many places, in *Leviathan* and other works, that all voluntary actions aim at happiness or at some good to the agent (I, 11, 80; I, 14, 105; I, 15, 114, 118; II, 19, 145; II, 25, 191; II, 27, 218). Since he defines good in terms of the satisfaction of any rational desires, and defines happiness as the continual satisfaction of desires, whatever their objects, this claim does not imply psychological egoism of an interesting narrow sort. The satisfaction of desires for the welfare of others would count as contributing to an agent's good on this view. On the other hand, there may be agents who care little for the welfare of others; and altruism, where it exists, is normally directed toward specific other persons to whom one is personally related, a basis altogether too narrow to support moral obligations generally. Hobbes wants to argue, not only that moral rules apply to non-altruists as well, but that they should be rationally motivated to obey them, motivated under a conception of rationality that does not demand impartiality between themselves and others.

He also accepts a version of the principle that 'ought implies can'. In arguing, for example, for the inalienability of the right to self-defense, he combines the broad egoist premise with the claim that one cannot be understood to be obligated to do what one by nature could not voluntarily renounce one's right not to do (I, 14, 110). These psychological and moral premises together entail that all moral obligations must at least accord with prudence, where prudence is understood as the adoption of the most efficient means to satisfy one's rational desires. But Hobbes also wants to argue for a stronger connection. As we shall see from his concept of natural laws, he holds that moral rules that determine obligations or what is right are themselves justified or determined by the long-range self-interests of each individual.

Before expanding on his concept of moral rules or laws of nature, we should note at the beginning, as Hobbes himself does, the immediate objection to the equation of moral rightness and rational prudence, the fact that it can sometimes be in my interest to harm others. Hobbes recognizes this fact in the state of nature, a pre-political condition, in which reason not only condones but requires non-cooperation and aggressive strikes against other persons and their possessions. Rational prudence in this condition is, however, self-defeating, in that all individuals remain worse off than they could be by doing the best they can in its terms. In this situation each individual would be irrational to accept unilaterally moral rules as guides to behavior, but all remain in a dire situation when all fail to do so. For Hobbes moral restraint becomes rational only in escaping from this condition into a political society; only then can the contradiction between individual and collective rationality be resolved. Since it is in the interest of all to resolve it, all have an interest in establishing the conditions in which moral restraint becomes rational.

Thus there are two major parts of the argument that equates morality with prudential rationality: the description of the initial paradox of rationality and its resolution, and the equation of morality and rationality that reflects this resolution. Let us first briefly review the first part of the argument. Hobbes, remember, holds that all agents desire power, defined as the means to satisfy other desires (I, 11, 80). Since the power of each individual is relative to that of others, the only way to insure the retention of the power one has is to prevent increases in power by others. And the only way to insure that is to attempt to gain power over them. Similarly, since one has no security in this pre-political condition against attacks by others, the best way to prevent such aggression is by pre-emptive attacks against them (I, 13, 99). Worse still, each, if rational, recognizes that others, if rational, will reason in the same way. Thus each must expect others to be more ready to strike in recognizing her own readiness, and for Hobbes the self-defeating character of the state of nature is also self-reinforcing. Finally, there are some who come to desire power for its own sake, and the presence of such characters renders the aggressive strategy even more dominant from the point of view of prudential rationality.

In this situation the fruits of co-operation are unavailable. Since all benefit from co-operation and the restraint that makes it possible, it might be in the interest of each to enter into agreements to co-operate and end the state of nature, or state of war, with particular other individuals. Unfortunately, according to Hobbes, it will not be rational to be the first to comply with such agreements in the absence of security that the other party will comply as well. Thus the paradox of prudence is simply repeated at this level. What is rational for each is irrational for all.

We see, then, that Hobbes is not only aware of the obvious objection to egoistic moralities; he spells it out with great specificity in his description of the natural condition for individuals in contact with each other. He points out that, in contrast to other creatures, the common good for humans is not a simple sum of their separate private goods (II, 17, 131). Thus, in pursuing my interest I do not automatically further the interests of others.

26

Rationality for me does not necessarily counsel selfishness, but it is committed to the maximal satisfaction of my coherent and informed desires. As such, conflicts between my interests and those of others are real, and I may even be rationally required to harm others in order to avoid harm myself.

But it is precisely because rational prudence is collectively self-defeating (at least initially) that this objection is not the last word on the equation of morality with this conception of rationality. Since, to put it mildly, all agents benefit from removing themselves from the state of nature as Hobbes describes it, all, if rational, should be motivated to institute a set of rules that would end the condition of perpetual threat and conflict. It is this set of rules that Hobbes equates with the set of moral demands on individuals. He argues that it is in the interest of all to establish the efficacy of such rules and then to obey them. Once they have been established as generally efficacious, the interest of each becomes compatible with the interest of all in the Hobbesian system, and the coincidence of prudence with moral behavior becomes more plausible. In order to see whether this equation holds ubiquitously even in the context of generally peaceful relations between persons, we must examine the operation of moral rules as Hobbes defines them in that context.

C. Laws of Nature and Moral Obligations

We have seen that for Hobbes, the universality of certain desires – for self-preservation, happiness, and power – leads not to harmony, at least initially, but to strife among rational individuals in conditions of moderate scarcity. If the fundamental right of individuals is, as Hobbes holds, the right to survive, and that right generates a right to anything necessary to survival, then in this context it implies a right to anything and everything, since here one cannot predict what will enhance one's (slim) chances of survival (I, 14, 103). This Hobbes calls the 'Right of Nature', which implies a lack of moral obligations in the natural condition.

We saw above that pursuit of self-interest in the state of nature is not conducive to the common good, and now we re-emphasize that it is not compatible with moral obligation or moral behavior either. But such pursuit is also self-defeating, so that prudent

27

individuals who recognize this should be motivated to generate constraints on the direct pursuit of maximal self-interest. They must seek to impose on themselves rules that will enable them each to reap the benefits of peaceful, co-operative interaction, benefits that are otherwise denied them. These rules Hobbes calls 'Laws of Nature', and he equates them with traditional moral requirements that determine right actions for individuals.

Each person's self-preservation and welfare depends on peaceful relations with others. Each therefore has an interest in imposing upon others rules that require and promote peaceful relations. If none can succeed in doing so without agreeing to such rules herself, then each is rational to agree to them. But we saw that for Hobbes the rationality of compliance is another more pressing concern. In the end he argues that not only agreement, but compliance, is required to reap the benefits of co-operative interactions. While it may be possible to be a free rider on occasion, to exploit the good will or productivity of others, one cannot rationally predict that one will benefit by attempting to do so. Thus it is prudent to obey those rules that require moral behavior toward others, if one can be reasonably certain that others will obey them as well. Once peaceful relations have been established, then each person's prudent adherence to those rules that make such relations possible promotes not only his own security, and hence other interests, but the security and other interests of other persons in his society as well. At that point each person's good is compatible with that of others, and rightness is reduced to long-range self-interest or prudential rationality.

Let us consider this second stage of the argument a bit more slowly. Hobbes's laws of nature state necessary conditions for peace, hence for self-preservation, our fundamental aim. The main clause of the first law of nature states simply to seek peace (I, 14, 104); the second, to renounce one's natural right to everything and accept as much liberty as one is willing to grant to others (I, 14, 104); and the third, to comply with one's agreements (I, 15, 113). Subsequent rules include the requirement to acknowledge others as equals and to grant them equal rights (I, 15, 120). All nineteen coincide quite well with what one would expect as a summary of the precepts of traditional Judaeo-Christian morality, prescribing justice, mercy, equity, etc.; and Hobbes summarizes them with (a negative version of) the Golden Rule (I, 15, 122; II,

26, 203). He acknowledges his traditonal view of the content of moral rules, seeing his contribution as the demonstration that these are to be themselves justified as means to peaceful coexistence and to the benefits of society for each individual (I, 15, 124).

While these rules promote the good of the group, Hobbes also holds that they promote the good of each individual, since each benefits from peace and co-operation within the group. In promoting my security I must promote the security of others as well. It is this congruence that allows the reduction of rightness to prudence or egoistic rationality for Hobbes. Acquiescence in the laws of nature is necessary for peace; peace is necessary for self-preservation (and co-operation); and self-preservation is necessary for the satisfaction of any other desires. Hence acquiescence in the laws of nature, given that others are restraining their behavior according to their requirements, is itself a necessary means for the satisfaction of whatever ends the individual may have. Although reason here serves desire, it opposes those passions and immediate satisfactions of desire that threaten peace, that on the longer view must be judged irrational. Morality equates with prudence, although not with all of it; and the right reduces to a part of long-range self-interest, that part that makes possible life within a co-operative society.

What seems uncontroversial (on reflection) in this brilliant account is that moral rules make possible co-operative relations within groups or societies, and that it is in each agent's interest to promote and support such rules on that ground. But the reduction of rightness to rational prudence, the equation of a property of rightness with the property of being in each agent's long-range self-interest (more exactly with a determinate part of that broader property), requires more. It requires at a minimum the truth of a more controversial claim: that it is always in the prospective interest of each agent to do what is morally required of her. Each and every moral obligation must reduce to a requirement of prudential rationality, and a necessary condition for that reduction is that every moral obligation must at least coincide with a requirement of self-interest. Assessment of this far more doubtful claim requires first a closer look at Hobbes's notion of moral obligation.

An immediate objection to the way Hobbes's view has been presented so far is that moral obligations cannot equate with commands of rational prudence, since moral obligations coincide with prudence only in certain conditions, not, for example, in the state of nature. But of course this is no real objection, since it is Hobbes's view that all moral obligations hold only conditionally. Actually, he speaks of obligations in several senses, and Hobbes scholars disagree about whether the laws of nature create moral obligations at all.[2] In some places in *Leviathan* he indicates that obligations arise only from voluntary agreements (as the laws of nature do not). On the other hand, the obligation to keep agreements itself rests on the third law of nature, so that laws of nature must at least be the source of genuine obligations. Hobbes also speaks of the laws of nature 'obliging' in two different ways: in conscience in the state of nature, and in effect when there is security that others will comply (I, 15, 122–3). This means that agents are always obliged (obligated?) to desire or seek that these laws be made effective, but are not obliged (obligated?) to obey them when they are not generally effective.

A unified interpretation can be achieved, I believe, by viewing all moral obligations as requirements of reason, and by recognizing that, for Hobbes, reason requires moral actions only when one expects others to behave morally as well. The fundamental obligations are those imposed by the laws of nature, but these are conditional, that is, cancelled when security is lacking for the compliance of others. Obligations of covenant are artificial, as opposed to the natural obligations of the fundamental laws, and rest upon the latter. Undefeated obligations are inconsistent with liberty (Hobbes says that obligation and liberty are inconsistent); but the conditional obligations imposed by the laws of nature are compatible with the complete liberty implied by the right of nature.

This interpretation of moral obligation in Hobbes is supported by the conditional way in which he states the first three laws of nature. Each contains a crucial proviso. The first is to seek peace, but, failing success, to defend oneself; the second is to relinquish the full right of nature, but only if others are willing to do so; the third is to keep agreements, but only if one can be reasonably certain that the other parties will comply as well. Thus in each case moral requirements are cancelled when it can be seen that it would be imprudent to obey them. At the same time it is always prudent to seek to make it prudent for all to obey them, that is, to seek to impose Hobbes's political solution to the paradox of prudence in the state of nature.

We need not conceive moral obligation here directly in terms of prudence. Rather we conceive it as a requirement of reason, and then conceive reason as prudential rationality in the sense defined above. The Hobbesian conception of practical reason is attractive in several ways in this context. First, it makes clear the connection between motivation and the recognition of a course of action as rationally required. Here we are motivated to do what we see as most reasonable to do because we are motivated to adopt the most efficient means to the maximal satisfaction of our informed and coherent desires. Motivation is easy to understand under this conception because it is desire based, although current desires do not always give us good reasons for acting (if they are irrational, for example). Second, and related to the first point, the action guiding aspect of judgments that certain actions are right is straightforward on this view as well. To say that an action is right is to say that each agent has the best reasons to perform it (at least under conditions of security), and the reasons are once more interpreted as above. This direct connection between the judgment that an action is right and the motivation to perform it may prove to be too simple upon reflection, but it has appealed to many philosophers and comes close to capturing the real connection.

The reduction of moral obligation or rightness to prudence again would carry entirely satisfactory implications regarding the possibility of moral knowledge on the model of empirical knowledge. We can achieve knowledge of those policies that are truly in our best interests to follow, although for Hobbes such practical wisdom comes only from experience, which teaches us the long-range effects of our desires and actions. Furthermore, as in the case of goodness, Hobbesian rightness will be a real property in the sense defined earlier. We might know *a priori* that we will have reason to do what is most conducive to the fulfilment of our fundamental ends, especially self-preservation, but what is so conducive is independent of our beliefs on the subject. We must learn through experience and the use of reason that moral obligation coincides with prudence. What we learn here is the truth of the Hobbesian argument: that we have reason to do what will maximally satisfy our rational desires; that pursuit of self-preservation is necessary to all our other rational ends; that peace is a necessary condition of (probable) self-preservation; that acceptance of moral restraint is necessary for peace and the benefits of co-operation; and that it can never be foreseen as prudential to threaten these benefits by breaking moral rules when others are complying with them. At least the latter stages of this argument express or rest on empirical claims.

D. *Objections*

A common objection to egoist moral philosophies is simply that moral demands are among those that typically oppose self-interest; hence the former are not to be identified with the latter. This objection might be telling against Hobbes if he had given us no way to identify moral rules other than as requirements of self-interest. But, of course, that is not so. He identifies moral rules and virtues according to common usage, according to what we ordinarily consider moral behavior and obligations, and then shows that these have a deeper prudential grounding. He accommodates the intuition of a clash between moral demands and self-interested desires by allowing that the former oppose immediate satisfactions of certain natural desires and passions. They equate only with long-range self-interest, in so far as they make possible peaceful relations with others.

A more serious objection is that moral obligations cannot reduce to requirements of self-interest since they exist in order to resolve conflicts among the interests of different agents. If conflicts among interests are real, then moral resolutions of those conflicts cannot maximally satisfy the self-interests of all the parties involved. Hence rightness cannot equate with what is in the maximal self-interest of each and every agent. Or so the argument concludes.

Hobbes's answer to this objection, as we have seen, is to agree that interests clash in the state of nature, but to argue that they coincide to the extent of supporting peaceful, co-operative relations when there is security that others will restrain their natural passions for the sake of these relations and the benefits they afford. Moral rules according to Hobbes express necessary conditions for peaceful interpersonal relations. Such relations can help to achieve the best that each agent can expect, given the interests of other individuals, and can help each agent to do better than she would do in their absence. But this answer is not sufficient as it stands. Hobbes's laws of nature do not exhaust the content of right actions or policies, and he recognizes this fact. Specifically, they do not in themselves fully determine how conflicts among interests of different individuals are to be settled. A complete account of the right must include a theory of distributive justice that will determine the ethically proper resolution of these conflicts.

Although Hobbes does not explicitly provide such a theory, he is not silent on the matter. The laws of nature are to be supplemented here by convention or political and judicial decision. We saw in the initial definition of 'good' that Hobbes allows representatives of commonwealths to decide what is truly good for their members. His sixteenth law of nature requires disputants to submit their conflicts to arbitrators, who will decisively settle them (I, 15, 121). The laws of nature must be implemented by governments or their representatives, and they can do so in different ways. But for Hobbes, however a particular government resolves conflicts among interests within its territory must be considered right there. To think that there are more universally applicable criteria of justice is an illusion; to try to oppose one's own view to the sovereign's decisions on such matters is to risk the greatest of evils, an end to peaceful and stable social relations (II, 29, 238–9; II, 30, 252).

This sort of relativism to some extent accommodates disagreement about what is right or just, as Hobbes's relativistic account of the good allows for differences in desires and disagreements about what is truly desirable. For him rightness, while always conducive to peace, is relative in its more specific content to particular groups, although not to particular individuals. Each individual has self-interested reasons for becoming a member of some such group, and these in turn give him reasons to act in ways determined to be right by the group or its representatives. This is not an implausible account of the source and scope of moral reasons. Nevertheless, the brand of conventionalism and relativism advocated here by Hobbes is unacceptable. We cannot accept that whatever a government determines to be right or just is truly so. (Even Hobbes himself cannot resist adding criteria by which to distinguish good from bad laws, although he avoids direct contradiction by refusing to distinguish just from unjust laws.)

Since this part of the account is unacceptable, there remains a major gap in the full account of rightness. One may have self-interested reasons for generally complying with fair agreements, or with social relations that might have arisen from fair agreements; but individuals will much more rarely be prudent to acquiesce in unfair distributive shares, even if their governments support such injustice. The Hobbesian argument that it is prudentially rational to comply with agreements made, or with existing social arrangements, if others are complying, must therefore contain a tacit appeal to fairness if it is to be plausible.[3] Second, unless either certain distributions are universally right, or we can find some way other than Hobbes's to relativize rightness to groups, we will be unable to specify a single property to which we all refer when we judge distributions right or fair, not even a relational property. The good for each individual may be what it is rational for each to desire. But since what it right must be so for whole groups, a similar account of rightness is far more elusive, given the conflicts within groups and no agreed way to resolve them such that the outcomes must be fair.

I shall return to this problem for the moral realist in later chapters. We may leave it now in order to press a more obvious objection to Hobbes's attempt to reduce moral obligation to prudence. Even if we could all agree on fair ways to resolve conflicts among interests of different individuals, it still seems that sometimes it can be in the interest of some individuals to violate the terms of these fair arrangements. There appear to be situations in which individuals can maximize their own benefits by free riding on or exploiting others, situations in which others are behaving properly, in which exploiters can violate the rights of these others and hence act wrongly, but can benefit themselves, can better satisfy their self-interested desires, by doing so. If it can be reasonable or prudential to break a valid covenant, then the third law of nature is not a rule of reason, or reason cannot be equated with prudence. The Hobbesian equation of morality with rational prudence then collapses.

Hobbes himself puts the objection succinctly in the mouth of his 'Fool', who questioneth, whether injustice . . . may not sometimes stand with that reason, which dictateth to every man his own good; and particularly then, when in conduceth to such a benefit, as shall put a man in a condition, to neglect not only the dispraise, and revilings, but also the power of other men. (I, 15, 114)

His answer here is to agree that wrong actions can be profitable, but to deny that they can be realiably predicted to be so. If we cannot realiably identify exceptions to the rule of thumb that acting morally (when others are) maximizes one's own benefits from social interactions, then we cannot be rational in adopting a policy of violating fair arrangements when we think we can benefit from doing so. If it is not reasonable to predict that such violations will be profitable, then it is not prudential to act on such predictions.

According to Hobbes, there are two reasons why we cannot reliably predict that we will benefit from breaking agreements with which others are complying. First, even in the absence of formal sanctions imposed by a political authority, one may be ostracized from whatever peaceful society or co-operative ventures may be formed if one acquires a reputation of defecting from such ventures whenever it might be perceived to be to one's benefit to do so. One will be excluded from civilized society if others find out about this pattern of behavior, and one cannot reliably predict that they won't find out. This is Hobbes's immediate answer to the Fool:

if he live in society, it is by the errors of other men, which he could not foresee, nor reckon upon; and consequently against the reason of his preservation; and so, as all men that contribute not to his destruction, forbear him only out of ignorance of what is good for themselves. (I, 15, 115)

This prudential obligation to act morally, keep agreements, or abide by arrangements that might have arisen from (fair) agreements, holds only in the context of security that others are acting similarly. This security can be gained in Hobbes's view only by the organization of political institutions with the power to impose sanctions for disobedience of law. But in the political context there is a second source of one's inability to consistently profit from wrongdoing: the effective threat of punishment for the attempt to do so. The formation of government thus plays two distinct but related roles in Hobbes's argument: it affords the security necessary for rendering agreements binding, and it does so by threatening punishments and thus providing additional self-interested reasons for acting in ways that maintain peaceful relations.

Hobbes seems to have thought that the threat of punishment for crimes should always be reliable and severe enough to more than nullify any prospective gain from criminal behavior:

> it is of the nature of punishment, to have for end, the disposing of men to obey the law; which end, if it be less than the benefit of the transgression, it attaineth not, but worketh a contrary effect. (II, 28, 230)

Given the difficulties involved in the detection and conviction of criminals, these threats would have to be severe indeed to have the deterrent effect for which Hobbes hopes. To the degree to which the probability of conviction for a particular sort of crime falls below 50 per cent, the severity of the punishment required for effective deterrence must exceed not only the absolute amount of prospective benefit from the crime, but also the severity of harm to be imposed on the prospective victim (assuming rough equivalence between the latter two amounts, as is common in crimes against property). But then questions arise about the fairness or rightness of carrying out such threatened punishments.

Hobbes seems to assume that an efficient government will make it impossible to rationally predict escaping detection:

> those that deceive upon hope of not being observed, do commonly deceive themselves, the darkness in which they lie hidden, being nothing else but their own blindness; and are no wiser than children, that think all hid, by hiding their own eyes. (II, 27, 220)

He is of course willing to tolerate a far more powerful and ever present government force than we would be willing to accept. The standard objection to his political philosophy at least since Locke is that his cure is worse than the disease of anarchy. Our problem here is that the self-interest of citizens would not be served by making the police and courts powerful enough to threaten and impose punishments sufficient to render it never in a prospective criminal's interest to act wrongly, even were this possible. The costs in terms of resources, loss of privacy, and increased probability of wrongful conviction would outweigh any gain from crime reduction. This would make it imprudent, hence irrational, to try to solve the problem of the rationality of wrongful behavior in this way.

In practice we tolerate a certain level of rational crime rather than attempting to tighten political controls and stiffen criminal penalties to the degree that might approach its elimination. We trade social order for privacy and liberty, reducing the costs of the former by tolerating some costs of the latter. But this reasonable compromise defeats the appeal to prospective punishment in the argument in support of the claim that the risk of wrongdoing can never be worth the projected benefit from the point of view of self-interest.

Hobbes appears to have held that his two prudential reasons for forgoing wrongdoing when others are behaving morally were separately sufficient to override predictions of benefit from such behavior. In fact they are jointly insufficient, since both rely on the probability of detection and future sanctions. whether ostracism or criminal penalty. Hobbes is simply wrong to believe that we never encounter situations in which we can reliably predict that our wrongful behavior would remain undetected and therefore unpunished. Let me illustrate this point again with a contemporary example.

You see an unlocked bicycle and verify that the owner is well out of sight. In fact you can see clearly that no one is in the vicinity. You do not presently own a car or bicycle, but love to ride and would save time riding rather than walking to appointments. We can also imagine that you are not presently in your usual neighborhood, can nevertheless ride there, and will not return to this neighborhood on the bicycle. It certainly seems that in this situation you can reliably predict that your present action will have no negative effects on your future opportunities; in fact your opportunities for future co-operative endeavors with others will be enhanced by your newly-found means of transportation. Your present action need not create a disposition to take imprudent risks in the future either. For one thing, there may be few material objects that give rise to temptations of a similar sort.

(Perhaps you really love bicycles but have been unable to buy one as good as this one; or perhaps your bicycle was recently stolen and you have an unusual and misplaced desire for revenge.) Granted that it would be wrong to take the bicycle; is it really also against your self-interest, imprudent to predict success, and hence irrational to take it?

Perhaps such situations are not very common (although given the rate of successful theft, I would assume that they are). How often we encounter them is irrelevant. As pointed out above, the reduction of moral rightness to (a part of) what is prudentially rational requires at a minimum the complete coincidence of the extentions of the two properties. If there are any cases of prudentially rational but wrongful action, then the reduction does not succeed. And this reduction is in turn necessary if we are to model moral knowledge on empirical knowledge, at least on empirical knowledge of the sort suggested by the Hobbesian account (knowledge of what is in our long-range self-interest, of what maximally satisfies our most coherent set of first- and second-order desires).

I have given an example of individually prudent but immoral or wrong behavior. The same problem for Hobbes's account can occur on a group level. Groups can sometimes trample the rights of members of other weaker or disadvantaged groups with impunity. Here it is generally not the secrey of the actions that protects their perpetrators, but rather their relative power. The extreme case of this sort involves actions or policies that have negative effects on future generations, where there is no question at all of possible retaliation against the present generation.[4] We might benefit from extensive use of resources now that can be predicted to leave subsequent generations in worse material conditions than we now enjoy. Many would judge policies having this long-term result to be wrong or unfair (although there may be problems in specifying to whom they are unfair, especially if they also may affect which individuals are born into later generations). Yet once more they do not seem to be imprudent on the part of those in the present generation; they do not seem to harm *their* self-interest. They conceivably might do so if members of the present generation care about their successors, say their children, and hence their children's children. But appeal to altruism or sympathy, here as elsewhere, cannot save a Hobbesian reduction of the property rightness, since Hobbes argues, and must argue, that moral behavior is prudent in the absence of such fellow-feeling, at least when others are behaving morally.

There is one other response possible to the kind of counter-example offered above, that rests on a different interpretation of prudential rationality. I have been attributing a maximizing conception to Hobbes, according to which it is rational to maximize the satisfaction of one's fullest coherent set of desires. Although this maximizing conception is commonly attributed to him by others as well, it is not entirely clear that this ascription is accurate. While his concept of reason is clearly one of prudence, there is some textual support for the claim that in his view at least the natural human condition requires not a maximizing, but a maximin or disaster avoidance prudential strategy. His laws of nature are justified not directly in maximizing terms, but in order to insure self-preservation, our fundamental motive in Hobbes's view:

> the motive, and end for which this renouncing, and transfer-ring of right is introduced, is nothing else but the security of a man's person, in his life, and in the means of so preserving life, as not to be weary of it. (I, 14, 105)

It is true that self-preservation is necessary for the maximal satisfaction of our other desires. But this point only leaves it open whether Hobbes is appealing ultimately to maximization or to disaster avoidance. In the state of nature both strategies call for pre-emptive action and lack of all restraint, but also for a willing-ness to promote peace and emerge from this condition if others are willing to do so as well. Hobbes's later political argument for unlimited sovereignty appeals more clearly to the idea of maximin or disaster avoidance. He argues that the worst situation under an all powerful sovereign is not as bad as the condition of anarchy that becomes more likely when sovereignty is weakened or divided (II, 18, 141).[5]

If we apply this alternative conception of prudential rationality in evaluating Hobbes's answer to the Fool, then his position appears to gain in plausibility. If agents are to aim not to maximize the satisfaction of their desires, but to avoid disaster; if they should not pursue policies with the highest expected values, but rather those with the best worst outcomes, or those with the lowest probabilities of disaster; then it will be wiser for them to play it safe and restrain their behavior within the rules of social order (once more assuming that others are doing so as well). The worst outcome is to be excluded from society altogether, or, in the political context, given sufficiently severe sanctions, to be caught and punished for violating the rules. Maximin or disaster avoidance would then require not simply reliable identification of situations in which there is a very low probability of being apprehended; it would require that there be no such probability at all (or at least none beyond the unavoidable chance of wrongful conviction), and absolute certainty of there being no such probability. Hobbes may well be correct in claiming that such certainty is not to be had for those who attempt to free ride, exploit, or violate reciprocal relations in political or even prepolitical contexts of interpersonal interactions. If you (as our potential bicycle thief) must avoid absolutely the chance of apprehension, then you had better leave the bicycle where you found it. Prudence interpreted in this way no longer counsels wrongful behavior, and the counter-example disappears.

Two additional objections nevertheless arise. First, although it may not be possible to be certain that one will not suffer the consequences of misdeeds directed toward others in one's society, collectively we can be certain of not being punished for worsening the lot of future generations. Thus, although one counter-example falls to this new interpretation of prudential rationality, the second does not. And there are other cases of a similar kind, for example, that of breaking a promise made to a dying man of which others are unaware. Remember that it does not take many cases of conduct judged wrong but prudent (according to the operative concept of prudence) to defeat the reduction of rightness to prudential rationality (or that part of it concerning relations with others).

The second objection is somewhat deeper and concerns the rationality of the maximin strategy itself. In conditions of dire threat and radical uncertainty, such as obtain in the state of nature according to Hobbes, it may be a reasonable policy to do one's best to avoid the worst possible outcomes, rather than gambling on doing better. But in the context of Hobbes's political society, where most citizens are behaving morally, it does not seem rational to adhere to this conservative strategy. It seems more rational in that context to maximize. Of course, this point presupposes some second-level criterion of rationality by which to assess first-level strategies. We need not beg questions, however, by simply stipulating a higher level criterion that will imply the result we want. Nor need we be concerned about the possibility of a regress here. Rather, we can appeal simply to what strikes us upon reflection as reasonable to do, or to those criteria we employ in deciding what is reasonable to do. We will assume here that whatever deepest criteria of rationality are implicit in our evaluations of agents and their actions are correct, or at least not incorrect. I shall have more to say on this subject in the chapter on Kant, where we will encounter a more controversial notion of reason than those implicit in Hobbes's discussions. Here we need only note that maximin does not afford a plausible criterion of reasonable action in normal conditions, in situations without dire threats. Lacking this criterion, the bicycle example and others like it become reinstated. It becomes yet more obvious once more that wrong actions can benefit their agents.

Hobbes's own reduction of rightness to prudence, and his argument to the Fool that supports that reduction, fails. Before abandoning this approach, however, we may survey some contemporary offshoots of the Hobbesian analysis of moral reasons.

E.   *Variation 1: Tit-for-tat*

Hobbes may have made his argument slightly more difficult than necessary (also more interesting) by holding that it is never rational to accept restraints, attempt to co-operate, or comply with agreements in the absence of security that others will do likewise. According to him, aggressive, pre-emptive strikes constitute the most rational defensive strategy in the state of nature. It is this claim that largely contributes to the prisoners' dilemma or self-defeating character of practical reason in this account of life without governmental authority. By following this strategy each individual loses the possible benefits of peace and co-operation, and collectively all thereby maintain a state of war. But if we accept Hobbes's claim, there is genuine paradox, since each agent at the same time maximizes his own expected value (or minimizes his risk of disaster), given what he can expect from others.

Some modern decision theorists disagree with Hobbes's assessment of rational individual startegy in conditions of uncertainty about the behavior of others. Let us define a set of such conditions more precisely. Assume that each agent has a choice of co-operating or attempting to take advantage of others; all can gain from co-operation as opposed to total non-cooperation; each can nevertheless maximize his own benefits by taking advantage in particular interactions; and finally, there will likely be repeated interactions with the same individuals over time (who therefore may retaliate for past defections). In these conditions initial non-cooperation in the face of uncertainty about others does not appear to be the best strategy. (The conditions as I have defined them do not include dire threats to life, but these dangers, even in the absence of formal threats of punishment, seem to be exaggerated by Hobbes.) Individuals do better in the long run by seeking the benefits of co-operation, at the same time being ready to punish those who attempt to take advantage.

In somewhat more technical terms, strategies that are 'nice' (agents who employ them are not the first to defect from co-operation), provokable (likely to retaliate for past transgressions on the part of others), and forgiving (co-operative again after retaliation) tend to do best in conditions as defined above.[6] One such strategy is 'tit-for-tat'. An agent using it co-operates in the absence of knowledge of those with whom she interacts. If she knows how others most recently acted, she acts likewise toward them. This allows her to reap the benefits of co-operation while discouraging others from taking advantage of her. She will thereby tend to do best over time when interacting with agents who are equally rational, especially if reputations for past behavior are likely to be accurate in her community. If such knowledge is widespread and influences opportunities for future interactions, then those who take advantage on particular occasions will tend to lose out in the long run, since the cumulative benefits of co-operation will likely outweigh the short-run gains from anti-social behavior.

The explanation for the success of tit-for-tat in conditions as defined is similar to Hobbes's argument to the Fool. But while Hobbes warns only against non-performance of covenants when the other parties have performed their parts, the tit-for-tat strategy calls for moral restraint and co-operation at all times, except when the other parties are known to have acted otherwise in immediately prior interactions. The latter therefore may seem to achieve a closer fit between prudence and moral conduct. An adherent will never be the first to act uncooperatively. Retaliation for past wrongdoing appears to be morally permissible as well, at least to the extent of non-cooperation in immediately subsequent encounters. The second feature of the strategy, together with the first, appear to support peaceful relations somewhat more strongly than Hobbes's laws of nature, with their provisos eliminating moral obligation in the absence of security. If we equate the rules of morality with support for peaceful relations, as does Hobbes, then tit-for-tat, despite its label, might be held to achieve the reduction that the Hobbesian seeks.

The problem here, however, is the same as that which ultimately defeated Hobbes's answer to the Fool. The intial conditions required for the rationality of tit-for-tat (or any nice or co-operative strategy), according to the self-interest maximizing conception of rationality, do not universally obtain. First a minor, but very puzzling, point that may seem to nullify the rationality of the tit-for-tat strategy.[7] It seems that its reasonableness depends upon the number of projected future encounters being open-ended (infinite?). If one knows that a particular encounter will be the last, then one will not be deterred by the thought of future sanctions for present behavior, and it will not pay to co-operate. But then if one knows that co-operation cannot pay on the last encounter, and one knows that others know this, then one also knows that co-operation cannot pay on the next to last encounter (since others are not going to co-operate on the last encounter anyway). The regress seems to entail that co-operation never can be rational. And it seems that knowledge that one will not interact with others infinitely suffices to begin this vicious regress.

If the last claim is not rejected, however, we land once more in genuine paradox. For if we accept the implication that co-operation is never rational, we lose all the benefits that co-operation on numerous occasions can afford, and again we all remain worse off than we could have been if we had co-operated. We might reject the requirement of infinite encounters by recognizing that reasoning on its basis depends on the assumption that others will reason in the same way. In fact, people do not generally reason in this way, and so the prediction on which the regress and its implications depend is normally false. It might be claimed that this response to the argument relies on people being irrational. It may seem difficult to argue for the rationality of co-operation based only on the assumption that agents will generally act irrationally. But before we label irrational those who do not reason according to the regress generated above, we should remind ourselves that each agent does better in the long run by ignoring it. In light of that, I believe we would be rational to ignore it as well, at least when agents do not know that their future interactions will be very limited in number.

There is a lesson to be learned nevertheless from the regress argument. It points once more to the same problem that plagued Hobbes's argument to the Fool, namely, that the rationality of moral restraint according to the self-interest maximizing conception depends on the likelihood of retaliation in the future for present misconduct, or upon one's inability to predict escaping retaliation. The truth of the claim that one cannot reliably make this prediction in turn depends on a host of empirical factors. If further interaction with particular individuals or groups is unlikely, if your present behavior is unlikely to be recognized so as to affect your reputation or future opportunities, if the psychology of present potential victims renders them unlikely to retaliate, if you can profitably take advantage now without becoming disposed to attempt to do so in less favorable circumstances in the future, if others are presently acting without restraint and not being penalized for doing so, if you can be reasonably certain that any or all of these conditions obtain, then you can profit from wrongdoing.

Much immoral and anti-social behavior occurs in circumstances in which there is no face-to-face interaction, and the behavior is likely to remain undetected. The bicycle example from the last section may be more trivial than most, but not atypical. The rationality of the restraining tit-for-tat strategy in many contexts, including those in which you are uncertain of the motives of those with whom you interact and uncertain of the probability of future interaction with them or others with whom they might communicate, is irrelevant here. In such circumstances you interact only in the extended sense in which you may harm or violate the rights of someone with whom you have no direct contact. Taking the bicycle will be a departure from your usually rational tit-for-tat strategy, since to your knowledge its owner has never harmed you nor anyone else. But there appear to be no self-interest maximizing reasons not to depart from that strategy here, and ample reason for doing so from the same point of view. Such examples once more defeat the reduction of rightness to this now enlarged notion of prudential rationality.

We have found little difference between Hobbes's conception of rational prudence in the absence of security and this contemporary variation in terms of the proposed account of rightness and its implications for moral knowledge. The extent of congruence between rightness and prudence continues to depend upon many contingent factors: the probability of recognition; the probability of future interaction within the same community; one's own psychology (for example the probability of guilt feelings or embarrassment); the psychology of others with whom one interacts and may interact in the future (for example their inclination to retaliate against wrongdoers); the present extent of moral rule violation; and so on. Complete reconciliation of rightness and prudence would therefore require a more radical departure from Hobbes's explicit argument.

F. Variation 2: Dispositions

Hobbes held that, given the proper generally peaceful context, it is irrational on each occasion to predict profit in the long run from violation of moral rules on that occasion. We have taken exception to that claim. Its falsity defeats the reduction of rightness as proposed by Hobbes. Another possibility, pursued in the contemporary literature by David Gauthier, is to focus the argument on general dispositions to behavior, rather than on particular occasions for action.[8] Although the probability of detection for each of several opportunities for taking advantage of others may be quite low, the probability of being apprehended at some time if one acquires a disposition to take advantage whenever the former probability is low, may be quite high. Perhaps, then, it can be held that the development of a disposition toward moral restraint is prudent, and that action based on a rational (rationally acquired) disposition is also rational. This two step argument might then succeed in the reduction we seek, where the earlier simpler argument failed.

According to this view, we attempt to maximize the satisfaction of our self-interest directly only when choosing which dispositions to acquire. Once we have the proper disposition, we are rational to act on it, even though on particular occasions when we do so, we will not thereby maximize our individual self-interests. This genuine constraint is justified by the long-term benefits (from co-operation) that acting on the rational disposition affords. For either tit-for-tat or Hobbes's strategy (co-operate only when others are co-operating) to be rational, we must expect present interactions to influence opportunities for later ones. This requirement is dropped in the new variation. An agent is to develop a disposition to co-operate on fair terms when the outcome of doing so is better than that for total non-cooperation. The prospective benefit of exploiting others is not to be taken into account on each occasion, and hence the probability of detection becomes irrelevant. Only in this way can individuals consistently reap the benefits of co-operative relations.

Here we have a real distinction in levels to which our maximizing criterion of rationality is applied, similar to the familiar difference between act and rule utilitarianism. For Hobbes there was no such distinction. Although he argues for the prudential rationality of obeying the laws of nature, the fundamental set of moral rules, and therefore has been called a rule egoist,[9] this label is misleading in that rule and act egoism coincide if his argument is correct. According to him, we are prudent on each occasion (given security) to obey the moral rules, because we maximize long-range benefits each time by doing so (at least we must predict this to be the case). The contemporary variation now under consideration denies this and applies the maximizing criterion only at the level of choosing dispositions.

Once more it seems that the variation might achieve a closer fit than the original between prudence (as now interpreted) and moral rightness. It is more plausible to claim that we are prudent in developing moral dispositions than to claim that we maximize self-interest every time we act morally (given that others are doing so). And if it is always rational to act on rationally acquired dispositions, then counter-examples to the latter view do not defeat the reduction of rightness to rational prudence. If a general disposition to moral behavior is rational, then so is each instance of acting on it. Unfortunately two questions must be raised. Is the disposition always to obey moral rules or comply with fair arrangements the rational one to acquire from the point of view of self-interest (assuming that we can acquire dispositions that we view as rational)? Is it always rational to act on dispositions that it is rational to acquire? Let us consider these in turn.

First, we must weigh the long-term satisfaction of self-interest derived from developing a disposition always to act morally (when others are) against other possible dispositions of this sort that we might acquire. I have admitted that the expected value of developing this disposition might well exceed that of the disposition to take advantage whenever the probability of escaping sanctions seems low enough to outweigh the risk on that occasion. Gauthier's argument in favor of the former strategy resembles at the level of choosing dispositions the argument in favor of the Hobbesian strategy of tit-for-tat at the level of choosing actions. It is that individuals disposed to demand more than their fair shares or to violate agreements or peaceful relations in attempting to exceed their fair shares will tend to be found out eventually and excluded from future co-operative ventures and from the benefits that might be derived from them.[10] According to Gauthier, individuals' dispositions need not be totally transparent to each other in order for it to be rational to acquire the disposition to moral behavior when others are restraining themselves. They need be only 'translucent', that is, the probability of one's disposition becoming known must be measured against the benefits from co-operation and losses from probable exclusion from co-operative ventures. This requirement is similar to the argument that present actions will influence later opportunities, but again it is applied only at the level of dispositions.

The question remains why, as rational maximizers of our own self-interests, we should restrict our attention to such rigidly defined character traits as the disposition to act always morally when others are (to comply always with fair agreements), or, at the other extreme, to take advantage whenever it seems profitable to do so. As admitted, the first of these may be more prudent to adopt than the second. If we tried to identify every exception to the rule of thumb that moral restraint is generally prudent, then eventually our immorality would probably be discovered and we might be excluded from certain groups and beneficial interactions. But we can refine our dispositions in this regard considerably by varying the epistemic level of certainty at which we are willing to attempt to take advantage or depart from fair arrangements. Thus, we might restrain ourselves except when we are almost absolutely certain that we will not harm future opportunities by taking advantage. The bicycle example again might illustrate a case of near absolute certainty. Restriction of immoral behavior to such cases can once more be profitable, and the cases would remain numerous enough to defeat the reduction of rightness to rational prudence, construed on the level of dispositions.

It might be replied that such complex dispositions as that just proposed are psychologically implausible, not real dispositions to respond in fixed ways at all. It rather seems to me that such flexible dispositions better reflect the behavior of real agents, especially that of clever self-interest maximizers who lack altruistic feelings toward strangers. More complex dispositions remain more opaque to others as well, making it less probable that they will be discovered.

It might be replied again that an individual so calculating as to adopt a complex disposition that would maximize his narrow self-interest would miss all the pleasures that can be derived from genuinely altruistic attitudes and actions, pleasures gained from the happiness of others. If so, then the self-interest maximizing conception of rationality as applied by the narrow egoists would be individually as well as collectively self-defeating. Two further counterpoints can be made to this reply. First, psychological dispositions can again be finer grained than the reply allows. Agents can derive pleasure from helping those particular other individuals whom they care about, without restraining their selfish maximizing behavior in relation to strangers. Similarly, they can co-operate within particular groups, while taking advantage of outsiders when doing so is profitable. In both cases gaps between self-interest and moral rightness will remain. Second, relying on the development of moral feelings brings us closer to a Humean account of morality than to a Hobbesian account. The former is the topic of the next chapter. But there is a point to be made here as well, namely that the development of genuine feelings toward others appears to be even less under agents' control than the development of dispositions to self-restraint. If so, then it cannot be a requirement of self-interest to develop moral feelings. This may be why Hobbes and Hobbesians intend their arguments to apply to non-altruistic maximizers too.

Finally, while it may not be possible to acquire directly sympathetic feelings for strangers, it might be possible to train people from a young age to have such feelings and, more important, to accept restraints on the pursuit of their narrower self-interests. Since all benefit collectively from the voluntary acceptance by others of such restraints, it is rational for all to institute, support, and publicly advocate a system of education that will aim at this effect. A rational agent will want to make such socializing and moralizing education effective, and, if she wants others to do the same, she will have to submit to it herself, and allow her children to be so educated. Even those for whom it is not entirely effective will then have to pay a psychological price for wrongdoing: publicly condemning how they behave in private. Those who do come to internalize moral norms through this process will then avoid ever-present internal sanctions by acting within the moral rules.

Unfortunately this final reply too remains unable to guarantee the coincidence of rightness and prudence required to reduce the one to the other. If an individual realizes the self-interested rationale behind this feature of the educational system (to encourage *others* to behave morally), then it is difficult to see how it could be effective for her. And if she wants the best for her children (in terms of maximizing their self-interest), then she will explain the rationale to them (when they are old enough to take advantage of opportunities to maximize directly). The psychological price of publicly condemning what she privately pursues should be softened by the recognition that this dual posture is rationally required. Her dispositions, if she is fully prudent and desires most strongly the welfare of herself and her family, will then remain more complex and flexible than the disposition always to act morally. The dispositional variation of the Hobbesian argument agains falls short of successful reduction.

It remains only to assess the second major premise implicit in this variation of the argument, the claim that it is always rational to act on a rationally acquired disposition. For the sake of a convenient and interesting test case, I shall focus on intentions rather than dispositions. This does not alter the question significantly, since the easiest way to acquire a disposition voluntarily, if indeed the argument is correct in assuming this to be possible, is to form an intention or set of intentions. This suggests that, if it is always rational to act on rationally acquired dispositions, then it is always rational to act on rationally formed intentions. But is it?

The issue is brought out most vividly by considering a hypothetical situation in the context of the debate over the policy of nuclear deterrence (a debate with many interesting Hobbesian features). Imagine (I do not believe this to be the case) that the United States can greatly reduce the probability of a first nuclear strike by the Soviet Union by threatening a second strike and maintaining a viable second strike capacity. Imagine also that bluffing is impossible. The only way to make the threat believable and maintain its effect is for American leaders actually to have the intention to launch a second strike in case of Russian attack. Soviet intelligence is too sophisticated for American leaders to fake having this intention (imagine, if you like, more developed methods of psychological analysis then are presently available). In these conditions, given sufficient lowering of the probability of a first strike as an effect, it seems rational for American leaders to form the intention to launch a second strike in case of attack.

Suppose now that our leaders have the intention in question. Suppose also that, despite the lowered probability, something has gone wrong in the Soviet Union, and a first strike has been launched against the United States. Realizing this, American leaders are now faced with the choice of ensuring the annihilation of the entire human race or of saving at least half of it by refraining from launching the remaining missiles. Absent the rationally-formed intention, there can be no question that launching the second strike would be totally immoral and irrational, an act of the same order of depravity as launching a first strike, perhaps worse in causing the end for all time of human civilization. But once the intention has been formed, can it really be rationally required and therefore moral to realize it in an act with this disastrous effect? Would it be irrational and immoral now for the president to change his mind and save the world?

If the intention had been formed on the basis of misinformation regarding the probabilities, then it would not have been rational, and so the leaders would not now be required to carry it out. Suppose that after the first strike is launched, it is thought that this error had been made. Then the president need not destroy the world. He heaves a great sigh of relief (despite his own impending doom). But suppose it is then discovered that the initial probability calculations were correct after all. Must he now once more reluctantly destroy the other half of the world's population?

These questions throw serious doubt on the claim that it is always rational to carry out a rationally-formed intention. And, as argued above, this makes it doubtful that it is always rational to act on the basis of a rationally-acquired disposition. The refutation of that claim, together with the earlier denial that it necessarily maximizes long-run self-interest to acquire a disposition to act morally always, defeat this final variation on the Hobbesian reduction of rightness to rational prudence.

G. Conclusion

There was much of use to our inquiry to be learned from Hobbes. I could find no fault in his reduction of goodness (in the sense of non-moral value in objects) to the rationally desirable. This account accommodates disagreement about what is good in a plausible way by relativizing it away. What is good for one person need not be good for another, although there may be some limits set by biology and psychology, as well as some universal goods, some things that must rationally be desired, in that they serve as means to the satisfaction of the widest range of other desires. This relativity of goodness to subjects with different sets of desires does not imply that each subject automatically knows what is good for him. Desires may be irrational in being misinformed or in failing to cohere with the subject's maximal set. Each of us can then gain knowledge of the good through experience, emotional development, and reflection, although this knowledge remains always fallible and subject to correction and expansion. The epistemological implications of Hobbes's theory of value are entirely plausible.

A realist about value can accept this account, if she is willing to accept the relativism and subjectivism. Judgments about the good are true if they correspond to objects rationally desired by the subjects in question. On the other hand, rationality itself is analyzed here in large part in terms of coherence among subjective states. The full property of goodness is relational, subjective, and complex, perhaps not what many realists about values have had in mind.

Hobbes's theory of moral obligation or rightness is in my view less successful, although once more there was much to be learned there. It is plausible that moral rules exist to make peaceful social relations and co-operative interactions among individuals possible. Each individual has self-interested reasons to join groups governed by such rules, and having joined them, also has reasons to abide by the rules in question. What is implausible is that these reasons always override others that a self-interested agent may have, that it can never be profitable for her to break the rules that generally are to guide her behavior toward others if she is prudent. For better or worse, it is possible in some circumstances to identify reliably exceptions to the rule of thumb that wrong-doing is usually not profitable in the long run. Where these exceptions exist, the reduction of rightness to rational prudence fails.

The analysis of rightness in terms of what is good for individuals (in terms of the universal goods of peace and self-preservation) does not succeed. What appears to be needed, if we are to give an account of moral knowledge similar to the account of knowledge of value suggested above, is a notion of rightness in terms of what is good for the group, or rational for the group to desire. Right actions or policies would be those that are conducive to the good of the group as a whole. The problem here, as we shall emphasize later, is that we once more encounter disagreement as to what is best for a given group. We cannot simply relativize the notion of rightness to groups, as Hobbes relativizes the notion of goodness to individuals, since there may be no agreement *within* the group as to what the proper distribution of goods there is.

Before giving up on the attempt to model moral knowledge entirely on the structure of empirical knowledge, we can re-examine the most plausible form of analysis of moral properties and the problems it encounters in Hume, and then turn to another attempt to analyze rightness in terms of rationality, now under a concept of rationality that may appear more adequate to the task, in Kant.

CHAPTER II

Hume: Subjectivism, Relational Properties, and Utility

We are presently looking at accounts of moral properties implicit in the theories of some of the most prominent ethicists in order to derive a model for an anlaysis of moral knowledge. Specifically, we want to know whether a coherent description of real moral properties can underwrite the model of empirical knowledge as a guide to a proper analysis of moral truth and knowledge. In the case of Hobbes, the view of the good or of (non-moral) value as the object of rational desire seemed plausible and promising as a start toward a full account of value and obligation. On the other hand, the equation of rightness with individual rational prudence failed, and we still lack a solid clue to the nature of a real property of rightness. Hume provides us with a utilitarian criterion that I shall evaluate briefly later in this chapter. But of equal or greater interest is the form of analysis he suggests for moral properties. While not entirely explicit, the implications of his arguments regarding the structure of ethical evaluations and the properties (if any) to which they refer are far more direct than in the case of Hobbes.

Hume is not primarily concerned with the nature of moral knowledge or moral properties. He is primarily concerned to demonstrate the psychological basis for ethical discriminations or evaluations. In keeping with his general epistemology, he debunks reason as a source of moral judgment, and argues that passions or sentiments underlie our evaluations. In his terms, such judgments are based directly, not on ideas or impressions of sensation, but on impressions of reflection, that is feelings. He is specifically interested in evaluations of character or character traits, that is, virtues and vices or what is called moral goodness and badness.

Moral goodness in persons is distinct from the non-moral

goodness of objects or states of affairs, what Hobbes analyzed as the object of rational desire. We cannot analyze good character traits simply as those rational (in the sense of prudence) for each person to desire in himself, since whether it is prudent to desire to be virtuous may depend on one's other desires. (So we concluded in arguing against Gauthier's Hobbesian position in the previous chapter.) Perhaps we could define virtues as traits rational for society to desire in its members, and in that way parallel Hobbes's account of non-moral goodness. But this definition would appeal to a problematic notion of societal desire, and in any case it is not the line that Hume takes. He instead appeals to the less problematic notion of approval, both individual and collective. Virtues are those traits that give rise to feelings expressed in approval; vices the contrary (T III, I, 2, 429).[1]

In general it is relatively non-controversial which traits are considered to be virtues, indeed which are virtues. Kindness, generosity, honesty, courage, and industriousness would be included in the list with little argument, although such traits as temperance, modesty, and chastity might generate somewhat more controversy. When we consider other broader or more specific dispositions that might be subject to moral evaluation, we must encounter the same degree of disagreement that occurs among judgments concerning rightness or just distributions. For one thing, a good or virtuous person is one disposed to act rightly; for another, justice itself is prominently included as a virtue both by Plato and Aristotle and by Hume. Disagreements about rightness will therefore coincide with disagreements about virtues. Even though Hume argues that we typically judge motives, hence character traits, more than actions when making moral evaluations (he ignores here reasoning involved in deciding how to act), we can translate what he has to say about the former into language referring to the latter. Indeed, many of Hume's arguments refer to the structure of moral evaluations and properties generally. And he does include a brief analysis of the notion of obligation to mirror his analysis of moral goodness: to say that an agent ought to perform an action or has an obligation to perform it is to say that her failing to perform it displeases in a certain way or elicits disapproval (T III, II, 5, 460).

Thus we may turn to Hume's arguments regarding the psychological sources of evaluations of character in order to draw their implications regarding the nature of moral properties generally.

A. *Arguments Against Objectivism*

In arguing that moral evaluations are based on sentiment, not reason, Hume implies (and indeed sometimes states directly) that there are no objective moral properties to be found in persons or situations (properties independent from our subjective states when we ascribe them). These two claims may be equated because Hume uses 'reason' in this context in a very broad sense, to refer to the apprehension of matters of fact, that is objective non-relational and relational properties, as well as the inference of facts or relations from others. If moral judgments are not based on reason in this sense, then they do not refer to objective facts, facts that obtain independently of subjective states of evaluators. The converse is also true.

Hume's first argument regarding the source of moral discriminations appeals to the motivating force of moral judgments, to what he sees as their intrinsically action guiding function. According to him, reason, the apprehension or inference of simple facts or relations among ideas or in the world, cannot in itself move us to action. Reason as the source of beliefs about objective facts, the apprehension of any objective state of affairs, does not motivate us without the presence of desire or aversion (I Appx. I, IV, 111). Knowledge of the existence of objects and their intrinsic properties, together with knowledge of relations among these objects and properties, is relevant to action in focusing desires and in informing us of the means to satisfy them. But desires and aversions themselves are the main motivating forces. Action results from factual beliefs plus desires, never from the former or from the faculty that is its source, alone.

The second premise of this argument is that moral evaluations in themselves do guide our actions. At least Hume appears to argue so. This nevertheless cannot be quite right as stated, since, according to Hume, moral judgments do not directly express desires or aversions, but rather feelings: sentiments of approval and disapproval. But we can take him to be arguing that such judgments are much more directly connected to motivations and actions than they would be if based on reason alone. The feeling of approval is pleasant according to him, while a negative moral judgment arises from a feeling that is unpleasant. He tells us that the impression we derive from contemplating virtue is agreeable and that from vice 'uneasy' (T III, I, 2, 424). A pleasant feeling leads us to desire the object that causes it, while an unpleasant feeling causes an aversion to the object that causes it. In this way moral evaluations naturally motivate, although only by means of the desires and aversions with which they are normally associated. On a deeper level Hume holds that moral judgments are based on sympathy, the ability to feel what others feel. When these feelings are unpleasant, they prompt disapproval of those who cause them in others and in oneself, as well as the desire to avoid such characters and character traits. In this way too Hume's account shows how evaluations can naturally motivate.

I have been trying to clarify Hume's claims that moral judgments move us to action, while reason itself does not. In doing so I have appealed to his theory of the sources of such judgments in order to show how they can motivate within his broader psychological framework. Of course his argument here runs in the other direction – from the premises about motivation to the conclusion regarding the sources of the judgments. He does provide independent support for the more controversial of his two premises, the claim that moral judgments in themselves move us to action. He argues first that, if such discriminations did not motivate and lead to socially beneficial behavior, we would not expend so much time and effort trying to teach and train people to make them properly. Second, he points out that moral philosophy, which attempts to elucidate the character of these judgments, has always been recognized to be practical, and not merely theoretical. Third, he claims that we often observe agents to be moved by moral considerations (T III, I, 1, 413–4).

Unfortunately, none of these points establishes the premise that Hume needs in his main argument. It is true that we try to train people, especially our children, to be moral, but this seems to involve not only teaching them to make moral judgments, but training them to be motivated to act in accord with moral requirements. Thus our efforts count against Hume's claim rather than in favor of it. The second supporting argument is little better. Moral philosophy may serve a practical purpose only for those already motivated to do what they come to believe is moral. The fact that philosophers (even of the caliber of Aristotle) have regarded ethics as a practical discipline certainly does not establish that it can have practical effect in the absence of prior motivation. Lastly, agents, of course, are often moved by moral considerations, and they can be perceived to be so moved. But the question remains whether moral evaluations in themselves move them, or whether their actions result rather from prior, independent desires or intentions to do what is right.

This last crucial question (for Hume's argument against reason as the source of moral judgments) is more difficult to answer than it might appear. It might seem that the numerous cases of agents failing to do what they know to be right, and indeed seeming indifferent to recognized moral requirements, defeat Hume's claim that moral evaluations intrinsically motivate. But he never denies that moral motivations can be overridden causally by self-interested motives. He claims only that there is some intrinsic inclination to be moral in all of us, based on the universal capacity for sympathy, for feeling what we perceive others to feel. In Hume's terms, the idea derived from observing another's feeling (or the behavior that signals the feeling) tends to give rise to a corresponding impression. But this impression and the desire to pursue or avoid what causes it may be relatively weak compared to other feelings and correlative desires. Thus the evidence of immoral actions, even seeming indifference to moral demands, remains compatible with Hume's thesis that moral judgments in themselves motivate. On the other hand, if we take seeming indifference on the part of professed amoralists at face value, take it to indicate genuine indifference, then we must relinquish Hume's claim.

In regard to those persons who are moved often to do what they believe to be right, it may seem inconsequential for Hume's position whether they are so motivated only in virtue of an independent desire to be moral persons. After all, he could still claim that, in virtue of their capacity for sympathy, they have a tendency to form such desires. But it is important for the analysis of moral judgments whether they arise from feelings immediately connected to desires and aversions, feelings of approval and disapproval resulting from other feelings that express the capacity for sympathy. For our purposes here, given the failure of Hume's independent supporting arguments for the claim that moral judgments intrinsically motivate, the main argument may be question begging. It seems to be Hume's view that reason is limited to the apprehension of objective facts and relations, and that such apprehension does not in itself motivate action, that leads him to deny that moral judgments can be based solely on reason (T III, I, 1, 414, 417). But we are interested in the claim that moral discriminations do not consist in the apprehension of objective facts or relations, implying that there are no objective moral properties (hence that empirical knowledge does not afford a model for ethical knowledge).

Fortunately, Hume provides another argument for the claim that interests us, one based on appeal to the phenomenology of moral evaluation. He points out that when we consider the virtue or vice manifested in any action, say an act of charity or willful murder (his example), we must know all the relevant facts *before* making a proper moral judgment (I A ppx. I, II, 108; T III, I, 2, 423). The evaluation of the act or of the character of its perpetrator does not involve the observation or inference of some additional objective fact beyond those (psychological) facts already observed or inferred. When we witness an act of gratuitous violence, we do not first observe the anger, cruelty, pain and harm and then observe or infer to an unobservable additional property of wrongness in the action. According to Hume, we simply react affectively once we grasp all the relevant facts.

This argument is strongly reminiscent of Hume's arguments earlier in the *Treatise* on physical substance, the self, and, most famously, on causality. He directs our attention to the experience involved in forming beliefs on these matters. He implores us to resist the misleading character of such experience and to attend closely to its sources and objects. We must in all cases resist the temptation to project subjective elements, feelings derived from the sequence of impressions, into the objective fabric of the world. In the case of causality, we perceive regular succession or constant conjunction among events and project a feeling of necessity derived from the natural progression of ideas. In contexts of moral evaluation, we perceive, for example, positive utility and project our feeling of approval.[2] By examining the sources of beliefs in all these areas, Hume claims to discover that they originate from additions to the objective data supplied by our sentiments or psychological processes. This recurrent theme in the *Treatise* might make one more suspicious of Hume's moral phenomenology (perhaps it is doctored to fit the general pattern); or, on the other hand, it might be taken to add coherence and support to the account.

In the case of ethical evaluation, Hume seems to be correct that all non-moral facts must be appreciated before a proper moral judgment can be made, and that this requirement makes it at least puzzling how that judgment could refer to some additional objective fact or property in the situation being evaluated. The contemporary version of this argument points to the fact that moral properties (or, not to beg questions, moral judgments) must supervene on non-moral properties or beliefs: there can be no differences among the former without correlative differences among the latter. Why should this be so, if moral judgments refer to properties beyond the non-moral properties of the situations under consideration? It seems that only some reductive analysis could explain this connection, at least if moral properties are conceived as non-relational or purely objective. But Hume explicitly denies any such identification when he argues that all the facts of the matter must be apprehended before we can make proper moral judgments. While he appeals to the phenomenology of the experience of evaluating in supporting this claim, we might also question why, if moral properties are to be identified so directly with objective properties, so much disagreement should persist at both the practical and philosophical levels as to the correct identification.

Hume provides a separate argument to the conclusion that moral properties cannot be identified with objective relations. According to him, lower animals and even inanimate objects can stand in all the same relations on which our moral judgments might be based. Since in these cases observation of the relations in question does not provoke censure or praise, moral properties cannot be identified with the relations in themselves (T III, I, 1, 418, 421, 422; 2, 425; I Appx. I, IV, 111). This particular argument is flawed by Hume's restricting its scope to those relations previously considered in the *Treatise*. But he does challenge us to specify some new relation to which our moral discriminations refer. If we restrict attention to purely objective relations, as Hume's argument here implicitly requires, then he seems to be correct that we cannot meet the challenge. What shows that we cannot is that the previous arguments regarding simple objective facts apply equally well to objective relations.

I have not yet addressed Hume's most notorious argument against identifying moral with objective properties, the passage on deriving an 'ought' from an 'is'. In fact I have given this passage the same priority given to it by Hume: it occurs as an afterthought. After presenting his other arguments against identifying moral judgments with apprehensions of objective facts, Hume notes that other moral philosophers often unwittingly pass from premises about the latter to conclusions couched in normative terms. He then writes:

> as this *ought*, or *ought not*, expresses some new relation or affirmation, it is necessary that it should be observed and explained; and at the same time that a reason should be given, for what seems altogether inconceivable, how this new relation can be a deduction from others, which are entirely different from it. (T III, I, 1, 423)

Thus Hume demands that such transitions be explained and holds it to be inconceivable that one could deduce moral propositions regarding obligations from propositions stating objective facts.

Obviously he is not simply pointing here to the truism that a term ('ought') cannot appear in the conclusion of a deductive argument without also appearing in the premises. First, 'ought' is not a predicate term of the sort involved in that fallacy. Second, the question is whether the moral term can be reduced to a predicate of that sort. Presumably, 'right' would do the trick. To say that an agent ought to perform an action is to say that the action is the right thing for her to do. But third, the question then becomes whether rightness is a property reducible to objective properties picked out by propositions containing 'is'. If so, then the deductions can proceed, although such identities will have to be made explicit before they will be perspicuous. Hume, of course, denies that such reductions will be possible, but he must rely here on his earlier arguments against this possibility.

He is not, I take it, opposing all transitions from claims about facts to claims about obligations or virtues. Indeed, he prides himself on his empirical, sociological method for deriving a correct moral theory. According to this method, by observing which character traits in fact elicit approval and which disapproval, we can discover the true virtues and vices and the true nature of virtue and vice. Exceptions are made for errors and incoherence, but these are also in a broad sense factual matters. If virtues are those traits that elicit rational approval, and if such approval is based on certain factual bases (mainly utility) and a universal psychological capacity (sympathy), then we can derive true statements about virtues from propositions referring to these facts. And if right actions are those that virtuous agents would perform, then perhaps we can also derive statements about obligations, those in the language of 'ought', in the same way according to Hume's theory. What he must be denying once more is rather the reduction of moral to purely objective properties. As he pointed out before, in the act of morally judging, we do not deduce or infer a further fact from those observed. Instead we react affectively. On the philosophical level, only by taking account of both the objective facts and our subjective reactions can ethicists develop the proper theory of moral judgment. But all these points rely on Hume's earlier arguments. The 'is-ought' passage at best obliquely summarizes them.

In the introduction I pointed out that 'ought' statements could be analyzed into statements about reasons for acting or believing. Moral 'ought' statements can be analyzed non-controversially into propositions ascribing the best moral reasons for action. This is not controversial precisely because it leaves open whether having such reasons is an objective, factual matter, or whether it depends on the subject's desires, attitudes, moral beliefs, or other subjective states. Hume could once more accept this translation as compatible with his arguments against objectivism.

I have found at least one of those arguments, as it was supplemented above, compelling. When we judge a person to be good or an action to be right, we are not *simply* noting some objective fact about him or some objective feature of the context in which the action is to be performed. We seem also to be expressing approval and perhaps recommending to others a similar attitude toward the person or intention to perform the act. Perhaps, then, the moral properties to which we allegedly refer can be analyzed in terms of relations between their objective bases and our subjective reactions. We may look to interpretations of Hume's positive view for further guidance in this direction.

B.   Varieties of Subjectivism.

In laying out his positive view of moral evaluations, Hume claims that they are 'derived from a moral sense' (T III, I, 2, 424). This might mislead some casual readers to liken his position to G. E. Moore's theory of moral intuition. Hume's claim that moral judgments do not express ordinary factual beliefs, since the latter do not move us to action, leaves it open that we might possess a special moral sense that intuits special moral properties in objects that do intrinsically motivate us. But apart from the queerness of this view, it is incompatible with Hume's other arguments against objectivism and with his statement of his own view. Hume, as we saw, argues that we must be aware of all relevant facts before evaluating, that an evaluation is not an inference or observation of any additional fact or property in the object itself, and that the immediate basis of moral distinctions lies in our sentiments, in feelings of approval and disapproval derived from contemplation of the objects of evaluation. These claims entail a subjectivist or relational view, but there remain several possible specifications of Hume's position. We must choose among them on the basis of clues in his writings and on grounds of intrinsic plausibility and usefulness, since he himself does not explicitly distinguish these possible interpretations.

Perhaps the simplest interpretation with some support in the texts is that, according to Hume, our moral judgments are reports of certain feelings we have when we contemplate the traits or actions under judgment. He writes:

> when you pronounce any action or character to be vicious, you mean nothing, but that from the constitution of your nature you have a feeling or sentiment of blame from the contemplation of it. (T III, I, 1, 423)

Later in the *Treatise* he says:

> The pain or pleasure which arises from the general survey or view of any action or quality of the mind, constitutes its vice or virtue, and gives rise to our approbation or blame. (T III, III, 5, 546)

The writing in at least one of these passages must be imprecise, since Hume is not quite consistent. In the first passage he seems to identify the viciousness of a vice with the feeling of blame that its perception causes; in the second, he holds that vice is constituted by the feeling of pain that gives rise to the feeling of blame. Perhaps these passages can be reconciled simply by noting that for Hume a sentiment of blame is itself unpleasant, so that there may be little to distinguish in the feelings to which he refers. In any case, these passages certainly suggest that moral judgments report feelings, and that moral properties therefore reduce to mental properties of persons at the time they are engaged in evaluating.

Before commenting on the plausibility of such a view and its compatibility with Hume's earlier arguments, we must immediately modify its statement to take account of Hume's reference in the second passage quoted to a 'general survey or view'. What is reported, it seems, cannot simply be what the evaluator feels at that moment, since she may be reacting personally to the action or trait being judged. She may be reacting primarily to its effect on her, but this is not what a moral judgment intends to convey. The feeling to which a moral judgment intends to refer must arise from an impartial perspective according to Hume (T III, I, 2, 426). The feelings involved in genuine moral evaluation arise from sympathy, not self-love, and they arise only when we consider character traits and actions in abstraction from all merely personal interest. Moral judgments for Hume, as for Kant and in contrast to Hobbes, must be impartial, and in the *Inquiry* he explicitly assigns to reason the task of correcting for personal biases and distortions of view. That this task is required is clear, according to Hume, because we intend to judge past and distant characters and actions, those which cannot have any effects on us personally, in the same moral terms as we judge our friends and enemies. Indeed we can recognize that our friends sometimes act badly and our enemies well. We can recognize that even when we would prefer the opposite, that is, when we feel negatively about it.

I argued above that the fact that personal feelings can dominate our affective response even at the moment we judge morally indicates that such judgment cannot simply report what we are feeling at the time. An alternative way to accommodate the requirement for impartiality is to hold that we can have both positive and negative, both moral and personal, feelings at the same time toward the same object, and that moral evaluation reports only on the impartial feelings. Another problem, however, for this view is that, according to Hume, moral judgments must be not only impartial or detached in the view they express, but must be also consistent and rational in their apprehension of the objective properties of their objects. He dismisses those moral judgments based on superstition and specifically condemns what he calls 'monkish virtues' – self-denial, abstinence, etc. – for lacking the usual objective grounds for positive evaluation (utility or agreeableness). Despite being praised by some, these are not genuine virtues. They may cause a sentiment of approbation in some evaluators, but this does not lead Hume to say that such traits are virtues for them. Thus a genuine moral judgment cannot be simply a report on whatever feeling is caused in the context. The attitude involved must be consistent with those that underlie other moral evaluations. It must not be based on false beliefs about the traits or actions that occasion it (such as the religious person's beliefs that the monkish virtues are useful for getting to heaven or agreeable to God).

Thus, if moral judgments are to be reports of feelings or attitudes ('sentiments', according to Hume), they must be reports of feelings that a rational evaluator would experience in the presence of the traits or actions under evaluation. In the *Inquiry*, Hume changes from speaking of expressing or reporting one's own attitudes to referring to the general approvals and disapprovals of those in the moral community. This may not be a significant change for him, since he believes that all persons share the same moral attitudes, based on the same objective features of actions and ultimately on the same capacity for sympathy. I have suggested that a more radical change would be more in keeping with his critical arguments, a change to speaking of hypothetical attitudes or feelings in rational evaluators. Knowledge of moral good and bad and of right and wrong on this view is knowledge of what arouses approval and disapproval when one is impartial, informed, and consistent.

This emphasis on rational evaluation may appear to be inconsistent with limitations that Hume places on the scope of rationality earlier in the *Treatise*. Although he uses 'reason' in a broad sense to include the apprehension of any objective fact, he limits what can properly be said to be reasonable to objective beliefs, to what can represent truly or falsely. Thus for him preferences or desires in themselves cannot be irrational or rational, and actions based on them are not to be directly judged reasonable or unreasonable either. Since moral beliefs are not reports of objective beliefs, the demand that these be evaluations of rational subjects may appear to be empty for Hume, to place no real constraints on their contents. But in fact he holds that actions may be indirectly unreasonable, if based on misinformation regarding their likely effects. This is one of the ways in which I have claimed that he views certain evaluative judgments as unreasonable too. His criticism of certain types of moral judgment indicates other ways as well. Purported ethical evaluations are to be dismissed if based on purely personal or self-interested reactions, or if they are inconsistent with (the non-moral grounds of) other settled moral judgments. Since Hume assigns to reason the role of correcting for personal bias, since inconsistency is a universally recognized mark of irrationality (although Hume does not explicitly emphasize or recognize this when it comes to preferences), and since he also allows that actions or sentiments can be derivatively unreasonable if based on factual error, he suggests that these constraints can indeed be captured by the demand that moral judgments report sentiments of rational evaluators. This demand is compatible with his attacks on reason as the sole source of moral judgment, with his arguments that such judgments are neither *a priori* or necessarily true or false, nor statements of objective facts. It is also implicit in his critical normative passages.

The modified subjectivist account is finally more plausible in itself, since it could explain moral disagreement and argument, as an analysis of evaluations as reports of actual personal feelings could not. The fact that your personal feeling is different from mine in itself provides little ground for argument, and reports of different feelings would not contradict one another. But differing reports on what rational evaluators approve do provide a basis for rational argument. Beyond this advantage, this account also might do better in explaining the connection that Hume assumes between evaluation and motivation or action. A report on a personal reaction might not move another person to action; and a report on what most people approve might not provide personal motivation, since one might be convinced that the majority is mistaken in its evaluation. But a report on how a rational evaluator would react should motivate one to react (and hence to act) likewise, at least if one is moved by genuine moral reasons.

Before suggesting another modification in the description of the most plausible Humean position, we must consider a different sort of view. The connection between evaluation and action, as well as Hume's denial that an 'ought' can be derived from an 'is', and his claim that evaluations are in some sense infallible (T III, II, 9, 491), seem to be captured better by the view that moral judgments express, rather than report on, feelings or attitudes. Hume does not distinguish this emotivist position from the view considered above. But the former is more in keeping with at least some of his explicit claims and arguments. The expression of a feeling might be more contagious and hence a better spur to action than a factual report on one's psychological state. If moral judgments are not propositional at all, then they cannot be deduced or inferred from factual propositions, and the general opinion (expression) on virtues and vices cannot be mistaken (as Hume says in the *Treatise* that it cannot). On the other hand, this last implication seems inconsistent with Hume's practice of criticizing certain sorts of evaluation, as described above. The emotivist view can ascribe a kind of derivative error in attitude or sentiment, if the feeling expressed arises because of a mistaken view of its object or of the object's effects. In fact, it can accommodate disagreement better than the view that evaluations report on (personal) feelings. Emotions or attitudes can clash, but reports by individuals of their feelings will not generate genuine disagreement.

There remain nevertheless more serious objections to emotivism, both as an interpretation of Hume's theory of evaluation and as an independently plausible meta-ethic. For one thing, I noted above that I can make a positive moral judgment even though I feel negatively about the person's having good traits or acting rightly (if he is my rival, for example). How then can I be expressing my feeling in so judging? The psychology here must be at least complex and its phenomenology misleading. Second, the emotivist view must accommodate not only disagreement in moral judgment, but rational argument that aims not simply at getting the objective facts right; and it must explain how we can take moral questions seriously, how we can wonder and agonize over what is the right thing to do.

Even when evaluators appear to agree on the objective facts of the situation, they may disagree in their evaluations. We may agree on the facts of fetal development and yet disagree on the morality of abortion, or agree on cases of past injustice and present qualifications and yet disagree on whether preference should be given to a black woman applying for a position in our philosophy department. This may not bother the emotivist who, unlike Hume, is willing to admit that different persons may have different reactions to the same facts. What is puzzling for this position, however, is that such persons may continue to engage in rational argument, pointing to analogous and disanalogous cases to support their positions and attack their opponents'. When not engaged in such argument against the views of others, we may still employ the same form of reasoning in trying to decide how to act in morally controversial contexts. In trying to decide for whom to vote for the position in my department, I may think of other cases in which compensation is owed to past victims of injustice and try to see how this case is like and unlike those others. I engage in such reasoning after becoming clear on the facts of the present case. I shall have more to say on the structure of such reasoning in later chapters. Hume himself seems to employ a variation of it when he dismisses the monkish virtues as inconsistent with our most coherent set of moral evaluations (as based rather on superstition).

The point here is that we apparently seek to discover what is morally right. We seek moral truth and knowledge as a guide to conduct, if we are interested in acting as we morally ought to. This cannot be a matter of trying to discover our own emotions, a kind of psychoanalytic exercise. Nor is it limited to the discovery of the objective features of the situation. The emotivist is therefore hard pressed indeed to accommodate this form of argument and inference. Indeed, it is hard to see how for him there can be moral knowledge at all. It is not simply that empirical knowledge won't do as a model. Moral judgments, not being genuinely propositional, cannot express truths or be known. This implication seems to be both far from Hume's intent and untrue to our ethical practice. At least it is far too early in this investigation to accept that skeptical outcome.

We must therefore seek to reinterpret Hume again in continuing to search for a plausible account of moral properties. In doing so, we may return to our modification of Hume's account of the sentiments or attitudes involved in moral judgments, but now with more attention to the objective contexts in which these reactions arise.

C. *The Relational View*

The most plausible version of the view of moral judgments as reports on feelings held that these feelings must be those that would arise in a rational (informed, impartial, and consistent) evaluator from the contemplation of the traits or actions being judged. In drawing the implications of such a view for an account of moral knowledge, it seemed necessary to speak of the relation between the traits or actions in question and the rational reactions of evaluators. Virtues are those traits that elicit approval from rational evaluators, and knowledge of virtues is knowledge of what does elicit such approval (and perhaps of why it does so). Here we must focus not simply on the affective reaction itself, but on what elicits it. Focusing on the relation rather than simply on the subjective side of it generates an account of moral properties that seems both more plausible in itself and truer to the Humean texts. After all, moral judgments appear to refer to the traits and actions being judged and not simply to our reactions to them. And Hume is very much concerned to discover the objective bases for rational subjective evaluations and to use this discovery as grounds on which to criticize certain moral judgments as irrational.

The textual support for this interpretation of Hume on moral properties (or on the referents of moral judgments) is more prominent in the *Inquiry* than in the *Treatise*. In the later work there is more emphasis on the role of reason (in the broad sense noted above) in moral evaluation. Hume points out that moral judgments differ from matters of pure subjective taste in that 'truth is disputable, not taste' (I I, 5). He notes explicitly that reason and sentiment co-operate in producing moral judgment (I I, 6). Whereas in the *Treatise* the emphasis seems to lie in refuting the rationalists in ethics, he seems more concerned in the *Inquiry* to expose the objective bases for moral evaluations. The shift is subtle, but it is reflected also in his explicit definitions of virtue and vice in the latter work:

> It is the nature, and indeed the definition of virtue, that it is a quality of the mind agreeable to or approved by everyone who considers or contemplates it. (I III, 8, 83) [Hume's hypothesis] defines virtue to be *whatever mental action or quality gives to a spectator the pleasing sentiment of approbation;* and vice the contrary. (I Appx. I, 1, 107)

Hume is clearly directing our attention here to the objects of evaluation and their properties, as these relate to our approvals and disapprovals. Being virtuous is being such as to elicit rational approval. Moral knowledge is knowledge of what features of traits and actions elicit such approval, and it is such knowledge that Hume is after. Some traits really are virtues and others are not, although they may sometimes be judged to be so. Whether a particular trait is a virtue depends on whether it shares the common grounds on which virtuous actions rest (utility or immediate agreeableness).

According to the present interpretation, moral judgments refer to dispositions in characters or actions to elicit rational approval or disapproval in virtue of certain of their features. They refer to relational properties of these objects, to relations between their objective features and our subjective rational responses (where a response is rational if informed, impartial, and consistent with others). Actually, this statement of the position is still oversimplified, since the features (utility and immediate agreeableness) on which our rational responses are based are themselves relational rather than purely objective. We might therefore think of moral properties as second-order relations, those based on other relations between objective properties and subjective reactions.

We may compare the plausibility of this account with that of the more purely subjective analyses on the grounds previously considered. These included the explanations of supervenience of moral on non-moral properties, of disagreement and rational argument in ethics, of the connection between evaluation and action, and of the connections between statements of objective facts and moral judgments (Hume's 'is-ought' argument). One might think that the relational account explains supervenience, since being such as to elicit rational approval reduces to having certain non-moral (objective or first-order relational) properties. But that is not quite true. The moral relational property depends also on subjective properties of rational evaluators, on their other subjective attitudes and capacities (for example, sympathy), and perhaps (as we shall see) on their moral beliefs. Supervenience therefore must be viewed here as a demand for consistency as part of the rationality of these evaluators. One is inconsistent in one's moral judgments if one judges persons or actions with the same non-moral properties differently. The demand for consistency may be linked also to the action guiding aspect of moral judgments. If moral evaluations are intended to suggest courses of action, and they are inconsistent in the way specified, then actions that follow these suggestions are likely to be self-defeating. We will be unable to formulate any consistent set of objectives for them.

These remarks are relevant also to an interpretation of Hume's position on 'is' and 'ought' according to the view now ascribed to him. From a description of the object of evaluation in itself, one cannot deduce how a rational evaluator will react. As pointed out, this depends on her psychology as well. Hume may have been referring in his argument to the impossibility of a deduction of that sort. On the other hand, if 'right' means such as to elicit rational approval, and such approval is based on common objective (or non-moral relational) bases, then we can derive 'oughts' from more complex 'is's'. We saw above that this possibility may not contradict Hume's intent in the argument in question. Indeed it is implicit in his method of arriving at the non-moral grounds for rational moral judgments. He argues only that such complex derivations require explanation, and that they do not consist in deductions of moral judgments from descriptions of purely objective properties. The relational view of moral properties provides the needed explanations.

The action-guiding aspect of moral evaluations (according to Hume) may seem to support an emotivist rather than relational account. At least the former will have the advantage here if the apprehension of properties in itself can never move us to action. We noted above that the expression of a feeling may be more contagious and more immediately connected to arousal of desires than reports on feelings. Reports on connections between non-moral properties and reactions may seem to offer little improvement in this regard over reports of feelings alone. But once more, if the property reported is that of being such as to elicit rational approval, if one wants to be rational, and if, as Hume claims, approvals, being pleasant, connect with desires for what cause them, or, finally, if one simply wants approval from rational peers, then the connection between moral evaluation and action may be close enough on this account to suit Hume and us.

Moral judgments as now characterized can serve both reporting and prescribing functions. In fact, the emotivist may lack any advantage in helping us to understand why an evaluator would want to spread his feeling to others. On that view the explanation would lie in his wanting to cause actions toward which he feels positively. But if he also believes that his reaction is rational (informed, impartial, and coherent with grounds for other judgments) in relation to features of the actions in question, and if he wants others to have similarly based attitudes and to act according to them, then he will have additional reason to seek to prescribe actions based on his attitudes.

Lastly, the relational account of moral properties, together with the demand for consistency in our evaluative reactions to non-moral properties, make comprehensible the nature of moral argument and reasoning. Reference to the objective or non-moral side of the relation explains why moral judgments must be fully informed; reference to rationality in the present sense entails the requirement of impartiality; and the demand for consistency explains why argument by analogy and difference is relevant to the quest for moral truth and knowledge. This appears to be the main advantage of the present account over emotivism, at least as the latter doctrine is normally construed. It also reflects the way in which this account accords with Hume's practice of validating and criticizing ascriptions of moral virtue.

Although Hume states this analysis most explicitly in the *Inquiry*, a comparison that he draws in the *Treatise* affords the best additional insight into the nature of moral properties as so defined. He writes:

> Vice and virtue, therefore, may be compared to sounds,
> colours, heat, and cold, which, according to modern philo-
> sophy, are not qualities in objects, but perceptions in the mind.
> (T III, I, 1, 423)

This passage can be extremely instructive if we emphasize Hume's appeal to secondary qualities as construed by 'modern philosophy', especially by Locke, and if, in light of the reference to a Lockean account of such properties, we ignore as loose talk (once more designed to contrast moral with purely objective properties) the characterization of these properties as (wholly?) in the mind rather than in objects. According to Locke, secondary qualities are not in the mind. Rather, they are powers or dispositions in objects, in virtue of certain of their primary qualities (or certain primary qualities of their 'insensible parts'), to cause certain ideas in us, that is, to appear to us in certain ways.[3]

What Hume describes here as the doctrine that secondary qualities are not in objects may be Locke's claim that no qualities in objects resemble our ideas of secondary qualities, that is, these properties as perceived – their phenomenal, sensuous aspects. In regard to this relation of resemblance, Locke holds that our ideas or perceptions of primary qualities differ from ideas of secondary qualities. Primary qualities themselves are non-relational, not to be analyzed in terms of ways they appear to subjects. But ideas of primary qualities resemble those qualities in objects, while ideas of secondary qualities do not. Despite this difference, secondary qualities as Locke characterizes them are equally real, at least according to our definition of real properties. Being such as to appear in a certain way under certain conditions is independent from actually appearing that way or being believed to appear that way.

One might question Hume's analogizing moral properties to secondary qualities as Locke conceives them, since the former seems to side with Berkeley in dismissing that account earlier in the *Treatise*. The view that secondary qualities (and perhaps primary qualities also) are just 'perceptions in the mind' may be closer to Hume's epistemological metaphysics than is the Lockean view described above. But Hume's moral philsophy seems rather to presuppose the realist's world that he questions earlier, and he admits even in the earlier discussion that such a position seems inescapable from the practical point of view. He makes it clear in the brief passage quoted that he is likening moral properties to secondary qualities as other philosophers conceive them. Despite misdescribing their view, it seems obvious that he is referring to such figures as Galileo, Descartes and Locke, rather than to

Berkeley. What makes this clear is the implicit contrast between secondary and primary qualities (only the former are mentioned in the passage), a contrast that Berkeley rejected as part of his dismissal of Locke's account of both.

Despite the analogy to which Hume points, there are ontological differences between relational moral properties and secondary qualities as characterized by realists. Secondary qualities consist in objects being such as to cause them to appear certain ways to normal perceivers in normal conditions. Positive moral evaluations are not perceptually caused, and moral properties are not those eliciting particular moral evaluations in normal subjects. Moral evaluations may be elicited by the thoughts of certain actions or traits whether in their presence or not; there is no moral sense akin to the perceptual senses. To ascribe moral properties relative only to normal evaluators would imply that the latter cannot be wrong in their evaluations in normal conditions, much as normal perceivers (at least as a class) cannot err in their color ascriptions in normal conditions of perception according to the relational dispositional analysis. But as individuals we do oppose the majority on moral issues far more often than we would oppose them in ordinary judgments of color (and not simply because of the relative importance of these judgments). I have suggested that we rather interpret Hume as holding that moral properties are those that elicit certain evaluations from rational evaluators, from those who are detached, coherent, and informed.

Despite these disanalogies, the important point brought to light by the general analogy between relational moral properties and secondary qualities is that neither side of the relation can be omitted from the analyses. Colors and other secondary qualities are not simply identified with the causes of the ways they appear. An identification of redness, for example, with properties of microphysical surface structures and ambient light would omit the phenomenal, sensuous nature of the quality as perceived. In addition, it would miss what is essential to being red, since the microphysical basis for red objects could change while the objects remained red, if the change were compensated by a change in our visual systems. To avoid this mistake, being red is understood here as being such as to appear that way, so that there is essential reference to the phenomenal property in the analysis. (On particular occasions, however, we might recognize a token identity between being such as to appear red on that occasion and the physical basis for the appearance. It is the quality as a type that cannot be reduced to a physical or purely objective type.) Nor, as is perhaps more obvious here, can we omit reference to the objective side of the relation, since, for one thing, we identify objects themselves by means of their colors and other secondary qualities.

Similarly, on the present view we cannot reduce moral properties to either objective properties or subjective attitudes or responses to them. The first section of this chapter made it clear that sentiments and subjective responses are essential to moral judgments for Hume. That character traits are good when the actions that result from them contribute to utility is contingent not only on the psychological make-up of the recipients of the actions, but also on that of evaluators. It is contingent on their approval and hence on the capacity for sympathy that underlies it. If persons were not generally sympathetic, moved by the plights of others, there would be no moral judgments as we know them at all. Since for Hume moral judgments do not state objective facts, it follows on his view that there would then be no moral properties either.

One might wonder again if this last inference is sound. Wouldn't actions conducive to social welfare be right, and those destructive of social welfare wrong, however evaluators reacted to these actions? It might appear so, but this is only because we as evaluators continue to approve of such actions, however we think other conceivable evaluators might react. The question is still whether in making moral judgments we are simply stating or inferring to objective facts to which moral properties reduce, or whether we are also normally expressing approvals and disapprovals and recommending courses of action or attitudes to others. Even if we reject Hume's view that moral judgments must always motivate evaluators themselves, it remains plausible that such judgments recommend actions to others and express attitudes of a certain sort. This alone, if an essential aspect of ethical evaluation, implies that we cannot eliminate the subjective side from an analysis of such judgments or of the properties to which they refer.

The analogy to secondary qualities indicates once again that a proper analysis of moral properties cannot omit reference to the objective (or non-moral relational) side of (second-order) relational moral properties. If evaluators began approving of socially destructive behavior and character traits, such reactions would not render these actions and dispositions right and good. For Hume, these could not be genuine moral judgments, since they would not express attitudes of impartial and sympathetic observers. The specification of impartial sympathy as the ultimate subjective ground of moral judgment ensures that only certain objective or non-moral grounds could elicit such judgments and serve as their (partial) referents. A judgment expressing the capacity for impartial sympathy could be prompted only by certain features of objects. Judgments not referring to traits that are useful or immediately agreeable are either not moral judgments, or mistaken moral judgments (if they purport to ascribe goodness or rightness). Despite occasionally holding the 'general opinion' infallible in moral evaluation (he might mean here only that the majority cannot always be mistaken in their judgments), Hume allows for mistakes when the non-moral grounds for positive evaluation are lacking. This in itself implies that moral properties must include this side of the relation as well. Indeed, in the *Inquiry* Hume sometimes defines virtues only in terms of the non-moral side of these relations:

> personal merit consists entirely in the usefulness or agree-ableness of qualities to the person himself possessed of them, or to others who have any intercourse with him.
> (I IX, 1, 98)

Moral judgments, like perceptual judgments about secondary qualities, thus direct our attention to features of their objects, as well as to their subjects' responses. This relational view is compatible with Hume's view that both sorts of judgment involve to some degree the error of projection.[4] I suggested above that his criticism of rationalism or objectivism in ethics parallels his critical discussions of causality and the self. In all these cases subjective responses are uncritically and mistakenly projected into the objective fabric of the world. We may add ordinary judgments about secondary qualities to this list. Here, according to the Lockean account to which Hume refers, subjects naively assume that qualities in objects resemble the sensuous aspects of secondary qualities as perceived. They mistake secondary for non-relational or objective primary qualities. Similarly in the case of moral evaluation, rationalists, and perhaps ordinary evaluators too, take themselves to be referring to purely objective properties.

One might think, if subjects project their responses onto objects and intend to ascribe objective properties not possessed by the objects, that all such judgments must be false. This would again imply that there cannot be moral knowledge. But despite this error of projection, we need not hold that all moral judgments (or all judgments of secondary qualities) are false in failing to ascribe correctly those properties intended. The objectivist account need not be construed as part of the meaning of these judgments, only as a naively assumed false metaphysical view of them. As noted earlier, Hume certainly thought that some moral judgments are true and others, a small minority, are false. The relational views of moral properties and secondary qualities, while allowing for the error of projection in dismissing objectivism, also allows for the intuition that these properties are in part objective and in an important sense real. The property of being such as to appear in a certain way is a real property of objects, albeit a relational one. A person's or action's being such as to elicit rational approval is similar in this important respect. These analyses may therefore seem more true to the phenomenology of experience and to the intuition of encountering properties to which our judgments must correspond than purely subjectivist accounts.

I conclude that the relational account of moral properties is both truer to the Humean texts and more plausible in itself than alternatives so far considered. If there are real moral properties, then they are likely to have this structure. Whether the view can withstand criticism remains to be seen.

D. Objection: The Non-moral Ground of Moral Properties

The sort of objection that I shall press against the relational analysis of rightness and corresponding virtues can be introduced best by returning to the analogy with secondary qualities. I shall first indicate a similar problem that plagues Locke's account of these qualities.

This account assumes that for each specific color, an object of that color will appear a certain way to normal observers in normal conditions. This holds not only for instantiations of broad color concepts such as that of redness, but also for more specific shades. We also assume that every red object is some more specific shade of red. But these assumptions may turn out to be together incompatible with plausible interpretations of the empirical data regarding color perception. Given the vast number of discriminable shades, and the many variables, both external and internal to perceivers, that affect apparent shades, it becomes overwhelmingly likely that normal perceivers will see slightly different specific shades on the same surfaces in normal conditions. Precise matching tests bear out the prediction that subjects have different matching functions, that they see different specific shades on the same surfaces in the same external physical conditions, even extremely artificial and controlled conditions.[5] It therefore seems that our everyday agreements in ascribing colors such as red to objects result from the breadth of such terms and concepts, the fact that they cover a very large number of discriminable shades.

If the less obvious facts are as described above, then we cannot specify in any non-arbitrary way a class of normal perceivers and conditions such that objects have those shades of color that appear to such subjects in such conditions. (We cannot pick those subjects who make the most discriminations, for no set of subjects is best at discriminating over the entire range of discriminable shades; and if there were such a set, those subjects in it might well disagree in some of their color ascriptions.) Any plausible way of doing so would have us ascribing incompatible shades to the same uniformly colored surfaces.

Thus we cannot understand secondary qualities such as colors in terms of objects being such as to appear certain ways to normal subjects under normal conditions. This account fails to capture a coherent set of properties. The set of properties specified is incoherent in that we are forced by the analysis to ascribe incompatible properties to the same objects. The empirical facts, together with some plausible assumptions about relations of inclusion and determinateness among color properties, seem to drive us to a non-realist position on colors, to the claim that colors qualify only the ways objects appear. Objects may appear differently in regard to colors to different normal subjects, without our being forced to ascribe incompatible properties to the objects themselves, if we limit the literal ascription of colors to the appearances or ways of appearing, rather than conceiving of these properties as objective *or* as relational.

We want to see whether a similar problem plagues the Humean analysis of moral properties in terms of relations between non-moral properties and subjective reactions (approvals and disapprovals). Can we specify a coherent non-moral ground for moral evaluations, or will this analysis drive us again to ascribe incompatible moral properties to the same objects? If rightness (or justice as a virtue) consists in actions (or dispositions) being such as to elicit approval from rational evaluators, then these evaluators must seemingly agree in the non-moral grounds that elicit approval from them. They must agree if we are not to ascribe both rightness and wrongness to the same actions according to this criterion. (Relativistic versions will be discussed below.) Hume holds that moral evaluations, at least those that are not to be dismissed as mistaken or based on superstition, form a consistent set over whole moral communities, and even across them, in that such judgments have common grounds. Subjects agree in their judgments, he holds, when they are informed and impartial, when they confront and recognize the same non-moral properties on which moral judgments are based. Let us critically examine this claim.

For the sake of this argument we may ignore the criteria of immediate agreeableness and usefulness to the person himself, which Hume perceives to ground some judgments regarding virtues. These properties do not ground judgments regarding specifically moral virtues, as Hume himself admits (although he notes the absence of a sharp line here). I shall be concentrating on judgments concerning justice, since they are the most crucial for determining a real (relational) property of rightness. Here, according to Hume, our approval of just actions and characters is based on utility, although the relation of utility to justice, an artificial virtue, is not as direct as in the case of natural virtues. Generosity, for example, is directly and almost universally useful to others, and it appeals immediately to our 'sentiments of approbation'. In the case of justice, by contrast, Hume blends Hobbesian elements into his account, and he is forced to modify a direct appeal to utility as the ground of all judgments regarding just actions and distributions of goods (he concerns himself exclusively with distributions of property).

He argues that it is in each person's interest to agree to a set of conventions that create stability in the possession of property. As in Hobbes's account, justice depends on a set of conventions to supplement such general precepts as that of rewarding industry. The gaps in natural precepts of justice must be filled in by positive law or precedent (I Appx. III, 125). Once such a system is in place, its effect is to increase social utility generally, and so we sympathetically react to just acts, policies and dispositions by approving. But Hume admits that individual just acts, those in accord with generally utility maximizing conventions for the regulation of property, may not in themselves maximize or even increase general utility. This constitutes an important problem for our assessment of the implications of his position regarding a real property of rightness or (perhaps more narrowly) justice. For actions that do not maximize utility but are perceived as just or right, as well as actions that do maximize utility but are judged unjust or wrong, provide examples in which we might expect irresolvable disagreement even among rational evaluators.

Some rational evaluators, we might think, may be hard core utilitarians. They may hold, for example, that property should be transferred whenever doing so will increase the sum total of satisfaction. Others will be advocates of individual rights, and they will hold that rights to property must be protected even when others could benefit more from its use. If such disagreement cannot be rationally resolved, and if rightness is being such as to elicit rational approval, then we must attribute both rightness and wrongness to the same actions and policies. As in the case of secondary qualities, the relational account of moral properties fails to specify a coherent set because of the facts of human psychology. In fact, dispute in ethics is more readily apparent than disagreement in regard to colors. This is because the breadth of such terms as 'right' adds to rather than hides, disagreement in the application of narrower terms and concepts. Can Hume's account accommodate such divergence in judgment, for example, when acts considered just lower utility, and conversely?

Actually, Hume evades this problem by holding that, while individual acts of justice may fail to maximize or increase utility, they must be supported, and hence can be approved, on utilitarian grounds. Just conventions must be observed on each occasion, he argues, because only in this way can the entire scheme, necessary for social utility, be maintained (I Appx. III, 121). He might be interpreted here as advocating rule utilitarianism: we must support and approve those acts required by utility maximizing rules; and we must not apply the criterion of utility directly to the evaluation of acts themselves. Indeed, in appealing to the ground of utility in the *Inquiry*, Hume builds in a principle of universalization that foreshadows Kant's requirement for impartial reason. He writes:

> we have every moment recourse to the principle of public utility and ask, *what must become of the world, if such practices prevail?* (I III, 2, 34)

In evaluating acts, it seems, we are to think of their universalizations, or at least of the rules that prescribe them. All and only acts required by utility maximizing rules are to be approved.

The reasoning that underlies the move from the natural application (to acts) of the principle of utility to its application only at the level of rules might be Hobbesian. It might echo Hobbes's warning to the Fool not to try to identify exceptions to the rule of thumb that moral acts are generally prudential as well. Here the rule utilitarian might reason that attempts to identify exceptions to utility maximizing rules (in this case conventions for just regulation of property) would err more often than not. But the problem with this argument is the same as that which defeated the equation of morality with prudence. It *is* possible to identify reliably situations in which acts will maximize utility but will be considered unjust, and perhaps in violation of utility maximizing rules (at least if these rules are stated simply enough to be usable). Consider an isolated case of theft when the thief is somewhat less wealthy than his victim and enjoys the gain more than his victim suffers from the loss (the latter being also insured, although not so heavily as to have any effect on future rates). It is simply false that one can never predict the balance of utility in such cases; yet the action will certainly be opposed by defenders of rights to property.

It is more promising for the rule utilitarian to avoid resting his case on epistemic uncertainty and instead to reason that acts which maximize utility in themselves may cumulatively threaten social order and hence utility itself. Each act in itself may have negligible effect on the general scheme, but cumulatively they may undermine those rules that protect social stability and increase collective welfare. This situation is common in diverse social contexts. It defines the problem of pollution, for example, and requires judges to rule according to law even when it is not morally optimal to do so. It seems in these cases that acts which maximize utility in themselves may lower it cumulatively. Individual acts of disposing wastes most cheaply, or the decision of a judge not to foreclose on the house of a poor widow, might fall into this class. Given the collective effects of these acts, Hume may seem right to insist that departures from utility maximizing rules be prohibited even when individually they maximize utility. Such acts seemingly must be disapproved in the name of utility itself. If so, then the rights advocate has no quarrel with the utilitarian.

To see that this argument does not succeed in reconciling these adversaries, however, consider that there must be some threshold for such actions beyond which they begin to have net negative effects on utility. This threshold might be very difficult to identify in practice. But it is the area well below it that interests us here. In that area it will remain possible to identify acts that maximize utility but violate reasonable conventions of justice. It is irrelevant to our present argument whether you or I consider such acts in such circumstances to be morally permissible. The point is that hard core utilitarians should disagree with others in evaluating actions that maximize utility but differ in this respect from similar acts in the vicinity of the threshold and beyond. If both hard core utilitarians and rights advocates can be rational evaluators, and if being right is being such as to elicit approval from rational evaluators, then once more Hume's analysis requires us to ascribe rightness and wrongness to the same actions and character traits (assuming also that moral persons are disposed to act rightly).

The examples here need not be limited to disagreements between utilitarians and non-utilitarians. One rational evaluator might take loyalty to family to have moral precedence over loyalty to country; another the reverse. One might hold that friends or clients may be favored over strangers; another may require impartiality in the same circumstances. Examples can be multiplied indefinitely, although those involving justice and utility are most pertinent to Hume's direct discussion.

It is interesting finally to compare non-moral goodness with rightness and moral goodness in regard to the problem of disagreement. In the previous chapter we suggested, following Hobbes, that value or non-moral goodness could be analyzed as the common property of objects of rational desire. Other properties of objects in the set of goods will constitute a diverse cluster, although common needs will produce some common elements among the goods for different persons. The common property so specified counts as real, since it is independent from our beliefs about it and even to some degree from our actual desires; yet its connection with motivation is readily apparent.

It is clear that (non-moral) goods defined in this way can conflict. They may not be all jointly realizable. But they remain in themselves all good. Conflicts will obviously occur in conditions of scarcity. Less obviously, even in conditions of abundance, different conceptions of the good may be equally rational yet not mutually attainable. This is because such conceptions will include among their objects not only material goods, but ideals of the good life that may inhibit their mutual realization. As claimed earlier, such conflicts do not defeat the description of all these objects and ideals as good in themselves. Conflicts within the same agents' conceptions of the good life are problematic; but such conflicts can be resolved by rational choices reflecting the fully informed second-order desires of the agents.

When we turn to accounts of rightness and moral goodness, conflicts among the interests of different agents become more problematic, as we have seen. The problem is that practices judged to be right or just often constitute ways of resolving or simply settling these conflicts. And there appear to be incompatible but equally rational ways of doing so. In the case of non-moral goodness, conflicts in meeting the desires of different agents do not force us to ascribe incompatible properties to the same agents or objects. But here we can have different rational evaluators approving of incompatible distributive schemes for the same groups. We cannot say that distributions approved of by any such evaluator are right, since, for example, a utilitarian and non-utilitarian distributive scheme cannot both be right for the same group. At least they cannot both be right if they are incompatible and rightness is a real property in the sense so far suggested.

What blocks the relational, realist interpretation of moral properties offered so far is precisely the same problem that blocks it in the case of secondary qualities: that the most plausible way of ascribing the properties under this interpretation leaves us assigning incompatible qualities to the same objects. Ironically,

Hume's analogy, although instructive, works against his account of moral properties, if disagreement is far more widespread in both contexts than he imagines. Before leaving Hume's account behind, we may consider one final variation on it that attempts to accommodate the sort of disagreements that we have found to be problematic for the realist.

E. *Variation: Relativizing*

We found in the previous chapter that differences in conceptions of non-moral goodness could be accommodated realistically by relativizing: what is good is what is good for particular agents, given their individual psychologies. We could not similarly claim that right or just distributions are simply those right for particular groups or communities, since both members of the communities and rational observers will disagree as to which distributions are right for them. But the inconsistency involved in ascribing both rightness and wrongness to the same distributions for the same groups might be avoided by a relational account that relativizes further.

It should be noted first that the relational accounts of both secondary and moral properties were already implicitly relative in another way. Normal perceivers and rational evaluators among humans, for example, may respond very differently from normal and rational members of other species. That red objects for us are green for Martians would not trouble the relational realist in regard to secondary qualities. Similarly, that rational evaluators who are not sympathetic to the feelings of humans would not share our moral judgments would not bother Hume or other relational realists in regard to moral properties.

More refined data on perception and reflection on moral judgment revealed possible differences among responses within the class of normal human perceivers and rational human evaluators. For Hume moral disagreements are superficial. Either they reflect ignorance, lack of impartiality, or inconsistency, or they arise from the fact that different practices may maximize utility in very different circumstances. The warlike virtues of the Romans may no longer be considered virtuous when they are no longer useful to agents themselves or to others. But such disagreement in different circumstances for Hume masks a deeper agreement on the non-moral grounds of the judgments (utility). He assumes that impartial, rational evaluators, basing their judgments on feelings resulting from sympathetic identification with others, will approve and disapprove similarly in similar circumstances:

The notion of morals implies some sentiment common to all mankind, which recommends the same object to general approbation and makes every man, or most men, agree in the same opinion or decision concerning it. (I IX, 1, 93)

We have noted possible disagreement that cannot be resolved by correcting for ignorance or partiality, and that cannot be explained by appeal to different utility calculations in different circumstances. The impartial point of view, although distinct from the personal viewpoint, is insufficient for generating moral agreement among rational and informed evaluators. While we might intend our moral judgments to apply to all (and while we might naively assume that they refer to objective properties), this does not insure that all sympathetic and impartial agents will accept them. In the face of such differences we must abandon Hume's relational account of moral properties, just as we must abandon Locke's account of secondary qualities in light of similar differences in perceptual judgments. But more relativistic variations might be available in both cases.

We can avoid ascribing incompatible properties to the same objects, actions, and agents by relativizing ascriptions to groups of perceivers and evaluators who agree among themselves. According to this revised analysis, when I say that an object is a specific shade of red, I mean that it is such as to appear that shade to perceivers who perceive as I do under normal conditions (assuming that I take myself to be a normal perceiver). When I say that a particular distributive scheme is just or right, I mean that it elicits approval from rational evaluators who share my moral framework. Once we relativize in this more radical way, seemingly incompatible ascriptions of relational properties are seen to be not genuinely inconsistent. Contradictions now occur not when we ascribe red and not-red to the same surfaces, or right and wrong to the same distributions for the same communities, but only when we ascribe red and not-red to the same surfaces relative to the same reference class of perceivers, or right and wrong to the same distributions relative to rational evaluators who share a moral framework.

When we refer to non-relational objective properties, disagreement implies error on the part of at least one party. But this, it may be said, is a mark precisely of the non-relational, intrinsic, or objective property, not of the real. The truth of judgments ascribing the former properties does not depend on subjective states of any sort. Realists, we have seen, may contrast such objective properties with relational, partly subjective properties while maintaining the reality of the latter. By narrowing the reference classes of the subjects to which their analyses refer, they can avoid inconsistent implications. The advantage for us of maintaining the relational analysis of moral properties by relativizing would lie in saving the availability of empirical knowledge as a model for moral knowledge. But the realist thrust of the analysis of moral properties at this point may become illusory. We must reassess according to our criterion of real properties and judgments that are to correspond to them.

I have defined real properties as those independent, not from all subjective states, but from beliefs or theories about them. The truth of beliefs about such properties is not determined by their coherence with other beliefs or methods of verification. This epistemic or semantic analysis of realism has become standard since it was introduced by Michael Dummett.[6] But relativizing the truth of moral judgments to evaluators who share moral frameworks or sets of judgments or beliefs violates this criterion for the reality of moral properties. We should note also, however, that satisfaction of the criterion, independence of the truth of judgments from beliefs, and hence the claim of a relational account to remain realist, should be construed as a matter of degree. The current relativized account still conceives moral properties in terms of being such as to elicit approval or disapproval from *rational* evaluators. The extent to which such properties remain independent from beliefs about them depends on the force of the demand for rationality (for being impartial, informed, and consistent), which depends in turn on the size of the class of evaluators to which moral judgments are relativized.

If rightness is being such as to elicit approval in rational evaluators who share my moral framework, then it seems that I can err in my ascriptions of this property. I can err by failing to be rational, that is, informed, impartial, and consistent, when I judge some action or policy to be right. An action can seem to me to have this property when it does not; hence whether it has the property is independent at least from my judgment or belief that it does. Since I am here referring to a (relational) property of the action about which I can be mistaken, it seems that the property to which I refer is (to that extent) real. Furthermore, that an action has this property can help to explain why I believe that it has the property. It can help to explain my belief by pointing to the fact that I am rational, and that rational evaluators who share my framework believe as I do in this case. We accepted above that if the truth of a belief prominently enters into the best explanation for its being held, then the belief counts as knowledge. When this truth is of the realist or correspondence sort, then empirical knowledge can be our model. Therefore, to the extent that my belief here must correspond to a real property of rightness, moral knowledge can be understood in much the way that we conceive of empirical knowledge.

The degree to which the moral property remains real on this account, however, is the degree to which it remains independent from evaluators' beliefs about it and from their other beliefs. This depends on the strength of the appeal to rationality in the explanation of moral beliefs. The nature and strength of the constraint on truth imposed by the requirement of rationality depends on the extent to which the truth of a rational evaluator's judgments depends only on her beliefs or on those of others. If those who share my moral framework constitute a very small class, or at the limit reduce to those whose moral beliefs are identical to my informed and consistent beliefs, then the constraint reduces to the demand to be informed and consistent. (Even the demand for impartiality loses its force if a rational evaluator can decide which differences among individuals are morally relevant, and can approve and disapprove in any consistent way.) But this demand becomes indistinguishable from the coherentist's or anti-realist's criterion for moral truth. Thus the import of the radically relativized relational account of moral properties cannot be differentiated from that of an anti-realist meta-ethic.

The point of asserting a realist position in regard to relational moral properties seems to depend on the size of the reference classes to which we relativize. Yet there may be no principled way to determine the extent of the relevant groups. Whether two subjects share the same moral framework and differ only in regard to particular judgments, or whether they differ in moral outlook or framework itself may not admit of an objective answer. We can determine whether, for the purposes of settling a particular seeming moral dispute between them, we should regard them as involved in a genuine disagreement. To determine whether their judgments contradict or whether their disagreement should be relativized away, we find out whether the parties are willing to reason from the set of judgments or principles on which they agree, to the solution most coherent with that body of data. If so, then for the purposes of that particular argument, they share the same moral framework. If not, then they do not. But relativizing this determination to particular moral disputes leaves it even more puzzling in what sense we can continue to characterize their assertions as referring to real moral properties.

We have seen that the point of this characterization varies with the size of the reference class of evaluators to which the truth of moral judgments is relativized. We have seen also that the size of these classes itself is relative to the nature of particular disputes and apparent disagreements. At this point it begins to look far more promising to seek to develop a non-realist account of truth for moral judgments and drop the appeal to empirical knowledge as a model for moral knowledge. It begins to look as if the constraint on evaluations that will determine their truth values is going to reduce to coherence in any case. For each subjective response to an object or action that we make, there is a correlative relational property that consists in its being such as to elicit that response from subjects like us. But there may be no advantage to saying that our responses refer to such properties. If the responses are limited to those of rational subjects, then appeal to relational properties can explain the rationality of our particular responses on given occasions. But a non-realist account of moral judgments can build in this constraint (in so doing it will depart from simple emotivism) as well. We can justify our evaluations by noting that they match those of rational judges without mentioning properties in objects at all.

It might be claimed that the relational realist account better captures the phenomenology of moral judgment. But this advantage is minimal. Our naive experience suggests that moral properties, like secondary qualities, are not only real, but non-relational or objective. Relational analyses ascribe Hume's error of projection, just as non-realist accounts do. According to both sorts of accounts, appeal to subjective responses does not simply fix reference to rigidly designated objective properties; it cannot be eliminated from an understanding of the judgments when made. Coming closer to capturing a naive and mistaken metaphysical intuition is of little or no advantage to a philosophical theory. We do not choose those spatial co-ordinates that come closest to capturing our intuition that the earth is flat.

F. Conclusion

The main significance of Hume's account for our inquiry, as I have interpreted his account, lies in its attempt to reconcile the partially subjective character of moral judgments with a realist view of moral properties, both moral goodness and rightness. In this chapter I have defended an interpretation of Hume as a relational realist, arguing that viewing rightness in terms of being such as to elicit approval from rational evaluators accords best with Hume's explicit arguments. It is also the most plausible subjectivist-realist position in itself.

Hume's subjectivism derives first from his internalism about moral reasons. A moral judgment is intrinsically motivating according to him. We saw reason to question this claim when it comes to first person moral assessments. The genuine amoralist who understands and uses moral discourse in first person evaluations in the same way as others constitutes a counter-example. But Hume also appealed to the phenomenology of evaluating to claim that the act of morally judging does not consist in noting an objective fact beyond those previously considered. Beyond referring to certain matters of fact, moral judgments appear also to express attitudes and recommend dispositions or courses of action to others.

The relational account includes these subjective elements, while maintaining the relevance of empirical knowledge as a model for moral knowledge. A person's or action's being such as to elicit rational approval can explain why particular evaluators approve of it and believe that it is good or right. This explanation is partly causal, but includes appeal to the rationality of the particular evaluators. If rationality itself can be unpacked in naturalist or empirical terms, then the explanations relevant to the assessment of claims to moral knowledge, while complex, do not differ in kind from assessments of claims to empirical knowledge.

The problem with the relational account, however, lay in Hume's assumptions regarding its objective side. Here he holds that utility constitutes the objective (or first-order relational) ground for strictly moral judgments, including judgments regarding justice in distributions of property. He recognizes that particular just acts may not maximize utility, and conversely, but argues that we morally approve of such acts on utilitarian grounds. We must support them because cumulatively they are required by utility. We noted exceptions to this general rule, however – cases well below the threshold where such acts begin to have negative utility. Here rational evaluators can seemingly disagree, depending on whether they are hard core utilitarians or strong advocates of individual rights.

Such disagreement, if not based on irrationality, could be accommodated within realist accounts of moral properties only by relativizing further to groups of evaluators who share moral frameworks. But at this point the realist thrust of the relational account, and the suitability of empirical knowledge as our model, begins to be lost. Once one must relativize to particular groups of evaluators, especially if these are not very large groups, the main constraints on moral judgments become those of consistency and avoiding factual errors (prior to the judgments). But these constraints can be captured more directly by non-realist accounts of moral reasoning and truth, which begin to look more appealing. Although simple emotivism fails to give proper place to the requirement of consistency or coherence, it might find central place in a non-realist, coherentist meta-ethical theory.

Before exploring this possibility and comparing further the advantages of realist and non-realist moral metaphysics for an account of moral knowledge, we must conclude this historical survey by examining the development of the notion of objective rationality in Kant. Hobbes equated moral rightness with prudential rationality; Hume suggested a different conception of reason and its role in moral judgment, but viewed rational judgments as based on considerations of utility. Neither account succeeded in specifying a coherent property of rightness. It remains to explore Kant's equation of moral action with that required by impartial or objective reason, where the latter eschews all appeal to utility.

CHAPTER III

Kant: Objective Rationality and Obligation

Superficially, Kant's account of rightness resembles in form those of Hume and Hobbes examined in earlier chapters. Kant is more careful than his predecessors to divide right actions into the permissible, the obligatory, and the morally worthy. The latter two categories can be derived from the former: actions are obligatory if their omissions are not permissible; and morally worthy acts are those that are performed because they are obligatory in some sense. (The closest that Kant comes to acknowledging supererogatory acts are his wide, imperfect duties, which do not require specific acts and are morally praiseworthy when performed.) If we equate rightness with the broader and more fundamental category of permissibility, as Kant sometimes does (F II, 56; MM, I, MEJ 25),[1] then we can say that for him, right actions are those that can be rationally willed. This appears similar to Hume's analysis in terms of rational approval, or to Hobbes's thesis that right actions are rational for the agent in the long run.

Kant, like Hobbes, holds that right actions are those that fully rational agents would perform, but the resemblance is superficial because the accounts of rationality differ sharply. Kant's analysis, while it incorporates Hobbes's, does not limit practical rationality to an instrumental role, to the adoption of the most effective means to personally desired or desirable ends (the totality of which constitutes the agent's happiness). His account builds on Hume's appeal to impartiality; but, whereas for Hume impartial, rational evaluators will base their judgments on sympathetic reactions to the utility of actions toward others, Kant emphatically rejects as bases for moral judgments the feelings that people happen to have and the effects of their actions on others. His rejection of all empirical grounds as criteria of rational willing renders his implicit account of moral knowledge entirely distinct from those of Hobbes and Hume. The proper model is no longer that of ordinary empirical knowledge.

We saw in the previous two chapters that Hobbes's equation of rightness with prudential rationality failed, that Hume's utilitarian ground for strictly moral judgments could be successfully contested, and that his appeal to sympathy did not suffice for indicating a coherent property of rightness to which sympathetic judgments refer. Hobbes's notion of personal or prudential rationality was relatively uncontroversial in itself (indeed it is captured as part of Kant's broader notion), but it was also incapable of capturing our ascriptions of moral obligation. Hume's description of rational moral evaluators as impartial moved in the direction of Kant's concept, but the ground of rational moral judgments remained subjective in a double sense. For Kant, the claim that purely rational agents necessarily will morally right actions implies an objective criterion of rightness. He provides an analysis of the contents of judgments of obligation that could be objectively binding, valid for all rational agents as such, irrespective of their subjective feelings and beliefs. It is entirely fitting and indeed required in light of our earlier conclusions that we turn now to this third major tradition in moral philosophy.

The more difficult and controversial account of practical rationality as objective or fully impartial must be explicated with the following questions in mind. Does complete rationality require full impartiality? Does this account of rationality capture ordinary judgments regarding rightness? Is the constraint it imposes on moral judgment sufficient to specify a coherent property of rightness independent from subjective moral frameworks? The latter two questions, remember, were fatal to the Hobbesian and Humean concepts of the right.

A. The Model for Moral Knowledge

As noted, Kant denies that rational approval or willing is based on any empirical ground. He agrees with Hume that there is no property of rightness given or apprehended directly in experience. But he disagrees with the claim that the truth of moral judgments is determined by a relation between empirically ascertainable properties and the affective reactions of evaluators. Knowledge of empirical properties therefore cannot be the model for moral knowledge. Kant's model is complex and in some ways idiosyncratic, deriving, as did Hume's, from his broader philosophy.

Just as a grasp of Hume's metaphysics, his arguments regarding causality, proved helpful in grasping his theory of projection in moral judgments, so a grasp of Kant's metaphysics and epistemology (to which I can only briefly allude here) provides an analogy for his positive position on moral knowledge. In the case of empirical knowledge, he holds that experience of the physical world is rendered coherent and intelligible, a possible source of knowledge, only through the operation of the forms of the sensibility and categories of the understanding. Experienced properties are structured in space and time, referred to substantial objects, and ordered in terms of causal laws. These forms and categories themselves are knowable *a priori*, apart from particular experiences, by noting the necessity of the structures they impose on experience. We know that all experience must be of objects in three dimensional space and of events in linear time, and this necessity is the clue that these structures derive from the activities of the mind.

In like manner, Kant's supreme principle of morality reflects the activity of practical reason in rendering moral intention and discourse coherent and intelligible. The principle can be known *a priori*, independently of experience, because it constitutes the necessary condition for objective moral knowledge. It states what is necessary for obligations to be binding on all agents capable of practical reason, regardless of the rest of their subjective make-up. The closest analogue of such foundational moral knowledge lies, as mentioned, in knowledge of the categories underlying empirical knowledge, although there are differences.

The fundamental principle of morality for Kant is determined by the formal structure of practical reason alone. We therefore might liken knowledge of this principle also to knowledge of the deductive and inductive laws of reasoning. We know what such laws must be if truth is to be preserved, conclusively or probabilistically, through their use. Cognizers must reason according to them if their conclusions are to be rationally obligatory. Similarly, agents can discern the principle of morality that must be recognized if moral obligations are to be binding on all (finite) rational wills.

There are further analogies and disanalogies with *a priori* knowledge of the categories, and with knowledge of their products in experience, that can throw additional light on Kant's complex concept of moral knowledge. As in the case of Hume, we may look to the analysis of causality. In Kant's system, the fundamental law of causality, that every event (which can be experienced) must have a cause, expresses a category of the understanding, the synthesizing activity of the mind. But particular causal laws, such as that friction causes heat, can be known only by subsuming particular experiences under that fundamental law. Similarly, knowledge of particular moral duties can be derived only when we subsume particular subjective principles of action, stating the reasons for which we act, under the form of the fundamental moral principle, which can be known *a priori*. Moral knowledge for Kant is therefore complex, part of it being more like mathematical or logical knowledge, part of it more like knowledge of empirical laws.

Some disanalogies with the empirical realm must be mentioned as well. According to Kant, practical reason issues regulative ideas rather than categories applicable to experience and verified to be instantiated there. We cannot know that moral obligations genuinely apply to us, since we cannot know that we have free choices. Thus the commands of practical reason cannot be deduced from the necessary character of action, as the categories are deduced from the necessary character of experience of the physical world. Nevertheless, we can know *a priori* what the fundamental principle of morality is, if, as Kant holds, it must be applicable to all rational agents who arc free. We know *a priori* what rightness is because we know what right, that is, fully rational and free, action would be if real, although we can never experience the property as such. We derive this knowledge from an analysis of what it is to will in a fully rational way, free from all non-rational influences.[2]

If moral obligations bind all conceivable (non-holy) rational agents, then they cannot depend fundamentally on the feelings that particular kinds of rational agents, such as humans, happen to have. For Kant, rightness does not depend directly on fulfilling or aiming to fulfill the desires of others, but on acting or willing to act for reasons that could be adopted universally, on making one's will coherent with the rational wills of all agents. The property of rightness is this property of coherence among rational wills. We may think of the truth of judgments regarding obligations as correspondence to this property, or we may think of it directly in terms of the coherence of judgments as expressions of rational wills. The latter is probably more in the spirit of Kant, for whom rightness seems to stand to practical judgments or acts of will as truth stands to empirical judgments. In the latter case, the judgments must be referred to existent objects in experience to which they must correspond. But in the case of moral or practical judgments, these must express only coherence among rational wills, the coherence of mutually realizable intentions.

It is crucial to note, however, that such coherence differs sharply from the non-realist, relativist view that moral judgments are true if they cohere with other beliefs within some moral framework. Kant holds that obligation is independent from agents' beliefs and fully objective in being the same for all rational agents. The claim that rightness is objectively determined by reason as the same for all in relevantly similar conditions is the crucial one for our inquiry, as reflected in the three questions raised above. To prepare for their answers, we may look first at Kant's arguments equating morality with rationality.

B. The Equation of Morality, Rationality, and Freedom

Kant's equation of right action with fully rational action can be seen to derive first from his complete rejection of consequentialism and of what we might call affective motivism (the view that acts performed out of love, for example, are morally good). Regarding consequentialism, not only does Kant deny that the morality of an action depends directly on the effects achieved; he denies also that it depends on the effects sought. The main argument supporting this rejection primarily concerns not rightness (alone), but moral worth. Actions, or the will that initiates them, cannot derive their moral worth from ends achieved or even sought, since the same ends can be sought for morally good, bad, or indifferent motives, and the same ends brought about by non-moral causes:

the moral worth of an action does not lie in the effect expected from it, nor in any principle of action which requires to borrow its motive from this expected effect. For all these effects – agreeableness of one's condition, and even the promotion of the happiness of others – could have been also brought about by other causes, so that for this there would have been no need of the will of a rational being. (F I, 18).

If good consequences are produced by actions done from bad or indifferent motives, as when a person helps others only to acquire a reputation so as later to be able to deceive them, then the actions lack moral worth. Hence their worth cannot derive from ends achieved or sought.

If the moral worth of an action does not derive from its effects, then we might think that it lies in the motive. For Kant, there must be a purely moral motive if moral action is real, but this motive cannot be that of aiming (primarily) at some end. Nor can it consist in an ordinary feeling that moves the agent to act, since, as we noted above, moral obligation (and therefore moral worth) must apply to all rational agents regardless of their feelings. The only pure moral motive is to will an action because it is right or obligatory. But if the moral worth of the motive or will does not derive from the ends sought or from the accompanying feelings, but rather from the rightness of the action willed, then the rightness of the action cannot lie in the ends sought or in the affective cause either.

Kant then derives the equation of morality and rationality by this process of elimination. Having eliminated consequentialism and affective motivism, he concludes that only the formal principle of the will, willing in accordance with practical law, or for the sake of moral law, determines rightness and moral worth respectively:

> Now an action done from duty must wholly exclude the
> influence of inclination, and with it every object of the will,
> so that nothing remains which can determine the will except
> objectively the law, and subjectively pure respect for this
> practical law. (F I, 18)

The moral law to which Kant refers cannot command particular ends, if the argument is not to lead back to consequentialism. Again by elimination, what counts must be only willing or acting in a way that conforms to the form of law, that is, in a way that could be willed universally. This, of course, is Kant's fundamental principle and criterion of right or permissible actions: to act only on principles (or for reasons) that could be willed to govern the actions of all agents. To act in a way that could be willed universally, such that one could intend all agents to act in that way, is to render one's action and will compatible or coherent with the rational wills of all other agents.

The equation of this criterion of rightness with a demand of practical reason itself requires the rationalist finally to show that reason demands such coherence among individual wills. It must be shown that rationality must be impartial, in that a genuine reason to act for one agent must be a reason for all in relevantly similar circumstances. And it must be a reason that a rational agent as such (or all rational agents) would will all to act on, thus removing all conflicts among rational wills. This central Kantian argument will be examined below, when we look more closely at his concept of practical rationality. Here I want to point out that the argument for the criterion of rightness from elimination, from the rejection of consequentialism and affective motivism, requires at least one additional (suppressed) premise.

Kant assumes that, if the moral worth or rightness of an action does not lie in the ends sought or affective cause, then it must lie in the congruence of the will with other rational wills, whatever their particular ends or ordinary motivating feelings. But this assumption rests on a deeper one, that there is some criterion which determines right actions in the same way for all agents, some coherent property of rightness singled out by that criterion. Kant attempts to show what the ground of obligation must be *if* it applies to all rational agents in the same way. He assumes the antecedent, which nevertheless has been, and must continue to be, a crucial question for us. The argument from elimination at best works only given the truth of this assumption.

His second argument for the equation of morality and (impartial) rationality appeals to a third term, freedom. The argument is simple in form: moral action is equated with truly free action, in turn equated with rationally caused action. For Kant, as for many other philosophers, moral obligation implies free choice. If the distinction between right and wrong is genuine, in the sense of determining real obligations for humans, then human action cannot be always determined by inclinations. It is not sufficient for genuine freedom that one does as one desires. Kant views desires or inclinations as thoroughly a part of the causally determined fabric of nature as we experience it. Free action is action not determined by desire, but performed on the basis of reasons. Inclinations may give one reasons, but may not in themselves determine behaviour if it is free.

But then free action is also rational action. It is not behavior that comes about haphazardly, by chance, or in the absence of law. Such behavior would be totally unintelligible. Free action is intelligible (although never experienced as such, according to Kant). It can be understood in terms of its reasons, in terms of the way it results in a lawlike way from the strength of reasons behind it. Free action, to be intelligible, must conform to laws, but these cannot be the causal laws of nature that would render such action determined rather than free:

> although freedom is not a property of the will depending on physical laws, yet it is not for that reason lawless; on the contrary, it must be a causality acting according to immutable laws, but of a peculiar kind . . . What else then can freedom of the will be but autonomy, that is, the property of the will to be a law to itself? (F III, 63)

To act or will according to law is to act or will rationally or coherently for Kant. Thus a free will is a rational will. Morality then implies freedom, which implies rationality, so that moral action must be rational.

The implications hold in the opposite direction as well for Kant. A rational agent cannot be propelled or determined to act by her desires alone:

> we cannot possibly conceive a reason consciously receiving a bias from any other quarter with respect to its judgments, for then the subject would ascribe the dermination of its judgment not to its own reason, but to an impulse. (F III, 65)

A rational person can accept that some of her desires give her reasons for acting so as to satisfy them, but she must act because they provide these reasons, not simply because they are her desires. Thus a rational person must be free from the determining force of desires. Thus full practical rationality implies freedom.

A person who is totally free from determination by inclination will also be impartial, according to Kant. Otherwise,

> the will does not give itself the law, but it is given by a foreign impulse by means of a particular natural constitution of the subject adapted to receive it. (F III, 61)

A free person, rather than being moved by objects that satisfy his particular desires, will act on grounds of reasons that must be equally reasons for other rational agents. And, if motivated primarily to be rational, he must also will that other agents act on the same reasons when they apply to them. Such impartiality is definitive of morally acceptable behavior for Kant. Thus, according to him, a totally free person will act morally. Thus full rationality implies (freedom, which implies) morally right action. Full practical reason and morality (willing in a morally permissible way) are shown to be equivalent via the mediation of the third term, freedom.

There are many problems with this argument. The concept of freedom itself is highly problematic, and there is not space to delve into all the complexities of the Kantian position, with its distinction between the phenomenal and noumenal worlds (things as they appear to us, as causally determined, and things as they are in themselves). Others have amply pointed to the difficulties in Kant's appeal to conflicts between desires and duties, given that the former operate causally within nature as experienced, and the latter apply only to the will beyond such nature.[3] Two points may be raised to the argument as stated above, however, without invoking or questioning that distinction. First, the claim that reasons can render actions intelligible by subsuming them under laws, when these are not causal laws, is at best difficult to understand. If the intelligibility derives from the regularities expressed in such laws, then on what grounds do we deny them the status of causal laws? Second, a person may be partial toward the satisfaction of her own desires without being determined (compulsively) to act so as to satisfy them. Thus freedom does not appear to imply that impartiality required to forge the link between rationality and morality.

To explore that supposed link more closely, we must turn to a closer examination of Kant's concept of practical reason.

C. The Kantian Concept of Rationality

For Kant, as for other philosophers, reason aims at and creates coherence within whatever domain it operates, and coherence is the mark and measure of rationality. In the Kantian system, the synthesizing activity of theoretical reason and its subordinate faculties renders experience and thought coherent by imposing universal forms upon the chaotic raw data. In parallel fashion, practical reason renders willing and acting consistent through its activity applied at several logically discrete stages. Once more Kant views this process of rendering chaotic data coherent as one of imposing universal principles upon the materials delivered raw or partially synthesized at some earlier stage.

In the case of practical reason or will, the data to be synthesized or rendered coherent by being subsumed under principles are not perceptual intuitions or sensory bombardments, but affective impulses or raw desires. The first stage of this process consists in the transformation of these into conscious and coherent interests, from which ends or goals of action can be formulated:

> The dependence of the desires or sensations is called
> inclination, and this accordingly always indicates a want. The
> dependence of a contingently determinable will on principles
> of reason is called an interest. (F II, 31)

The will to which Kant refers here is not for him as yet fully rational, since its principles develop from and refer to contingent desires. These are initially rationalized when they are recognized as providing general reasons for acting whenever they occur in similar conditions. This recognition already entails acting according to principles, although as yet only contingent principles based on desires.

Once certain ends are willed, in order to be coherent one must also will the means necessary to achieve them. This requirement of reason is expressed in what Kant calls 'imperatives of skill' (F II, 34). The requirement to will whatever means are necessary to the fulfilment of one's accepted ends (and perhaps the most efficient means available) may be conceived as the next level in the process of rendering one's intentions and actions coherent. The third stage consists in adopting whatever goals and means will be conducive to one's happiness as a whole. Here, according to Kant, the overall end is abstractly given (necessary for humans), but cannot be concretely conceived by the individual, so that reason can issue only advice or 'counsels', rather than commands (F II, 35–6). But presumably one requirement here is to blend one's ends in order to achieve a coherent set that will not result in self-defeating pursuits.

The activities of practical reason summarized above echo the conception of prudential rationality that we found in Hobbes. Kant's major break with the tradition lies in his crucial final step. For him, in order for an individual's will to be fully coherent, not only must she intend to act on the same reasons in the same conditions, not only must she will means consistent with her ends and make her ends consistent with each other, but she must also make these goals consistent with those of other individuals, at least as they rationally will their own ends. This last sort of inter-personal coherence among wills is expressed first by the formula of universalizeability. An intention to act that conflicts with other intentions of rational agents, especially with those general ends that rational humans (including oneself) must have (such as happiness), cannot be willed universally, since one cannot rationally will inconsistent ends. But the demand is expressed most clearly in the formulation of the basic principle that requires willing as a lawmaking member of a 'kingdom of ends', where the latter phrase refers to a community in which individual goals are rendered compatible or mutually supportive.

This final stage of rational willing takes one beyond 'conditioned' principles, those that express ends arising from contingent desires, to the unconditional moral principle, which requires coherence with rational wills whatever their particular ends. This step is therefore discontinuous with the earlier ones; general ends are now set by reason itself (for example, the happiness of others), rather than posited by desires (CP I, 65–6). In one sense there is continuity from willing single ends coherently (recognizing them as repeatable reasons), to blending all one's ends into a harmonious life plan, and finally to blending these ends with those of others. In another sense, the last step is radically different, at least as a proposed requirement of reason. Beyond the discontinuity, this requirement is also far more controversial than the earlier one. That impartiality (to the degree of making one's will and actions compatible with the reasonable ends of others) is a demand of morality is intuitively plausible, although we must see below whether it captures all and only those duties that we take to make up obligation or rightness. But that such impartiality is a requirement of reason is much less immediately intuitive.

Despite this lack of obviousness, Kant to my knowledge provides scant argument for his crucial claim regarding practical reason. The main argument seems to be the one summarized in the previous section, appealing to the link between rationality and freedom. Kant views complete freedom as total independence from inclination. A being totally free from all inclinations might well be impartial, although if all members of a community were equally free in this sense, then there would be no general happiness to adopt as an end. Furthermore, as noted above, the notion of freedom is in itself suspect. A being may be causally undetermined without being free from all inclination or impartial. Kant thinks of free agents as giving laws to themselves, and he thinks of such laws as having to bind all rational agents as such, independent of all contingent desires. Laws of the latter sort might again require impartiality; but that what is rational for us (humans) must be rationally required of all rational agents, as such, is once more an assumption that must be established rather than posited, if Kant's main argument is to be complete.

Kant's view of practical reason as positing a 'kingdom of ends' as its necessary regulative ideal is coherent with his view of reason in its pure or theoretical guise. Reason for him always aims at a complete harmonious system; the full coherence of all elements in its domain is always the regulative idea or ideal. In the cognitive realm the goal is that of a unified and complete science of the natural universe. The parallel in the practical domain is not a unified social theory, but rather an actual kingdom of ends or fully harmonious society of rational agents. In both cases, however, coherence among originally disparate elements is achieved by subjecting them to universal principles.

This symmetry nevertheless does not provide a cogent argument here. The kingdom of ends, in which all individual pursuits are compatible and even mutually supportive, may be an attractive ideal for moral or social theory and practice, especially if the compatibility or coherence of wills preserves the rationality and autonomy of each individual, as in Kant's ideal society. But that pursuit of such an ideal must function as a limit and perhaps goal of each rational agent's behavior, if that agent indeed is to qualify as rational, once more must be established by argument rather than posited. The aesthetic symmetry with the theoretical goal of a fully unified science, expressed in the general idea of system or complete coherence of all individual elements in a domain, while a pleasing image, is insufficient to establish a rational requirement in this respect of each individual.

We may seek to supplement Kant's explicit arguments here. For this purpose we may borrow from contemporary Kantian rationalists. To begin, we must return to the basic notion of a reason for acting. Different individuals, of course, may have different reasons for acting. If I like chocolate ice cream, then I have a reason to go to the supermarket where it is on sale. If you do not like that flavor, then you do not have this same reason. But if my reasons in the circumstances are sufficient for justifying my acting in a particular way, then they must be sufficient to justify any agent in relevantly similar conditions (including desires) acting in that way. That is simply what it means for reasons to be sufficient for justifying actions.[4]

If we think, as Kant does, of subjective principles of action (or maxims) as determining which factors, including desires, count as reasons in various circumstances, then the conclusion just reached on logical grounds implies that such principles must be the same for all rational agents. This is the first premise of the argument for the impartial conception of practical rationality. It is not yet sufficient to establish that rational agents must be impartial, since as yet we have derived no implications regarding motivations toward other individuals. Thus, for all we have said so far here, it might be rational for every agent to act only in pursuit of her own self-interest. We have implied only that, if pursuit of self-interest is a rational subjective principle for one agent, it must be so for all.

The pivotal premise regarding motivation is the focus of the argument of Stephen Darwall, a contemporary Kantian ethicist.[5] The initial point is that a purely rational agent (or rational agent as such) will always act on the strongest reasons he has, just because they are the strongest reasons in the circumstances. That is, a rational agent as such will be primarily motivated to do what he does because it is the most reasonable thing to do. He will be motivated first and foremost to follow rational principles, which, as we noted, are the same for all. But if this is his primary motivation, then, according to Darwall, he will also desire or will that all other agents act on the same principles.[6]

In order to see why this claim is initially plausible (Darwall seems to think it self-evident), we should notice that motivation to act on one's strongest reasons is already in an important sense impersonal. One wills to act on these reasons simply because they are one's strongest reasons at the time, because they would move any purely rational agent in the same conditions. It is not because these reasons relate in any particular way to one's own desires that one is motivated to act on them. They may or may not arise directly from desires, but it is the fact that they would move purely rational agents that counts. Of course, in some sense reasons must be my reasons in order for me to be moved to act on them. But they are not my reasons because they further my self-interest or the satisfaction of my desires, rather because I am in those conditions in which they would move any purely rational agent to act.

If a rational agent's primary motivation is to act on rational principles that are the same for all, and if this motivation is impersonal in the sense indicated, then it is plausible that such an agent would will all other agents to be rational as well, to act on the same principles. But then Kant's conception of rationality is established: a rational agent must act only on principles that she would will universally. This *is*, of course, sufficient to rule out the pursuit of self-interest as a rational, general, subjective principle. An individual who wills the pursuit of her own self-interest primarily would not generally will that others act on the same principle, since their so acting will not in general be in her self-interest. On the other hand, moral principles can be willed universally without contradictory implications.

Thus Darwall seeks to establish the impartial conception of practical rationality by emphasizing the normative or motivational aspect of reasons and the concept of a rational agent. Reasons are what ought to move agents in so far as they are motivated to be rational; and rational agents are moved to act on their strongest reasons simply because they are their strongest reasons. They then will that all agents adopt these same attitudes toward what ought to move them. Another contemporary Kantian, Alan Gewirth, emphasizes not the normative aspect of reasons, but what he sees as the normative requirements of action.[7] According to him, as a rational agent, I must demand as a right those conditions (freedom and material prerequisites) that are necessary for successful action of any sort. But if I must demand these as rights simply because they are the necessary conditions for successful agency, then I must, if rational, recognize the same demands as made by other rational agents. Therefore I must grant them the same rights that I must demand myself, and I must recognize that, simply as a rational agent, I ought not to interfere with the freedom of others, as reasonably exercised.

On both accounts, then, a rational agent must intend only actions that he could rationally will for other agents as well, those actions which, if performed, would not violate his fundamental rights that he must will to have respected. This, of course, is the central Kantian claim. The main argument in this section for the conception of rationality that underlies this claim appealed to the motivations of a rational agent as such. Before seeing in more detail how Kant's basic principle, rationally required according to him, functions as a criterion of rightness, I want to look more critically at this conception of rationalty, especially as it relates to the motivations of rational agents.

D. *Motivation and Rationality*

The main argument in the previous section for the conclusion that practical reason must be impartial (that rational agents must act only on principles that they would will for all others) appealed to the claim that a rational agent as such is motivated to do what she does primarily because it is the most reasonable thing to do in the circumstances. In this section I want to ask first whether this is a plausible conception of rational motivation. Are normal agents, those who would not be deemed irrational in ordinary contexts of evaluation, moved to act on the deepest level by the recognition that their acts are the most rational among possible alternatives?

It might be thought that this question is irrelevant to a philosophical analysis of rationality. One might argue that it is not important how agents in fact act. The central point, it might be held, is only that, in so far as they are rational, they ought to act on the strongest reasons they have at the time, and they ought to do so because these are their strongest reasons. Two responses may be offered to this objection to our question. First, we may accept as a tautology that an agent ought to do what he has most reason to do. This follows from plausible analyses of 'ought' and 'reason,' and it is not my purpose here to question it. If we try to ask why an agent ought to do what he has most reason to do, then we seem to be asking why he has reason to do what he has most reason to do, and that question lacks point if not sense. But the conception of rationality as impartial is more controversial, and a premise in the argument for that conception was that rational agents are moved to do what is rational primarily because it is rational. The latter again constitutes a stronger claim than the tautology recognized above, and it is relevant to the evaluation of the argument for the Kantian conception.

One may still wonder why, if an agent, in so far as she is rational, ought to do what she has most reason to do, we cannot equally say that she ought to do so primarily because it is rational to behave in that way. If this ought to be a rational agent's primary motivation, then isn't the empirical question about how agents in fact act again irrelevant? This requires a second and deeper response. It may be that, rather than basing our actions on certain factors because we take them to be reasons, we take these factors to be reasons because we normally base actions on them: they normally move us to act. There may well be constraints of consistency on what we can count as genuine reasons in various circumstances. But our main question at present is whether rational consistency requires impartiality; and in evaluating the argument for the claim that it does, it is important to decide whether we are motivated to act on reasons because they are reasons, or whether they are reasons because we are normally motivated to act on them. Only the former thesis lends plausibility to the crucial lemma that rational agents will all other agents to act on the same reasons or subjective principles as those on which they base their actions.

Is it the case, then, that, in addition to being motivated to do what they take to be rationally required, agents are motivated to act as they do primarily because they view such actions as rational? As (I hope and believe) a fairly typical or normal agent, I am motivated to satisfy my own desires, to try to achieve and obtain what I consider good (the objects of my coherent set of desires). I am also motivated to share with my spouse, provide for my children, help my friends when they need help, contribute to worthy projects, and so on. In none of these cases (if I can trust introspection here) am I motivated primarily or most deeply by the thought that doing these things is rational. If my spouse or children thought that I am moved to provide first for them primarily because I perceive this as the rational thing to do, they would be repelled by my peculiar psychology. We would dismiss any conception of rationality that did not hold these things reasonable to do; we are not guided by an independent conception of rationality or of a rational agent as such in wanting to do them. It is true that I am motivated to avoid doing what I consider irrational, but that is because clearly irrational behavior is normally counterproductive in my attempts to satisfy my first- and second-order other desires, not because my deepest desire is to be a rational agent. (Indeed, I remain unsure that I have a concept of a rational agent apart from that of someone who tries efficiently to satisfy desires that humans ordinarily have.)

The hypothetical objections of my wife and children mentioned above have been recently voiced by other philosophers against those, such as Kant, who would require that acts be done for moral reasons if they are to have moral worth.[8] Such acts as providing for my wife and children, or helping my friends, if performed out of a sense of duty rather than because I care for them, would represent a kind of interpersonal alienation, a peculiar and almost inhuman kind of personal detachment. This is similar to the objection I have raised against the view that rational agents are primarily motivated to be rational. In relation to Kant's theory, the objections are both directed against the demand for impartiality in motivation, although, at this point, I am questioning the argument that leads to the conception of rationality as impartial, rather than its implications for morality.

This sort of objection can be answered, however, from within the Kantian framework itself. Attention to Kant's own language in many passages suggests a reply. We can think of the motivation to be rational, as well as the motivation to be moral, as a limit or accepted constraint, as a fundamental motivation only in a counterfactual sense, rather than as a force that ordinarily directly moves us to act. It need be only that a person would not perform an action if it were immoral or irrational for rationality or morality to be an overriding motivation in this sense. A person who satisfies this counterfactual description certainly qualifies as rational and moral in his behavior. Such a person need be neither abnormally preoccupied with rationality and morality, nor peculiarly detached from his personal projects and interpersonal relations and commitments. He need not have the constraining demands constantly in mind while engaging in everyday actions. If he has sufficiently internalized them, they will operate as constraints when required without intruding constantly into consciousness. In the same way, a good driver does not have to always think about obeying traffic laws in order to do so, and a good reasoner is not conscious of the rules of deductive logic when arguing.

As noted, Kant himself suggests this interpretation of the primacy of the motive to be rational and moral. Basic formulations of the fundamental principle are stated as limits, and even the formulation that speaks of an end, speaks of it as a limit rather than as a positive goal:

> So act as to treat humanity, whether in thine own person or in that of any other, in every case as an end withal, never as means only. (F II, 46).

The idea here is that, when we do use other persons as means to our ends (in business, sex, and so on), we must limit those ends to those shared by or rationally willed by the other persons involved. The first formulation, which requires willing in a way that could be universalized, dictates only the form that subjective principles must be capable of assuming and posits no ends at all. To function as a criterion of rightness, principles that posit ordinary subjective ends must be filled in. Hence, because of its lack of substantive content, the primary formulation of the fundamental principle of practical rationality and morality can express only a limit on the subjective ends of agents. Elsewhere in the *Foun-*

dations, Kant explicitly speaks of his principle as 'the limiting condition of all our subjective ends' (F II, 48), and he notes that the supreme end of rational nature itself is 'conceived only negatively' (F II, 54). This at least suggests that we should conceive of the motivation to obey the command of impartiality as also limiting in the sense defined.

It is true that in the *Metaphysics of Morals* Kant writes of other ends posited by reason itself, ends that do not function solely as limits, namely the happiness of others and the cultivation of one's own abilities. The necessity for the latter, however, follows from the requirement to will the means to any ends one may adopt (MM, II, DV, 51); and the former, if suitably weak, may be required to secure the means for ends that require co-operation (MM, II, DV, 53, 121). Kant views the duty to contribute to the happiness of others, to make their ends one's own, as imperfect, leaving great leeway for personal pursuits:

> a maxim of promoting another's happiness at the sacrifice of
> my own happiness, my true needs, would contradict itself
> were it made a universal law. – Hence this duty is only a *wide*
> one. (MM, II, DV, 53–4)

Thus, once more, it is permissible, indeed inevitable, that ordinary desire-based motivations normally move agents to act, that the motive of being rational and moral functions as a limit or counter-factual constraint.

Kant seems to find it mysterious how respect for impartial law can function as a motive at all. But this is because he refuses to recognize it as an ordinary causal factor on a par with other desire-based motivations. If, however, we avoid his idiosyncratic dualism of reasons and causes (the one operating in the noumenal, the other in the phenomenal, world), we should have no difficulty in explaining the motivation to be rational or moral as a product of social training. The individual's susceptibility to such training might be given a deeper biological explanation in terms of its value for the survival of kin. Given these explanations, if we interpret the motivation to be rational or moral as a limit to more immediately desire-based motives, it need not render a Kantian ethics vulnerable to the objection that it requires a peculiar and repellent moral psychology.

We must remember that we questioned the claim that a rational agent as such is primarily motivated to be rational in her behavior, as that claim functioned as a premise in the argument that practical reason must be impartial, that a rational agent acts only on principles that she wills for others. Our question now, therefore, is whether the primacy of this motive interpreted counterfactually or only as a limit suffices to establish the controversial conclusion. The constraint expressed, interpreted in this new more plausible way, remains impersonal. It therefore may seem that an agent who would not act on ordinary motives or subjective principles unless he considered them rational would still thereby will that all other agents act on the same principles.

But this can be contested.[9] Might not an egoist acting on the principle of furthering her self-interest not do so if she were convinced that it was irrational to do so? And might there not be such an egoist who satisfied this counterfactual constraint and yet, being convinced that the principle of self-interest is rational, yet not will that others act on it (since that would work against her self-interest)? I am not sure. If there could be such an egoist who was primarily motivated to be rational (in the counterfactual sense), then the argument from rational motivation for the impartial concept of rationality fails. But the existence of such an egoist is questionable. It at least seems doubtful that someone who always acts on a principle of furthering her own self-interest would not be more strongly inclined to do so than to forgo doing so if she became convinced of a conflict with canons of rationality. It is more plausible that such a person would never become convinced of such a conflict on the practical level, since she would naturally conceive as rational those deepest motivations on which she takes herself to act.

More importantly, the latter seems true of us all, egoists or not. The person who naturally provides first for his wife and children would be unlikely to become convinced that such behavior was irrational or immoral. It could happen, nevertheless. Huck Finn, for example, was convinced that his behavior, especially that behavior that we find most admirable, such as his loyalty to Jim, was immoral. Still he persisted; and that seems to return us to another question suggested in the previous paragraph, namely, whether normal agents would override their ordinary motivations were they to become convinced that they were irrational. Is the counterfactual constraint ordinarily satisfied? Again it is hard to tell without hard psychological evidence, especially given how rarely such conflicts would be perceived. Once more, however, the real question for us is whether a rational agent as such satisfies this constraint, and that seems more clearly plausible. On the other hand, couldn't an agent in fact be rational, normally act in a rational way, even though he would persist in such behavior if, like Huck Finn, he became convinced that it was irrational to behave as he does? Then such an agent might be rational without satisfying the counterfactual constraint.

Perhaps we should surface from such deep psychological waters to ask a simpler question: whether our ordinary concept of rationality implies impartiality in the Kantian sense. Must I as a rational agent will that all other agents act on the same subjective principles? This seems very doubtful in cases where I do not normally will or act impartially in the ordinary sense. Consider my preferring my children's interests to those of other children. When the interests of my children conflict with those of others, and it is not a matter of depriving other children of important rights or needs in order to make mine trivially more content, then I prefer that the interests of my children be satisfied. Must I therefore will that other parents act on the same principle in these circumstances and prefer the interests of their children? It seems rather that I could rationally prefer that they be impartial, for example. In fact, my willing that they prefer their children seems incompatible with my preferring the interests of my children when those interests clash with the interests of their children.

The only response for the Kantian rationalist here seems to be to claim that my preference is itself irrational, unless perhaps grounded in some deeper impartial principle, such as that all parents should prefer their children because all children tend to do better when all parents do so. But this is certainly not the reason why I prefer my children. Is my preference therefore irrational? What, then, of my preference for the satisfaction of my own desires, as opposed to those of total strangers, when these conflict? It seems that here I can give a reason (of sorts) for this preference (if, indeed, I need a reason in order to qualify as rational in this preference). I will enjoy the satisfaction of my own interests and desires in a way that I will not enjoy the fulfilment of the desires of strangers, and this appears to give me a reason for my preference. I can recognize that others have the same reason for preferring their interests, just as I can recognize that they will prefer those of their children. But once more I cannot consistently will that they do so. Thus I cannot consistently will that others act on the same principles as I do, and yet the principles in question appear to be rational.

The examples here need not appeal to a full egoist principle of always acting to maximize my self-interest. To assume that principle rational would be to beg the question against the Kantian. The weaker principle of preferring my interests to those of others when doing so does not violate their rights will suffice as an example of a principle that appears rational and yet cannot be consistently willed universally. Other examples as well seem to make clear that I can rationally will that others act irrationally. (It might be possible even to will rationally that I act irrationally in some conceivable circumstance; but that is more problematic in conception, and I will not pursue it.) Suppose that I survive a plane crash, and I am stranded on a desert island. I know that rescue planes have searched the area for survivors for several days. It would be irrational for them to continue searching the same area, and they have other pressing business to attend to. Yet I would certainly (rationally) will that they continue to do so.[10] Thus I rationally will that they act on an irrational principle.

Since the argument from motivation was highly dubious, and there are other reasons for doubting that practical rationality requires impartiality in the sense of willing that all agents act on the same principles, we may conclude that Kantians have not established that reason must be impartial. This shows once more only that morality is not rationally required of each agent. It remains to be seen whether Kant's conception of morality as impartiality captures our conception of rightness, and whether the demand to grant others the same rights that I claim for myself indicates a coherent, objective property of rightness to which our moral knowledge can refer.

E. The Criterion of Rightness

We have now answered our first key question for this chapter negatively. To begin to answer the second, we must first examine more closely how Kant's criterion of moral permissibility functions in practice. I have emphasized his view that morality consists in respecting the autonomy of others, limiting one's will to coherence with their rational wills. Incoherence is indicated by an individual's inability to universalize the subjective principle of his action. Kant's test for moral permissibility requires avoidance of two sorts of contradiction in attempting to universalize. Some principles contradict themselves (or the means necessary to realize them) when universalized. According to Kant, these violate narrow and perfect duties, which require specific actions, generally toward specific other individuals, and which can be enforced through law (and obeyed irrespective of motive). Other principles do not become self-contradictory when universalized, but they contradict or nullify means to ends that the agent must rationally have, thereby once again rendering his intentions incoherent. These violate wide and imperfect duties, requiring only unspecified actions, not matched by rights and not properly the object of civil legislation. (I ignore other permutations on these categories here.)

Some general objections to Kant's test for right actions as it works in practice can be answered simply by applying it correctly. Some critics have thought that by specifying the maxim of an action narrowly enough, one can render it immune from disqualification by this test. I have no trouble, for example, in willing that everyone named Alan Goldman at my university steal or lie when it is convenient to do so. But the objection is lame, since obviously only relevant factors are to be built into the statements of subjective principles, and the notion of relevancy can be determined internally, from a sympathetic interpretation of the Kantian system itself. Subjective principles refer only to factors that the agent counts as reasons for her actions in the circumstances. Clearly my name and place of employment do not count as reasons for most of my actions, and would not normally enter into reasons why I might steal or lie. To be somewhat more precise: reasons are those factors that make a prima facie difference in a rational agent's intentions. They need not constitute necessary conditions for her acting as she does, but they must raise the antecedent probability of her doing so. Because of this probabilistic relation, they help to explain why a rational agent acts as she does. Subjective principles that specify only reasons in that sense cannot be trivialized in the way this objection would have it.[11]

On the other hand, that Kant's test leaves much room for

controversy in the way it is to be applied, and in its implications once applied, is clear from his own notorious illustrations of its use, first in the examples from the *Foundations*. The most plausible application relates to narrow duties to others, specifically a promise to repay a debt. Kant points out that if we were to universalize the policy of breaking promises whenever in some difficulty, the institution of accepting promises would be destroyed (F II, 39; I, 20–1). Hence in willing this policy universally, I would both will that my promise be accepted and that it not be. I would remove the means to the success of the very maxim on which I act, hence will incoherently. There may not be a strictly formal contradiction here, since it is contingent that people would no longer accept promises so easily broken; but in willing the probable loss of means to the success of my policy, I do appear to be caught in conflict and irrational intention.

Kant's applications of the test to generate wide duties and supposed duties to oneself are far less convincing. Here, as noted, the contradiction is to arise not between the very maxim in question and its own universal instantiation, but between the latter and other ends that are presumed to be rationally required for each agent, or between the maxim universalized and the means to realize those ends. Kant holds, for example, that if I try to universalize a policy of not helping others in need, I will contradict my will in other circumstances in which I need the help of others (F II, 40–1). This contradiction in will must arise, apparently, because my own happiness is a necessary end for me, and because I cannot always pursue this end with any chance at success without the aid or co-operation of others. But the argument fails. Even granting that no one is self-sufficient (or that a truly self-sufficient person, for example a hermit, would not need to help others), not all agents require charitable help. If I can reliably predict that, being rich, I will never require aid in the form of charity, then I can be confident that no contradiction will ever arise within my will from the universalization of the policy of not donating to charity. If never doing so is wrong, then Kant's test as he applies it here proves to be too weak in failing to require it. (Alternative ways of applying the test of universalizing will be considered below.)

His applications of the test to show duties to oneself – to develop one's talents and not to commit suicide when future pain appears to outweigh prospective satisfaction – are yet more muddled. Both arguments appeal to 'Nature's purposes', Nature having given us talents to develop and use, and having given us self-love to improve life, not destroy it (F II, 39–40). This dubious metaphor can perhaps be removed from the premises here, however. It might be argued in line with the previous example that always failing to develop talents will contradict my will in those cases in which I might require their development for success in my other ends. In those cases I will intend the ends but not the means for their achievement, a form of practical incoherence. Similarly, it might be argued that suicide removes a necessary means, life itself, for any ends (necessary or otherwise) I might have. Hence willing it will be incoherent with the fulfilment of other ends I might or must will.

But these modified arguments also fail. As Kant himself realizes when he calls upon us to limit our ends to respect the autonomy of others, I can modify ends toward which I am naturally inclined in order to make them coherent with other ends and means at my disposal. Hence, rather than developing my talents as means to ends I will, I can achieve coherence by lowering my aims to match my lack of developed talents, remaining content with a life of relative idleness. That happiness is a necessary end for me does not entail that I must have developed talents in order to achieve it. Thus Kant fails to show that the universalization of my negative maxim will conflict with ends I must have, or nullify the means to the fulfilment of those ends. Similarly, if I will no other ends for myself, then suicide may be a rational act, especially if happiness is clearly no longer within my reach. In conceivable dire circumstances it might even be required as a means, perhaps the only means, to lessen the suffering of myself or others.

These last two examples might be damaging only to Kant's application of his principle, not to the principle itself or its proper use as a test of permissibility or criterion of rightness. If we do not believe that we have these duties to ourselves (as I do not), then we cannot fault Kant's principle for failing to show us that we do. Our question now is whether the principle captures our common conception of rightness, and using it to try to demonstrate unrecognized duties will not provide an answer. Nevertheless, we have also seen that its failure to generate a duty of charity may be more telling. We must look at examples beyond those provided by Kant to decide whether the test is indeed too weak or too strong, or both.

Other critics have suggested that the test is too strong in prohibiting practices that seem morally unobjectionable and perhaps even required. Consider as an example of the former, celibacy.[12] This, like homosexuality, could not be willed universally without willing the destruction of the human species and perhaps of existing rational nature, which Kant describes as a necessary end for rational beings. Yet most would hold that celibacy, if not homosexuality, is morally acceptable. These appear to be examples of practices that are morally permissible only if not everyone (or a very large number) engage in them. Perhaps failing to vote in a national election is another such example. If there are such practices, then the test of universalizing appears to be too strong. Other examples seem to generate even more counter-intuitive implications of Kant's test, which seemingly prohibits morally obligatory practices. Suppose that I oppose bigotry or help the poor. If these practices were universal, then there would be no bigotry to oppose or poor to help.[13] Willing them to be universal might appear to be self-defeating in much the same way that Kant holds the universalization of a policy of breaking promises to be self-defeating. If so, then so much the worse for his criterion.

But these purported counter-examples may be refuted by paying careful attention to our rule for the proper formulation of maxims to be universalized. Recall that genuine reasons why actions or policies are adopted are to be built into these formulations. A priest who is celibate for religious reasons can coherently will that all those who have these reasons remain celibate. Similarly, that all those with exclusively homosexual (or simply without heterosexual) desires refrain from heterosexual intercourse can be willed without willing that the human race die out. Contrast these cases with those in which a practice may be harmless if rare, harmful if widespread, and almost universally desirable in itself. Polluting or not paying taxes are examples of this sort. Here reasons for engaging or not engaging in these activities are themselves almost universally shared, so that universalizing the maxims that express them will conflict with other ends (for example happiness) that agents must have, or with the means to fulfil them (assuming that we require public services in order to be happy). Hence the implications of Kant's test are acceptable in both sorts of cases.

The examples of helping the poor and opposing bigotry can be handled as well, although somewhat differently. Here I can will without contradiction that all help the poor, so that *thereafter* there will be no poor, and similarly for victims of bigotry. Although the fulfilment of my universalized maxim will remove the means (or the necessity) for its further use, it is not part of my intention or will that these conditions continue to exist. I can, if you like, reformulate the maxims as that of helping the poor when they exist, and that of opposing bigotry where it exists.

Although these examples fail to prove Kant's principle too strong, it still faces the charge of being too weak, as indicated by its failure to generate a duty to be charitable. Other, more stringent negative duties may slip by this test as well. Consider our old example of the bike, and your moment of moral weakness in being tempted to steal it. Here, unfortunately, attention to the reasons that can be legitimately built into your maxim may be damaging, rather than helpful, to the successful application of Kant's test. Suppose that you are tempted to steal only bikes, so that its being a bike (rather than some other object) that you can take without fear of apprehension is among the reasons why you would take it. The general institution of private property would not then be placed in jeopardy by the universalization of your maxim to steal the bike in your circumstances. Thus universalizing would not be self-defeating in just the way it was claimed to be in the case of breaking promises. It is true that were your maxim to become universal practice, bikes might be more closely guarded or securely locked than they are now. But it is almost universally true now (at least in Miami) that unlocked and unguarded bicycles are stolen, and yet some owners persist in leaving them unlocked out of carelessness or laziness. Thus here the universalization of your maxim would not necessarily destroy the means to its fulfilment, and Kant's test fails once more to rule out your immoral policy.

Whether you would actually will that all those in a similar position to do so steal bicycles, given that you will to do so yourself, is another question that is sometimes confused for Kant's formal test. Kant does claim that immoral agents attempt to make exceptions of themselves rather than willing their maxims universally; but he once more seems to be making a point about being unable to universalize immoral principles coherently, rather than making a psychological point (F II, 41). We might think of the empirical counterfactual question as an alternative test for permissible actions, a variation on Kant's criterion as he applies it. Here an agent asks not whether he could will his principle of action universally, but whether he actually would do so. Even this alternative test might not rule out the immoral practice in regard to bicycles, however, since a thief might be indifferent to its universalization if he were always careful to lock any bike he might possess.

Having seen that Kant's application of his test (whether the individual, given her ends, the ends she must have as a rational agent, and the means required to realize them, can coherently will the universal form of her subjective principle) proves too weak, we might pursue further variations on it to see whether they fare better. One clearly stronger test would be to require not that the individual actually will the universalization of his maxim (which also turned out to be too weak), but that all agents will a given maxim. For Kant, of course, there is no distinction between the question whether an agent can coherently will the universal form of her maxim and whether all agents can, since in both cases the real question is whether this form contradicts the maxim itself or other ends that all agents must have. But the empirical questions are clearly distinct. While the empirical test applied to one individual was too weak, applied to all it is quite easily seen to be too strong. There are few actions or policies that all individuals would will, especially not policies that involve or attempt to resolve conflicts among individual interests.

There are further variations that fall between these two. We might ask whether a given agent would will his maxim from all relevant positions, for example, as recipient or victim of the action, rather than as agent. This test is weaker than the one which requires that all would will the maxim, since this test restricts the question to an agent with a single set of values, not requiring him to adopt the values of those in the other relevant positions. There are two problems with this new variation. First, while it may seem plausible as a criterion of subjective rightness, it would fail to specify an objective property of rightness as the same for all rational agents. It will fail to do so if a person's values, including what will bring her happiness if successfully pursued, affect what she wills (as prudentially rational) and differ from the subjective

118

values of other agents. The test therefore would lack Kantian implications regarding the possibility of objective moral knowledge, our main concern here. Second, while designed to be weaker than the variation that requires that all agents will the maxim in question, this test proves again to be too weak. The oft cited fanatic Nazi, for example, who wills the annihilation of non-Aryan groups, might accept his fate, given his present values, if he were non-Aryan himself.

The final variation that we shall briefly consider here is a generalization of Rawls's requirement that just distributive rules must be acceptable to (willed by) all when all are ignorant of the morally irrelevant differences among them.[14] Ignorance of these factors blocks agents from building them into their reasons for acting or choosing, and renders their wills impartial to that degree. This requirement, if imposed on all subjective principles, is the closest to Kant's own, since, according to him, fully rational agents would not will to act on the basis of morally irrelevant differences. At least they would not try to take advantage of such differences, and this is what Rawls's veil of ignorance is supposed to prevent. Here, by adjusting those factors of which agents are to be ignorant, and, on the other hand, by allowing them knowledge of certain of their values and other aspects of their psychology, we might generate the proper degree of impartiality (operating as a constraint on the pursuit of self-interest) to produce only morally permissible principles that pass the test. At least, if each individual or morally significant group were allowed to design a veil of ignorance that barred knowledge of just those factors that the individual or group took to be morally irrelevant, and that allowed knowledge of those reasons for action that were taken to be morally permissible, then no individual or group would perceive any discrepancy between applications of the test and intuitive judgments regarding rightness.

The charge against this variation of Kant's test therefore cannot be that it is inherently too strong or too weak, that is, too strong or too weak to match whatever considered moral judgments we happen to share. But two other related objections arise immediately. If we consider only the veil of ignorance designed by a particular individual or group, even one which shares our own moral framework or coherent set of beliefs, then we must recognize that the classification of acts as permissible or impermissible that results from the application of this group's test reflects only its own shared set of prior moral convictions.[15] Once more, therefore, the test would lack any claim to objectivity. The implication, central to Kant and to our reading of him, that we can have objective moral knowledge grounded in *a priori* principles of practical reason, is lost. On the other hand, if we consider various tests of this sort, applied by different groups, using different veils of ignorance that reflect their own view of morally irrelevant factors, then there is certainly no guarantee that judgments regarding rightness implied by these tests will agree. The tests taken together predictably will leave us with no coherent view of what is permissible and what is not, especially in regard to morally controversial matters.

This brings us to our final question in this chapter, whether Kant's approach can claim to capture an objective property of rightness, or a set of moral constraints that is the same for all agents.

F. The Objectivity of Rightness

We have seen that for Kant rightness consists in coherence or compatibility of ends among rational wills; right actions are those which do not violate the autonomy or frustrate the ends of other rational agents. This requirement is reflected first in the test of universalizing subjective principles of action, the idea being that principles which conflict with themselves or with other necessary ends or means when applied to all express only incoherence among rational wills. The concept of coherence is expressed more explicitly in the model of a kingdom of ends, where human purposes and endeavors will be jointly realizable and even mutually supportive.

We saw in the previous section that, while Kant's test may constitute a necessary condition for moral action (from the agent's point of view), it is too weak to capture even our shared convictions regarding rightness and wrongness. But if Kant's ideal model of the kingdom of ends is viable, if, to be more precise, conflicts among individual ends and interests can and must be resolved in a way required by reason so as to result in only compatible purposes and intentions, then his fundamental insight would be sound even if his test for right actions is not. According to Kant, the kingdom of ends is 'only an ideal' (F II 50), a regulative idea of reason, but it is a viable ideal if we are indeed free to modify our desires in the direction of social coherence, as we are required to do by reason. Our final question, then, is whether there is some way of resolving conflicts among individual interests that is required by practical reason, such that actions are right if they fit the system that results from this resolution.

Unfortunately, Kant himself offers little clue beyond the metaphor of the kingdom of ends itself how these conflicts are to be resolved. Of course, the list of duties generated by the test for permissible actions expresses partial resolutions, or resolutions of particular kinds of conflict. If breaking a promise, for example, would be convenient for me, and in that sense would serve my self-interest, but at the same time would harm the recipient of my promise, then the conflict is to be resolved in favor of the other person. Each duty toward others implied by Kant's test represents a resolution of this sort. The problem is that prima facie duties generated in this way, and therefore prima facie rights as well, themselves can conflict. In fact such conflicts constitute the interesting moral questions. In our day the issues of abortion, reverse discrimination, the allocation of professional services, and redistributive taxation (to name but a few) all involve conflicts among prima facie rights and duties of different groups and individuals.

Kant offers very little guidance on how to resolve conflicts among duties and rights, and what little he does offer counts as much against as in favor of use of his theory for this purpose. His notorious prohibition of lying no matter what is at stake on the other side is a case in point (MM, II, DV, 155). A defender of the Kantian framework might maintain plausibly that Kant is simply applying his principle wrongly here, which is no refutation of the principle itself. He should have recognized that one can universalize a principle to lie when that will prevent the violation of a basic personal right. If one lies, for example, in order to prevent a physical assault, then this reason is properly built into the maxim to be universalized. If people always told lies for this reason, that would not prevent others from believing them (since others would not necessarily know that they were lying for this reason, hence would not necessarily know that they were lying at all). Thus the universalization of this maxim would not be self-defeating in the way in which it would be self-defeating to will universally breaking promises for convenience (a more pervasive reason that would destroy the institution) or after having borrowed money (a matter of public knowledge).

This is all well and good for showing that the example of lying to prevent violations of seemingly more important rights fails to reveal Kant's test as too strong (as it would be if applied as he applies it in this case). But the problem here is that it seems equally possible to will without contradiction that assaults be permitted in order to prevent lies (when lying is the only way to prevent assaults). Perhaps you or I would not will that this priority be universal; but there appears to be no contradiction either in conception or will in our doing so. Since it need never be the case that we will be potential victims of assaults that are preventable by lies, willing the odd priority universally need not involve us in contradictory wills. (For all I know, you may be a more likely assaulter than victim, although I would like to think better of readers of ethics books.) If we rely instead on the variation of Kant's test that asks what agents would actually will if they were made to will universally (as lawmaking members in a kingdom of ends), then unfortunately I believe we would find only disagreement in just those hard cases that interest us most. Some individuals or groups, for example, would will that abortions always be available on demand; others would will that they never be available at all.

Kant's general statement on this matter is simply confusing. He writes:

> a conflict of duties and obligations is inconceivable. It may, however, well happen that two grounds of obligation, one or the other of which is inadequate to bind as a duty, are conjoined in a subject and in the rule that he prescribes to himself, and then one of the grounds is not a duty. When two such grounds are in conflict, practical philosophy does not say that the stronger obligation prevails, but that the stronger ground binding to a duty prevails. (MM, I, MEJ, 25)

Kant's distinction between ground and obligation here may be similar to the newer distinction between prima facie and overriding obligations. He would probably have resisted the notion of an obligation that is merely prima facie, since he holds that all obligations bind rational agents necessarily, rather than some-times, or only in the absence of certain competing factors. Never-theless, ignoring this idea of necessity, we might view Kant's test as generating prima facie obligations to be weighed as he would have us weigh 'grounds'.

Unfortunately, he provides no explicit hint as to how this is to be done so as to objectively resolve these conflicts. In the *Doctrine of Virtue*, he raises certain questions of moral casuistry that involve weighing competing moral factors, for example whether it would be permissible to end one's life in order to save one's country (MM, II, DV, 86), or to say what is not true for reasons of etiquette or politeness (MM, II, DV, 95). But he does not explicitly answer these specific questions, let alone indicate a perfectly general method for doing so.

The general Kantian framework nevertheless does fit better with certain ways of augmenting it for this purpose, and there are some implicit suggestions in this direction in his writings. It is clear, for example, that the utilitarian way of weighing benefits and burdens in resolving conflicts among interests would be soundly rejected. In *Theory and Practice*, Kant provides an example of a person who has been entrusted with money by a dying man for his heirs, unbeknown to them. The person's family would benefit far more from the money, being presently in dire want. Kant makes it clear that duty nevertheless requires that the money be turned over to the rightful heirs, despite the balance of utility (TP I, 53).

Further implicit clues as to how to extend the Kantian frame-work so as to resolve conflicts among interests, duties, or rights can be gleaned from his political philosophy, specifically his position on justified legislation. He holds that if law is used as an instrument with which to maximize aggregate happiness, then conflicts will be inevitable and irresolvable, since human concep-tions of happiness differ greatly (TP II, 58). Rather, freedom is to be limited only to the degree necessary to make the freedom of each compatible with the freedom of all. The basic right of humans is to freedom compatible with that of others (MM, I, MEJ, 43–4), and coercion is justified only when it prevents viol-ations of this right (MM, I, MEJ, 36). As should be expected, autonomy is the fundamental guiding value here.

Kant is explicit and clear that criminal laws properly prevent violations of perfect duties to others. He is less unambiguous on forced redistribution of goods through taxation. A student of his ethics would expect that he would disallow such governmental intervention in free market distribution, since he holds that charity is an imperfect duty for individuals, and in general that imperfect duties should not be enforced through law. But that student would be surprised. Kant writes:

> it follows from the nature of the state that the government is authorized to require the wealthy to provide the means of sustenance to those who are unable to provide the most necessary needs of nature for themselves. (MM, I, MEJ, 93)

He appears to view this obligation on the part of the wealthy as contractual, the existence of all members of a state depending on their agreement to commit themselves to mutual support. He might also have pointed out here that support of the needy is not for the purpose of increasing their happiness, but rather to provide the material means required for their exercise of autonomous choice, to which they have a basic right. The problem is that it can be argued from the same Kantian framework that agents have rights to the fruits of their autonomous activities, and, once more, that imperfect duties are not to be enforced through law, since that would violate the right to choose when and how to fulfill them and call into question the moral worth of the actions that do fulfill them.

The issue of redistributive taxation affords a good example of how opposing positions can be equally supported within the Kantian framework. Excellent evidence of this possibility is the face that views as diametrically opposed on this issue as those of Rawls and Nozick both claim to derive from fundamental Kantian assumptions.[16] From a variation on the universalization test, in which contractors unanimously choose rules of distributive justice from behind a veil of ignorance that bars knowledge of morally irrelevant differences, Rawls concludes that a rule would be chosen that maximizes goods to the worst off. From a fundamental right to autonomy, to lead one's own life and not be used as a means to the welfare of others, Nozick concludes that no one has a right to the fruits of another's free economic agreements and activities (as long as the latter violated no rights at the time).

Neither argument contains obvious errors, and both are distinctively Kantian.

It is true that Nozick emphasizes autonomy and the second formulation of Kant's principle, while Rawls relies on a variation of the first formulation. But had these emphases been reversed, the conclusions of these latter day Kantians might well have remained the same. After all, allowing the poor slowly to starve while collectively they support the economy can be construed as using them merely as means. And, as noted, they will in effect lack the right to lead their own lives if they lack the material prerequisites for its exercise. On the other hand, the wealthy might not be able to will significant redistribution universally (in the absence of threats), since this might well nullify the means to their happiness. Even if we estimate what would be willed under a veil of ignorance that blocks knowledge of social and economic positions, choices of *laissez-faire* and maximally redistributive rules appear to remain open, to be determined by the psychologies (attitude to risk) of the hypothetical contractors. The former would be chosen by those with a gambling spirit, unwilling to settle for a mediocre share of goods and willing to take chances in the face of uncertainty; the latter, by those more conservative about risking their life prospects. General levels of affluence, how much one could expect in different economic strata, might also affect the choice.

Thus the emphasis on autonomy does not in itself distinguish between these diametrically opposed positions on this morally and politically crucial issue. If at most one of these positions can be right, then the Kantian framework appears unable to specify coherently a single property of rightness or set of moral constraints the same for all. Even if we grant (as we did not in an earlier section) that rational agents must be motivated to honor in others the same rights that they claim for themselves, this does not suffice to indicate universally correct solutions to moral conflicts. There will remain different and incompatible ways to limit the autonomy of some in order to protect the autonomy of others. Which necessary conditions for free choice and action are viewed as more important will depend on the evaluators as well as on those whose actions or practices are being evaluated. Thus Gewirth's neo-Kantian position mentioned earlier, which requires recognition of universal rights as means to freely chosen actions, remains, like

Kant's own criterion, unable to specify a rationally required set of universal constraints that will resolve moral conflicts.

Once more the prospect of finding this set of universal moral constraints looks even dimmer when we adopt a critical attitude toward this framework and refuse to be limited to consideration of its fundamental value. In weighing conflicts, the effects of actions on capacities for autonomous choice may not be the only morally relevant consideration, or even the deciding factor. Pain or suffering caused to agents (apart from its effects on their autonomy), or even suffering caused to sentient beings who lack the capacity for autonomous choice, may sometimes be viewed as overriding. Conflicts among genuine interests do not all reduce to opposing effects on the freedom to act; and once more there will be incompatible ways of weighing different morally relevant factors, including, but not limited to, this one.

Returning for a moment to the example of distributing or redistributing material goods in society, the most intuitively acceptable position to most present day Westerners might be some compromise between the views of Rawls and Nozick. If so, the Kantian might respond to the problem posed here by saying that this compromise must be worked out in practice by political means. She may consistently hold that different distributive schemes may be right for different societies, and that any may be right for a particular society if it has emerged from a political process that reflects a social consensus. This may actually be close to Kant's own view on this issue. He held that a moral state must embody the principle of equality before the law, which implies equality of opportunity. But he also held that the latter is compatible with any inequalities in possessions, and that the test for just law is whether it could be willed by all coherently, not whether all actually agree with it (TP II, 60–61, 65, 67).

One may wonder how the notion of rightness can remain objective or even coherent, how a Kantian can maintain that moral constraints are the same for all, if he allows that different distributive rules may be right for different groups. Doesn't this imply a moral relativism directly at odds with Kantian objectivism? Not necessarily. Relativism of this sort once more need not conflict with realism about rightness. Right rules here are not relative to the beliefs of evaluators as evaluators. In fact, the relativism here may not be properly characterized as moral relativism, since there are universal criteria for right distributions. All right distributive rules share the property of reflecting the general will or political consensus, and of being coherently willable universally. Furthermore, there is a single constraint imposed in political contexts of acquiescing in authoritative political decisions as long as they could be rationally willed by the populace.

This position does not ascribe rightness and wrongness to the same distributions for the same groups and societies (which would, of course, be incoherent), and the fact that different distributions may be right for different societies is compatible not only with moral realism, but perhaps even with objectivism, at least in Kant's sense. Right rules are those that could be rationally willed and are coherent with the general will, whatever it may be (although what it is will depend on the subjective states of its members). The Kantian can still claim that knowledge of what such rules are is grounded in *a priori* principles of practical reason (the demand for impartial or broad coherence).

It might then appear promising to accept this political solution to the objection that the problem of distribution exemplifies, the objection that Kant's system cannot generate a non-relativist, objective notion of rightness on which to base claims to moral knowledge. But the response, I believe, results in an impoverished domain of application for moral concepts that fails to do justice to the use and functions of moral discourse. Agreeing that any solution to an apparently serious moral issue is right if it enjoys a political consensus prevents one from judging the socially accepted arrangements to be wrong. This, as is obvious and was argued in the chapter on Hobbes, is an unacceptable implication.

The Kantian might respond that, when we criticize a particular view dominant in our own society, we normally do so on the ground that this view fails to cohere with more fundamental values of the group with which we identify. To return to the question of distributing social goods, if this sort of objection is raised to an actual distributive scheme, then it amounts to the claim that this scheme fails to reflect the general will, or its rational version, in the deepest sense. But then, the Kantian can point out, it fails to meet his (objective) criterion for an acceptable scheme or set of social rules. Hence, he will say, he does have a way of criticizing the status quo in moral terms, and of accommodating differences among social arrangements for different societies, while

127

maintaining the criterion that preserves the conception of rightness as universal.

At this point, however, our erstwhile Kantian has slipped into using a criterion for right distributions for his society that is no longer political. Whether a scheme reflects the general will is no longer to be determined in terms of an empirical determination of the social consensus. Rather, the criterion is itself moral, a matter of coherence with the group's fundamental moral values, which, it is now admitted, can differ from those of other groups. Thus the objectivist, realist thrust of the notion of rightness has now been relinquished. Right distributions are relative not to political acts, but to particular moral frameworks of societies, and of evaluators as members of those societies. The coherence criterion itself is no longer universal, and the distinctive feature of Kantianism so far as we are concerned is lost. Just as the relativization of Hume's notion of rightness destroyed its realist pretensions, so this relativistic version of Kant's criterion of rightness fails to retain Kantian implications for the possibility of moral knowledge (of universal moral constraints).

The difficulty for Kant illustrated by the problem of distributive justice could have been posed as well by analysis of any of the other moral issues mentioned above. We must therefore answer the third question for this chapter negatively as well: the constraint he imposes on moral judgment, that it be impartial or coherent with the wills of other rational agents, either cannot be satisfied (if put in terms of actual willing by all), or is too weak to specify a property of rightness independent from subjective moral frameworks (if put in terms of the possibility of coherent willing).

G. Conclusion

As in epistemology, Hume's moral philosophy set the stage for Kant's, when the former emphasized the difference between moral evaluations and judgments of ordinary empirical fact. But for Hume the model of empirical knowledge and inquiry, broadly construed, remained proper in ethics as well, since he located the ground of moral judgments in affective reactions of observers in certain frames of mind to certain features of their objects. Kant, on the other hand, sharply differentiates practical decisions and moral judgments expressing them from perceptual judgments of both outer and inner sense. His model for moral knowledge, I suggested, is partly mathematical and partly that of knowledge of scientific laws, themselves grounded in *a priori* principles of the understanding. Therefore he is far more explicit and emphatic than was Hume about the rational constraints on moral judgments that distinguish them from matters of mere taste or sentiment, or from purely affective reactions. The fundamental constraint imposed by reason itself is that of coherence, which Kant views as subsumption of data at each level under principles that aim at complete universality.

We saw that for him, the coherence of one's will with those of all other rational agents is a demand of reason itself. It is irrational not to make one's ends compatible with those of others, to violate their autonomy in one's choices. This is not because such action is imprudent, as Hobbes claimed, but rather because reason demands a broader coherence (amounting to impartiality) than the coherence of personal ends and means to which the concept of prudence refers. Aside from analogy and metaphor, however, the main argument that I could reconstruct for this claim appealed to a psychology of motivation for rational agents that I rejected (and that Kant himself found mysterious).

I rejected also the claim that the requirement of impartiality captures a single conception of rightness as the same for all agents. Even if we find the emphasis on autonomy an attractive ideal or expression of our own fundamental value, we must recognize that there remain different ways of limiting various freedoms in conflict, ways endorsed by different ideologies or moral frameworks within our own culture, none of which is willing to accept all of them as right. We are driven once more by these fundamental divergences in value orientations to relativize judgments of rightness to particular frameworks, an anathema to the Kantian rationalist.

On the positive side of the ledger, I did not find Kant's requirement too strong a constraint on an individual's moral judgments: each evaluator is required to find a morally relevant difference for each difference in morally judging cases (this amounts to the demand that such judgments must be intended to apply to all in relevantly similar circumstances, circumstances which determine the reasons for action). It may well be, as I suggested in the section on motivation, that what we count as reasons for acting or for evaluating are what we are naturally inclined and socially trained to count as reasons. There is no independent conception of rationality to guide us here. Nevertheless, the constraint on coherence in moral judgment is a real one, even if relativized to an individual's or group's set of evaluations. This we can accept from Kant without accepting the stronger claims that it is irrational not to will or act morally, where moral action obeys a set of constraints or obligations that are the same for all agents.

If we combine Kant's notion of coherence within a set of moral judgments with Hobbes's emphasis on moral rules as necessary for the survival and flourishing of groups, then we will relativize the demand for coherence to sets of evaluations within groups, members of which share moral frameworks or fundamental values. An individual will have reason to adhere to the maximally coherent set of evaluations within groups with which he identifies, although such reasons need not always override others. The truth of ethical evaluations can be determined by such coherence; and an evaluator will have moral knowledge if her judgments are explained (in part) by the fact that they cohere in this way. This sort of explanation is not causal in the way that ordinary empirical judgments are causally explained by the presence of the properties to which they refer. But our historical survey, now complete with egoists, utilitarians, and Kantian rationalists, has proved unable to identify a property of rightness akin to empirical properties that could enter into such explanations.

CHAPTER IV

Realism, Emotivism, Coherentism

A. Summary

Our inquiry thus far has centered on the question whether empirical knowledge constitutes a suitable model for an account of moral knowledge. In the case of empirical knowledge, properties instantiated independently from our beliefs about them causally help to explain the beliefs that we do have about them. If moral knowledge is cut from the same model, then we ought to be able to specify the nature of moral properties (of rightness and goodness) and give some account of how their presence can help to explain causally our moral beliefs. In regard to knowledge of non-moral goodness or value, Hobbes's relativist, subjectivist, relational concept suggested a plausible account. The good for each person is the object of his rational desire. A desire is rational if its fits an informed and coherent set of ends and means to realize them. That an object is good in this sense can help to explain causally why, for example, a person feels satisfaction in its possession; that something is bad for someone can causally explain why its achievement or possession brings only frustration. Regarding knowledge, that something is good in this sense can help to explain why a rational person comes to believe it so, although its being so is not dependent on her believing it to be.

Our historical survey failed to reveal an equally coherent analysis of moral goodness (of persons) or rightness. Hobbes himself provided a plausible account of the origin and function of moral rules and moral reasons, the latter in terms of indirect or modified self-interested reasons. Individuals have reasons of self-interest to join various groups and enter into co-operative endeavors. They then have reasons to obey the coherent set of

131

norms making possible and governing co-operative enterprises within these groups. What Hobbes failed to show is that these reasons must always override other more direct and narrow self-interested desires that agents may have, that it can never be in the long-run interest of any individual to violate moral rules (or to develop a disposition sometimes to do so). The equation of moral obligation with rational prudence failed to capture our common notions of both, as Hobbes intended.

For Hume, moral goodness and rightness consist in being such as to be approved from a more impartial perspective, expressive of the universal sentiment of sympathy. He provided arguments against purely objective moral properties, pointing out that we must apprehend all relevant objective properties in situations before making moral judgments, which serve also to recommend actions and express attitudes and social norms. Although the anti-objectivist strain here is obvious and, I believe, sound, I argued that Hume should not be interpreted as a pure subjectivist or emotivist. According to him there are real relational moral properties, consisting in objects being such as to elicit approval. Neither side of this relation can be eliminated. Moral properties are second-order relations between first-order relations (of utility) and rational, sympathetic responses to these first-order relations.

More important than my interpretation of Hume for our present purposes were the arguments in that chapter that the realist, relational view of moral properties seems more plausible on several counts than simple emotivism, the view that moral judgments express attitudes without referring to real properties of objects or events and without having truth values. I briefly argued there that emotivism seems not to account for moral argument and reasoning beyond apprehension of the non-moral facts and that it does not capture our intuition, when we are engaged in such reasoning, of seeking truth and knowledge as a guide to conduct (when we are concerned to act morally).

Despite these advantages of the realist, relational view over simple emotivism, Hume's version of realism led to contradictions. In his view utility primarily constitutes the non-moral side of relational moral properties, the basis for sympathetic approval. It seems instead that informed, impartial, and sympathetic evaluators can disagree on whether policies that maximize utility should be approved. This disagreement forces the Humean realist to ascribe rightness and wrongness to the same policies for the same groups. Disagreements of this sort appear more damaging to the realist view than those regarding non-moral goodness. Non-moral goods need not be good for all people, but all such goods will share the property of being the object of rational desire for some person, even when they cannot be jointly realized. In the case of rightness, however, the question of distribution arises. Unless we relativize the truth of judgments concerning rightness to groups of evaluators and thereby relinquish moral realism and the empirical model for knowledge, we cannot say that right policies are those approved by any rational evaluator (and wrong policies those disapproved by any rational evaluator). Since some policies will be approved by some and disapproved by others, this account is incoherent. If instead right policies are those approved by some and wrong policies only those disapproved by all, then the account is far too weak to capture our negative moral judgments. (I will review relativist realisms below.)

Kant resolves such disagreements by entirely eschewing utilitarianism. He holds that a proper appreciation of the requirements of impartial reason shows that moral worth and rightness cannot depend on ends sought or achieved, but only on the coherence of the agent's will with those of other rational agents, on his ability to will universally. Kant's rational constraint, however, proved too weak to capture a full set of moral obligations, too strong as a general demand of practical reason (as opposed to a demand on moral reasoners), and, like Hume's account, unable to prevent or resolve fundamental conflicts among evaluations satisfying it.

In light of the failure of our historical survey of dominant moral traditions (and their more contemporary offshoots) to produce a consistent account of real moral properties, it remains to develop a relativist, coherentist analysis of moral knowledge that construes the truth of such judgments in terms of coherence within moral frameworks. Before embarking on that task in the final chapter, I shall in this one canvass in a less historical but more systematic way the merits of the most plausible form of moral realism as opposed to emotivism and coherentism as meta-ethical theories.

I have defined moral realism as the thesis that the truth of moral judgments (ascribing properties of goodness or rightness) is independent of evaluators' moral beliefs. Properties real in this sense could causally explain beliefs about them, and the possibility of such explanations makes empirical knowledge the proper model for an account of moral knowledge. Emotivism is the thesis that moral judgments express attitudes and so lack truth values entirely. Coherentism, of course, holds that the truth of moral judgments lies in their coherence within a moral framework (the notion of coherence will be elaborated in the next chapter).[1] Explanations for beliefs expressed by such judgments will not appeal to real moral properties as causes, since according to this view there are no moral properties independent of evaluators' beliefs. It is important to compare all three views in their most sophisticated versions. Some advantages that realism enjoys over simple emotivism it may not enjoy over a coherentist account of moral truth and knowledge, or for that matter over a more sophisticated non-cognitivism.[2]

The grounds on which these positions are to be compared have been implicit in my criticisms of the historical accounts considered, and indeed in some of their attacks on rival positions. First, we must note implications regarding connections, if any, between moral judgments and motivations to act. Second, we require explanations for moral conflicts and disagreements and an account of arguments and reasoning to resolve them. In regard to moral reasoning, we seem to require some notion of truth in order to account for inferences and for the goal of moral knowledge beyond apprehension of the non-moral facts. Finally, we need to explain the apparent supervenience of moral properties on non-moral properties, or alternatively the requirement that we not make different moral judgments when we cannot find differences in non-moral properties (and furthermore, that we take the latter differences to be generally morally relevant). We need to explain this phenomenon while also accommodating the inability of realists to identify types of moral properties with types of non-moral properties.

This inability is what leads me to view as the most plausible realist analysis the kind that we considered in the historical analyses. This analysis might identify particular instantiations or tokens of moral properties with the non-moral bases that elicit rational approval or will, but it types the properties according to relations which include these evaluative reactions. Accounts of this sort, we saw, must answer the charge of incoherence in the face of fundamental disagreements in evaluations based on the same non-moral bases. In light of this problem, emotivism gains plausibility by dropping the non-moral side of the relation as inessential to the typing of moral judgments. I shall argue, however, that coherentism enjoys the sources of plausibility for both its rivals without their liabilities.

B. *Morality and Motivation*

An argument dating back to Hume against (objective) realism is that moral judgments intrinsically motivate, or at least that they connect more directly to motivation and action than do factual judgments. The argument, if its premises are accepted, works only against belief in objective moral properties, not against the relational realist who includes evaluative responses as part of the relation. These responses are themselves linked to motivations. The more traditional realist who believes in objective moral properties can respond as well. He can point out that various factual or non-moral judgments also entail, or at least suggest, proper attitudes toward their objects. To say of a higher animal that it is alive (or dead), or in pain, or starving, requires or suggests the propriety of certain attitudes and actions toward it. And yet these are clearly factual judgments. To say of a sentence that it is true, or false, or ambiguous, or badly formed, suggests or expresses attitudes of acceptance, dismissal, or puzzlement.[3] Thus, moral judgments too might refer to objective facts, or at least to facts independent of the evaluator, and still express or suggest attitudes and appropriate actions.

Realists of either stripe can dismiss the major premise of this argument and thereby turn it against the emotivist position. While normally we intend to recommend a course of action to others by saying that it is right or ought morally to be done, we need not be motivated ourselves to do what we recognize as right. Denying any necessary connection here is compatible not only with the recognition that moral judgments ordinarily recommend actions to others, but also with acknowledgment that first person moral reasoning too usually aims at eventuating in decisions how to act. We normally engage in such reasoning only when we are interested in doing the right thing. A person might reason morally, however, because she wants to avoid censure, and she might give advice as to what is moral in order to aid a friend or cohort in avoiding censure.

I have analyzed the concept that one morally ought to do x in terms of one's having moral reasons (overriding at least any contrary moral reasons) to do x. Reasons, it seems, must be linked in some way to motivation. The idea of a reason to act in a particular way that could never motivate anyone to act in that way seems useless if not senseless. But this does not establish that moral judgments analyzed in this way intrinsically motivate. We can say simply that a moral reason is a factor that would motivate a rational moral agent, someone interested in acting morally. Similarly, a reason generally is what moves a rational agent, a prudential reason what moves a prudent or self-interested agent, and so on. This analysis of moral reasons leaves room for a coherent notion of an amoralist, a person who can make judgments about what is right and wrong but is not in the least moved to do what is right because it is right. It also allows us to say that such an agent ought not to do certain things.

The amoralist, as others have pointed out,[4] constitutes a problem for emotivism. *He*, at least, does not seem to be expressing a positive attitude, intended to guide actions, when he notes that an action is right or morally required. The emotivist has two possible replies. The first is to say that those called amoral, if they nevertheless use moral terms sincerely, are somewhat positively disposed to actions they judge right and negatively disposed to actions judged wrong. These attitudes, although linked in the usual way to motivations, are always overridden by stronger self-interested or anti-social motives. However, although this psychological explanation would account for the amoralist's apparent lack of interest, the explanation itself is ad hoc and lacks evidential support. Why think that he is motivated or disposed to be moral when there is no sign or any such motive at all?

The second response for the emotivist here is to say that an amoral person, when using moral language, expresses no attitudes herself, but refers to what others approve or disapprove. This response entails that such a person must use moral language in a deviant way; her terms lack their usual meanings. Again there is no evidence, independent of the theory in question, for thinking that people who lack the desire to be moral must mean something different by their uses of 'right' and 'wrong.' It might be argued that their very lack of motivation to act in accord with their judgments constitutes the required evidence. But differences in such direct connections to action are not generally evidence for differences in understanding or meaning, and the first person avowals of amoralists and their seemingly unambiguous debates with moralists constitute counter-evidence to the thesis that amoralists understand and use moral terms differently.

Another related problem for the thesis that moral judgments intrinsically motivate (the thesis sometimes called 'internalism') is that it seems to make the question 'Why be moral?' always lame if not without point. In some contexts this question seems both pointed and difficult to answer. It is ambiguous as stated, and the kind of reason sought must be specified. If one seeks moral reasons here, then the question is indeed pointless, inviting only regress. But one may well seek prudential reasons, which may exist and may not. The emotivist too may want to know whether such reasons reinforce or oppose the motivations or attitudes expressed by moral judgments. But for her there will always be some motivating reason to be moral, the reason intrinsically expressed in moral judgments themselves, so that the question cannot have the sharp point it seems to have from the mouth of the amoralist, for example. So the emotivist seems to make the question too easy to answer.

That factual statements may be action guiding, and that moral judgments may not be, appear to give the realist account an advantage over emotivism. But while the emotivist posits too intimate a relation between moral judgment and motivation, the non-relational realist, who simply identifies moral properties with psychological properties such as utility, misses the connection that exists. It is an important feature of moral judgments that they ordinarily recommend or dissuade from courses of action. The judgment that something is the (morally) right thing to do is ordinarily a positive appraisal of the action, and essentially so (or importantly so, if you do not believe in essences). Relational realism is plausible here in noting the connection to motivation for normally moral agents. It captures this connection in its claim that judging an action right is judging that it is such as to be approved or willed by rational moral evaluators. Normal evaluators are motivated to act in ways that rational evaluators would will or approve.

As yet, however, we have compared the realist position only with emotivism on this issue, not with a plausible coherentism. The realist may appear to have a different sort of advantage over the coherentist. It lies in the fact that obligations appear to be independent of the desires and beliefs of evaluators. From the first person point of view, they appear to come from outside me as moral judge. Coherentism allows that particular obligations exist independently of their bearers' beliefs that they do. Obligations exist if positing them coheres better with the fullest, most coherent set of evaluators' beliefs than denying them. But it may appear that particular obligations are more strongly independent of their bearers' beliefs, independent of whole sets of beliefs as well. I cannot evade a moral obligation by rearranging my set of moral beliefs so that acceptance of the obligation no longer coheres with the new set. The realist captures this intuition by holding that rightness is a property independent from my beliefs about it as moral reasoner. He might charge that the coherentist cannot do the same.

The intuition in question can be captured by the brand of coherentism that I shall endorse here, however. That is because the sources for sets of evaluations or norms with which particular moral beliefs must cohere are those groups in which individuals interact. As Hobbes argued, moral norms exist to settle conflicts of interests among individuals in groups engaged in co-operative enterprises. Individuals have self-interested reasons, more strongly, deep psychological needs, for commitment to and identification with various social groups, groups defined in part by their moral norms. Given the rationality of such commitments, individuals will acquire reasons, independent of their other desires if not of their moral beliefs, for moral restraint, and these reasons will be reinforced by further socialization into group practices.

I hesitate to say that such reasons or obligations are entirely independent of individuals' moral beliefs, since these beliefs will normally derive from norms applied to the individuals from an early age, usually by their parents as spokesmen for certain groups. Moral reasons and obligations derive from the same norms. The sound part of the intuition underlying the realist's point remains intact, however – obligations are indeed imposed from without, although ideally internalized by moral individuals. An individual cannot avoid or nullify moral obligations by rearranging her set of beliefs because beliefs are not so easily rearranged and because it is the informed and coherent evaluations (and norms they express) of the social groups of which she is a member that determine her particular moral obligations. While making this point, we must allow that an individual can criticize the norms and shared moral beliefs of such groups. I shall have more to say on this below, but clearly one ground for criticism of dominant evaluative judgments according to the coherentist is lack of coherence with more central sets of values.

Thus coherentism of this sort does not deny an external source for moral obligations, although it does deny that this source consists in a real property of rightness. It recognizes that there is no unique coherent set of norms or judgments that could be used to fix reference to such a property, that there can be incompatible sets of this sort that determine obligations for their adherents. This position, like relational realism, posits a contingent but genuine connection between moral judgments and motivations. Normal individuals are motivated to follow the norms of the groups with which they identify, although this motivation may be overridden by conflicting self-interest or more partial reasons. The amoralist, who lacks this normal disposition, is the person who fails to identify with the social values of any group. Fortunately he is relatively rare, but certainly not inconceivable. He need not be conceived as one who contemplates real moral properties yet remains unmoved by this spectacle. Instead, he is the true loner, alienated from genuine social connections that would provide normal moral motivation.

The coherentist's explanation for this phenomenon too is at least as plausible as the (relational) realist's. Thus these positions share an advantage over emotivism on the issue of moral judgment and motivation (ironically, since emotivists have typically criticized realism on this score). To distinguish further all three meta-ethics, with their implicit accounts of moral knowledge (or of its non-existence), I turn to our second criterion: the ability of each to explain conflicts and disagreements within and across moral frameworks.

C. *Conflicts Within Frameworks*

I have located the central problem for a realist account of moral properties in fundamental disagreements between internally coherent moral frameworks, disagreements that are indicative of incompatible non-moral bases for moral evaluations. Others recently have questioned the very idea of a coherent moral framework, or set of beliefs and values they express, that could always guide behavior in morally charged contexts, and that could fix reference to non-moral bases for consistent moral judgments. The questions arise from phenomena characterized as moral dilemmas.[5] If such phenomena indeed reveal that all moral frameworks which attempt to guide behavior must be, or are very likely to be, internally incoherent, then this finding would be damaging not only to realism, but to coherentism as well. It would be problematic to characterize truth in this domain in terms of coherence within a framework, if all frameworks must contain inconsistent judgments (and so be incoherent). The interpretation of moral dilemmas to which I refer therefore has been seen to support a non-cognitivist meta-ethic. In this section I shall briefly summarize and criticize this interpretation.

Moral dilemmas as so characterized arise when an agent has conflicting moral reasons such that neither set overrides the other so as to cancel completely its force. Reasons conflict when they support different courses of action that cannot be jointly undertaken. When they do conflict in this way, we might appear to have situations in which agents ought to do A, ought to do B, and cannot do both. If we accept that 'ought' implies 'can' and that, if one ought to do A and ought to do B, then one ought to do A and B, then from these premises we can derive the contradiction that one ought to do A and B and that it is not the case that one ought to do A and B.[6] We can drop the conjunctive principle and the implication from 'ought' to 'can' and still derive a less formal conflict. From the principle that one ought not to do what will prevent his doing what he ought to do, it follows in this sort of situation that one ought to do A and ought not to do A.

If these ought judgments are supposed to refer to a real property of rightness, then there is an obvious problem here for the realist. Although there can be conflicting imperatives or desires, all of which retain force, contradictory judgments cannot all correspond to the presence of real properties. An action cannot be both right and not right, where this property is not to be relativized so as to remove the contradiction. There is a problem here too for even the relativist kind of coherentism, since the contradictions apparently arise within sets of evaluations made by particular individuals or groups. It will not help to relativize the truth of moral judgments to frameworks, to interpret truth as determined by maximal coherence within frameworks, if each is incoherent in containing implicitly or explicitly contradictory judgments.

Bernard Williams, who first raised the problem in this form, seems to take it as an argument against any form of cognitivism, against the thesis that moral judgments express genuine beliefs capable of truth or falsity.[7] He points out that even when one decides that one of two conflicting ought statements overrides the other, the former often does not cancel the force of the latter. In Williams's view this contrasts moral judgments with genuine beliefs, rendering such judgments similar in this respect to desires. When a person acts on one of two conflicting desires, she may continue to feel the unfulfilled desire; but when a person decides that one of two conflicting beliefs is true, she deems the other false and no longer regards it as a guide to action or attitude. In the case of conflicting moral oughts, Williams holds that an overridden obligation may nevertheless continue to require reparations and feelings or attitudes of regret and even guilt. These requirements indicate that it continues to be a genuine obligation.

In responding to these arguments, I wish to deny neither that moral considerations within a framework can be evenly balanced for and against a given action (or for two incompatible actions) nor that an obligation that is overriden may then require reparation and regret. Some ethicists would hold that virtual ties between conflicting obligations are inevitable because different values of a single culture or individual may be incommensurable, incapable of being weighed against each other at all.[8] I cannot think of any two values that cannot be weighed so as to give a clear verdict in at least some contexts. And it is difficult to think of any value in a moral framework like ours that cannot be outweighed by some others, when those others are more centrally at stake. A framework or value orientation that places great emphasis on loyalty to family, for example, may nevertheless recognize that fairness to strangers may outweigh trivial interests of family members. Dilemmas, or at least virtual ties, instead arise because the same value can pull in opposite directions (for example, one can save only one of two lives in danger) and because diverse values, at stake to different degrees, may fail when in opposition to generate clear verdicts on overriding obligations.

We cannot deny that conflicting reasons may tie; we must rather deny that virtual ties imply contradictions within moral frameworks. One way to avoid formal contradiction is to relinquish the principle of conjunctivity (that if one ought to do A and ought to do B, then one ought to do A and B). Indeed, the denial of this principle is plausible whether moral judgments express rational beliefs or rational attitudes or desires. In regard to desires, it may be desirable to eat a dish of chocolate ice cream and desirable to eat a piece of chocolate cake, but not desirable to do both; it may be desirable to play tennis and desirable to jog, but not desirable to do both. In regard to rational beliefs, it may be rational to believe each sentence that I write in this book, but not rational to believe them all. Thus, whether, in Williams's terms, moral judgments are more like beliefs or more like desires, it may not be possible always to conjoin them.

Denying this principle does not completely solve the problems here for realism and coherentism, however. We saw that, if we describe ties among opposing moral reasons in terms of conflicting ought statements, and if we accept that a person ought not to do anything that prevents her fulfilling an obligation (that is not overriden), then we must conclude that sometimes an agent ought to do an action that she ought not to do. This conclusion in itself raises doubts about a real property of rightness and about the coherence of a set of moral beliefs that implies it. We must therefore refuse to describe ties among conflicting moral reasons in this way. Fortunately, there are alternative descriptions with equal or greater plausibility.

We need not say, as some realists might, that there is always one overriding obligation in cases of apparent ties, although we may not know in such situations which obligations override. In some cases this claim might gain plausibility from the fact that we seek moral advice in difficult situations that involve conflicting reasons. We assume that such advice might guide us toward a proper resolution of the conflict; that is, we assume that the opposing moral reasons are not really tied, although we do not know ourselves which reasons determine the single right course of conduct. In other contexts, however, the realist's appeal to ignorance is implausible, here as elsewhere in ethics, because we have no idea what further information could be relevant to the resolution of ties. Indeed, it may be clear that there is no further information to seek, as in the case when a person can save only one of two threatened lives.

In cases of real ties, we still need not say that agents ought to do both of the incompatible actions. Remember that I analyzed 'ought (morally) to do x' as 'has overriding (moral) reasons to do x.' In the case of genuine ties, neither set of reasons overrides the other. Nevertheless, reasons on both sides outweigh any other (third) set of reasons that the agent may have. Therefore, the most plausible account of such cases is that the agent must (ought to) perform one action or the other, but may perform either.

When an agent does perform one such action, he may properly feel regret for not having been able to do the other as well, and he may owe reparations to those whose prima facie rights went unfulfilled, especially if he helped to create the situation. The appropriateness of regret does not show that he ought to have done the other action, only that as a sensitive person he ought to feel badly when others are harmed, especially perhaps if he was personally involved. A person could equally regret not having been able to prevent harm because of physical disability. A feeling of guilt, as opposed to regret, over the action not performed is not entirely appropriate and certainly not required of a morally sensitive person (unless he created the situation). But we can certainly understand why such a person might feel guilt, having been socialized to take moral reasons very seriously and in the normal course of events not to ignore those that have not been overridden. Even if we admit that it is better (in terms of moral consequences) that agents be disposed to feel guilt whenever serious moral reasons remain unheeded, this admission does not imply the problematic interpretation of tics in conflicting moral reasons that ascribes incompatible oughts. As I shall argue further below, optimal moral consequences are no sure guide to the truth of meta-ethical theses.

We may similarly deny Williams's other inference here. The appropriateness of regret, indicative of the fact that an overriden obligation is not entirely cancelled, does not show that moral judgments are more like desires than beliefs. For the relational realist moral judgments are beliefs about relations to appropriate attitudes: approvals, disapprovals, and presumably positive and negative feelings such as regret linked to these. For coherentism of the sort to be defended here, moral judgments are beliefs about reasons that normal agents are motivated to follow (and regret not following). Either view accommodates the appropriateness of regret in the unfortunate situations under discussion.

Thus conflicts within a single moral framework give no advantage to the emotivist over realism and coherentism. I should point out now that I am not interpreting a single moral framework as the set of moral beliefs of an individual or group. Individuals may belong to different groups with incompatible sets of norms and values, and groups too may endorse incoherent sets of moral judgments (in a sense of coherence to be elaborated in the next chapter). Instead, a single framework consists of a coherent set of moral judgments that might be endorsed by a rational individual or group. I have shown in this discussion that sets of judgments can be consistent despite apparent moral dilemmas. The serious problem for realism lies, I believe, in conflicts between frameworks as so defined. But I shall argue that this issue favors coherentism, not emotivism.

Before turning to accounts of moral disagreements themselves, I shall note implications of the three meta-ethics regarding appropriate attitudes toward both one's own beliefs and the beliefs of those who oppose them when disagreements arise.

D. Fallibility

How should one regard the moral judgments of others with whom one disagrees? When should one be willing to interfere in order to prevent actions based on those judgments? On the one hand, when actions are harmful to others who do not share the judgments on which they are based, one may feel justified in interfering no matter which meta-ethical theory one holds. On the other hand, actions that appear harmful only to those who acquiesce in them because they share the moral judgments on which they are based, as well as self-regarding actions that appear to harm only the agent himself, may elicit distinctions among the three categories. Suppose, for example, that the members of a certain sect or persons from another culture are being punished for dancing or displaying affection in public, or suppose that some member is punishing himself by fasting for having violated a rule that prohibits such activities. Assume also that these punishments could be prevented by interference. Do the different meta-ethical views capture our normative beliefs in such cases?

One generally recognized justification for paternalistic interference is ignorance on the part of the agent. If someone is about to harm herself by an action based on factual error, then, absent the opportunity to prevent the harm by correcting the error through education, others may be justified in preventing it by more coercive measures. If laymen desire to take drugs to cure their ailments when in fact the drugs would have the opposite effects, then laws preventing their acquiring drugs without prescriptions appear to be justified. On the other hand, paternalistic interference cannot be justified every time someone thinks that an action of another is harmful to that person or foolish. Constant intrusions against personal liberty must be prohibited. One way to achieve a reasonable compromise on this issue is to invoke the distinction between factual error and disagreement in value judgments. Would be paternalists are not justified in interfering to prevent actions that they perceive to cause harm to the agents or to others who consent in the actions, when the potential paternalists perceive these actions to be based on foolish or misguided values rather than on straightforward factual errors. Thus, while preventing people from taking drugs when they are ignorant of the effects is justified, interference in the actions mentioned in the previous paragraph would not be justified.

One need not claim that it is always clear how to distinguish factual from evaluative beliefs as bases for actions in order to hold that paternalistic interference is justified when self-harm would otherwise result from verifiable factual error. The moral realist's problem is that she cannot draw this distinction in these terms at all. When she disagrees morally with another person, she simply perceives that the other person has made a factual error. Moral judgments for her are factual judgments; they are true or false by corresponding or failing to correspond to real properties. Because she interprets them as factual judgments, she has no obvious way to distinguish them so as to protect actions based on them against paternalistic interference.

Of course, even for the realist, moral judgments constitute a distinct class of factual judgments, and so she could simply single them out for such protection. But this would be *ad hoc*. She lacks any principled way to draw a distinction here that results in a reasonable position on paternalism. The coherentist, on the other hand, can recognize that a moral judgment on which an action is based may be true for the agent although false for him (the evaluator). If the action is harmful to others, he may still wish to oppose it with force, since his own moral judgment normally will be action guiding for him. But he may refrain from interfering with actions based on (alien) coherent moral evaluations when these actions affect only those who share the evaluations. The emotivist too might refrain from imposing his attitudes on others, when there are no unwilling victims of their actions. But according to realism, an opponent's moral views cannot be true for him; they are simply mistaken.[9]

The realist might reply that he need not adopt a dogmatic or intolerant view of the moral opinions of others, if he has a properly modest or fallibilist view of his own opinions. As mentioned, according to him, when two persons disagree in their moral judgments, one must be mistaken. In holding his own moral beliefs on a given issue, he will assume that an opponent is mistaken. But he need not make this assumption dogmatically or with sufficient zeal to prompt constant interference in the affairs of others. Although the realist's moral judgments express genuine beliefs in his view, he can certainly recognize his own fallibility in these beliefs. What he lacks here, however, as I argued above, is a principled way to distinguish moral beliefs as *more* fallible then others. He therefore cannot draw the distinction that underlies the reasonable position on paternalism defined above.

If it could be claimed that moral judgments refer to real, unobservable properties, then perhaps the fact that moral beliefs are not observational would indicate why these beliefs should be more fallible than others. But this claim would render the normal action guiding aspect of these beliefs problematic. It is implausible that inference to properties that can never be observed directly guides actions. As Hume argued, the phenomenology of moral judgment also provides evidence against the claim that it consists in such theoretical inferences. If we consider the type of realist analysis that seems more plausible, say that the rightness of an action lies in some relation between its consequences and its approval by rational evaluators, then perhaps the special vulnerability of these beliefs could be held to lie in our difficulties in estimating consequences, or our lack of knowledge of the nature of rationality. The problem with this claim is that we often can estimate consequences reliably and can specify the characteristics of a rational evaluator. In addition, it is not only when we are uncertain of consequences that we may be rightly loath to interfere in actions of others based on alien moral beliefs.

The moral or prudential effects of believing an empirical theory do not constitute evidence for its truth. Meta-ethical theories are kinds of empirical theories, true if they correspond to real properties of normative moral systems. Thus the moral implications of a meta-ethical view, if there can be any such implications, must be irrelevant to its truth. Furthermore, a coherentist meta-ethical theory should not in itself have genuine moral implications. These points appear to make this argument regarding meta-ethics and paternalism problematic. The point of the argument, however, is not that each meta-ethic directly implies what would-be paternalists ought to do, but instead that coherentism allows for a distinction that we naturally draw in reflecting on paternalistic interference and that many evaluators utilize in their moral frameworks. This distinction is not readily available to the moral realist. Meta-ethical theories must account for features of normative theories, and realist meta-ethics seems unable to account for a distinction that is part of our normative framework.

Despite this disadvantage on the issue of attitudes toward the moral beliefs of others, the realist might claim an advantage at least over the emotivist in being able to recognize his own moral fallibility.[10] An emotivist knows that she approves of some sets of moral judgments themselves more than she approves of others. She also knows that her set of judgments is subject to change and revision. She can picture that her present set of evaluations will evolve into another set, which, of course, at that later time she will endorse as better. In this sense she can perhaps approach a notion of fallibility for her own moral judgments.[11] But, since her present attitudes constitute her present standards for evaluating, it is hard to see how she can now regard her moral judgments as (now) possibly wrong. In judging beliefs possibly wrong, it seems that we must use actual standards for evaluation, not possible standards (standards that we might adopt at some later time). As we saw in the chapter on Hume, there is another sense in which an emotivist might hold moral judgments mistaken, namely, when they are based on mistaken factual beliefs. But I believe that we want to be able to view moral judgments as fallible even when we are certain that we have the non-moral facts right. Our tendency to seek advice despite being confident of the non-moral facts in a morally difficult situation expresses recognition of such fallibility.[12] It is this kind of fallibility – possible error by current standards – that an emotivist meta-ethic seems unable to capture fully, while realism and coherentism can.

Thus far in this section we have seen that coherentism and emotivism are better able than realism to capture a distinction that is useful in considering justified paternalism, or interference in self-regarding or consensual actions when we morally disagree with others; while coherentism and realism are more believable when it comes to attitudes toward our own controversial beliefs. There is a further difference between coherentism and realism here, in that the latter can claim to be more strongly fallibilistic. But I doubt that the truth of this claim would really favor the realist. Given his test for truth, a coherentist can certainly recognize that any particular moral belief could be false. I shall argue in the next chapter that he can assess whole moral frameworks as well. He cannot, however, conceive of falsity in an ideal moral system, one that is internally coherent, universally shared and endorsed, and under which society clearly flourishes and none of its members are dissatisfied. It is a mark of realism, with its non-epistemic view of truth, that it can conceive that even our best verified theories at the Peircean end of inquiry, those theories that meet all operational tests of the relevant kinds, could yet be false, at least in part. This test can be applied to normative moral theories or systems of moral beliefs. If all humanity were to converge on a single set of moral views that was operationally ideal, the realist no doubt would hold that the truth of these views entered the best causal explanation for this convergence. But truth would be equated neither with the final agreement itself, nor with the other features of the moral beliefs that render them operationally ideal.

This criterion for a realist metaphysics has been emphasized by Hilary Putnam.[13] He has argued against metaphysical realism in regard to science and the physical world on this ground. According to him, we cannot conceive that an ideal scientific theory, one that meets all our theoretical and practical tests for good theories – one that is perfectly predictive, simple, fruitful, and so on – might yet contain falsity. His argument (in a nutshell) is that any reference scheme that mapped the terms of such a theory on to objects so as to satisfy all these constraints and have the theory come out true would be a correct reference scheme. Model theory tells us that such a reference exists. There could be no grounds for thinking this scheme not correct, since it is a part of the ideal theory of the world. But if the reference scheme does all we could want and therefore is correct, then the overall theory would be true not simply according to it, but true *tout court*.

I believe that this argument can be answered in defending realism for empirical theories. To answer it, we have to picture reference (to unobservables as well) in terms of some real or natural relation between terms and their objects. If this reference relation is real, then we can be mistaken in the ways we conceive referents. We will be mistaken if our beliefs fail to correspond to the presence of the relation in question. This property must help to determine reference 'all the way up', that is, it must determine the reference of terms within a theory of reference as well, so that once again we can get such a theory wrong. Given this determination of reference, in terms of causal or other real relations, I have argued at length elsewhere that we can imagine falsity in those theorems that purport to refer to theoretical entities, even in an operationally-ideal scientific theory.[14] The reference scheme that maps theoretical terms on to objects so as to make the theorems true may not be the correct scheme, the scheme determined by the real reference relation.

Can we in a similar way imagine falsity in an ideal moral theory or framework? Remember that we are speaking now not of meta-ethical theories, the implications of which we are testing here. Those theories, I take it, are true or false in corresponding or failing to correspond to features of normative ethical frameworks. If realism is true as a meta-ethical theory, then normative theories, and particularly operationally ideal normative theories, should meet the test now being applied. They will meet this test if their terms refer to real moral properties, and if reference is determined as pictured above. Assuming that reference within theories interpreted realistically is grounded in some real relation, causal or otherwise, we want to know whether we should interpret normative moral theories in this way. One way, perhaps, to determine this is to determine whether we can conceive falsity in an operationally-ideal normative theory.

There is a further problem, however, in applying this test to normative ethical systems or sets of theorems or principles. We must specify what are to count as operational tests for such theories. Suppose, for example, that some normative system simply captured all particular moral judgments and choices based upon them. In that case we clearly might still judge the theory false – if, for example, consensus in its favor had been reached only as the result of brainwashing. It is part of the realist's argument against coherentism that such coherence between particular beliefs and principles is not sufficient for truth in moral judgment. However, such coherence is not the only ideal feature of a normative theory that makes it operationally ideal. This feature is similar to predictiveness for empirical theories, but in both cases theories must meet further operational tests. In the case of a moral framework, we must picture as before that we have a predictive theory under which society flourishes, all its members are happy, productive, and treated fairly according to everyone's critical appraisal that is free from extraneous influences and rationally arrived at.

It is not clear that we can conceive as false a moral framework, or set of coherent moral principles and judgments, that is ideal in this stronger sense. If, by using the terms 'right' and 'good' according to the criteria implicit in this framework, by recommending policies according to this usage, we achieved the happy results envisaged, it would seem entirely gratuitous to claim error about the nature or presence of goodness and rightness. Our inability to conceive such an ideal theory false might appear to count against moral realism. It seems to indicate that the truth of moral judgments is not independent of (all) moral theories, as realism requires. But we must be still more careful in characterizing operational tests for moral theories and the notion of independence that the realist invokes.

He claims that the properties of goodness and rightness are

independent of evaluators' beliefs and the theories built on them. He need not hold that these properties are independent of our practices and the interests they serve. As we have seen, he can interpret moral properties as relational and view the non-moral bases for our evaluations as involving the satisfaction of our interests. Uses of 'right' and 'good' so closely connected to individual and social well-being as described above will indeed be correct uses that generate true moral judgments, but this does not refute the reality of moral properties as we earlier defined it.

Thus, given plausible operational tests for normative theories, it is not clear that Putnam's test favors any of the opposed meta-ethical views. All three would hold the ideal theory as described true, but for different reasons. For realism and coherentism, this truth does not lie in the fact that accepting the theory has good moral consequences. Truth and epistemic justification are distinct from moral justification. The realist judges the ideal theory true because individual and social well-being, which are partial referents for the theory's moral terms, also constitute plausible non-moral bases for relational moral properties. The coherentist holds this theory true because it is not only internally coherent, but also meshes as a system with non-moral norms, including epistemic and psychological norms. (I shall argue in the next chapter that a coherentist can and must take such coherence with non-moral evaluations as part of what determines moral truth.) The emotivist would endorse this ideal theory too, because he and others approve it is morally best, the closest that he comes to a notion of moral truth. Thus there seem to be no grounds for distinction in the truth value that each meta-ethic must assign to the ideal theory.

From the coherentist's perspective, if a normative theory that is operationally ideal in the sense defined could be considered (partly) false, this judgment would have to be made from the point of view of some other coherent framework. I have so far in this discussion assumed convergence on a single ideal framework (as part of its ideality). It is this assumption (together with other operational tests) that prevents Putnam's test from differentiating realism from non-realism. If we instead picture two incompatible frameworks, each ideal in securing rational convergence within a particular society, then our old problem of incompatible non-moral bases for moral judgments arises again for the realist. He is again unable without contradiction to ascribe truth to all the judgments of these normative systems. I can see no reason why incompatible theories could not be ideal in the sense defined, if all members of different societies happened to converge internally on particular schemes, say one that was more collectivist and one that was more oriented toward the protection of individual rights. The problem for the realist would then be not that he had to assign truth to the judgments of ideal theories, but rather that he could not do so.

Before refocusing on that problem, we may conclude this section by reiterating that coherentism seems more plausible than its rivals when we combine implications regarding proper attitudes toward both one's own beliefs and those of opponents when in disagreement. The coherentist can distinguish between those judgments of an opponent that are true for her and those that are not (whether because based on factual errors or because incoherent with her more fundamental values); and he can be more inclined to interfere with actions based on the latter judgments. He can also distinguish (as perhaps an emotivist cannot) an agent who performs wrong actions despite knowing them to be wrong from one who acts immorally without knowing that he does so. The coherentist can blame agents who act in violation of their own moral frameworks more harshly than others. In regard to his own moral judgments, or those norms and implicit evaluations of a group with which he identifies, there are three grounds on which he might criticize these or come to hold them false. First, particular judgments within such sets can be incoherent with others, with the principles that capture these judgments and the values they express. Second, the values of any particular group can be criticized from the point of view of another, especially a broader, group. It was pointed out that individuals typically identify with several diverse groups of differing scope. Third, a reflective individual may develop from the social inputs her own conception of an ideal moral framework, although, if genuinely moral, this conception will always refer to ways of settling conflicts of interests within groups.

I shall have more to say about coherence, falsity and error in moral reasoning in the next chapter. We turn now to descriptions of moral disagreements themselves and of ways to resolve them.

E.   *Disagreement*

I have been maintaining all along that a relativist coherentism in regard to moral truth can accommodate seemingly irreconcilable disagreements in moral judgment. This appears to be a major advantage of the view over relational realism, which seems forced by such disagreements to ascribe rightness and wrongness to the same actions and policies. The relativist-coherentist simply admits in the face of interminable dispute that what is right in relation to one moral framework may not be right in relation to another. But the availability of this response raises a host of other questions. Does this tack imply that we need never recognize genuine disagreement on an ethical issue? Can the relativist account for seemingly genuine disagreements over the truth of certain moral claims? Can he oppose on moral grounds an action by an agent with a different set of values and moral judgments; can he say without equivocation that the other person ought not to act that way? Can such disagreements ever be resolved through rational debate?

If these questions all must be answered negatively, then the advantage claimed by relativism in accommodating interminable lack of agreement seems outweighed by the realist's ability to allow for genuine dispute among those whose views differ not simply on the single issue, but, as is more likely, diverge in other ways as well. For the realist, widespread differences in the moral beliefs of two individuals do not prevent their referring to the same properties when using moral terms, or from genuinely disagreeing about the presence of these properties in various contexts. He can make use of a causal theory of reference, according to which we refer to what causally explains certain of our uses of terms, whatever our beliefs about those referents might be. Real moral properties can enter such causal relations, hence becoming the topics of genuine disputes irrespective of the extent of moral disagreements between the disputants.

It is incumbent similarly upon the coherentist who allows for incompatible coherent frameworks to show how genuine disputes can arise and be settled despite varying degrees of genuine moral disagreement or divergence in beliefs. In order to do this, she must show first how those who diverge in moral beliefs can nevertheless share referents, or at least disagree about the same topics or genuinely contradict one another. She must show second when disputants can be considered to argue from the same moral framework and third how, in terms of that background, they can resolve their dispute.

When faced with a morally abhorrent practice of some alien group, say a group that practices human sacrifice, we want to say that they are wrong in doing that and that they ought not to do it. But I have analyzed the concept that one morally ought or ought not to do *x* in terms of one's having moral reasons for or against *x*. Moral reasons are factors that would motivate rational moral agents. If, as seems plausible, a person's moral reasons derive only from the moral frameworks to which she subscribes, then it becomes problematic to say that an alien group has moral reasons not to practice human sacrifice, if nothing in their framework prohibits it or implies its prohibition. If they have no reason to desist, then, under the analyses given, it is equally problematic to say that they ought not to engage in this practice. If it is not the case that they ought not to engage in this practice, then how can one say that the practice is wrong? Once more relativist coherentism faces a major problem in making sense of judgments that seem genuinely to oppose the actions of those with widely divergent moral beliefs. For both the realist and the emotivist, moral judgments do not vary in meaning or intent when directed toward agents with generally different moral beliefs, and this appears to be a decided advantage.

The relativist-coherentist nevertheless can reply. As an opener, she can point out that she can oppose the actions of those operating within different moral frameworks with at least the force that can be mustered by an emotivist. All three sorts of meta-ethics can recognize the normal action guiding function of moral judgments, although only for non-cognitivist views is this a matter of entailment or necessity. For all three, opposing moral judgments will normally suggest different courses of action, and my own judgments will require me to act according to them. I need not always be tolerant of the practices of those with widely different views, although, if I recognize that some action is right according to their framework, I may be more reluctant to interfere. My reluctance presumably may be overridden by a perception that unwilling victims are being harmed.

Thus the three views differ little in their implications (or lack of them) regarding practical or active opposition to alien practices, at least those involving unwilling victims (see the discussion of paternalism in section C of this chapter). The problem that the realist poses for his rivals is that we also want to say sometimes that people with divergent views disagree about the truth of a particular moral judgment and can argue the matter in an attempt to resolve their dispute. Coherentists, like realists, can think of meaning in terms of truth conditions (the meaning of a statement is determined by whatever makes it true). If so, they must either view those who ascribe rightness and wrongness from different moral frameworks as meaning different propositions by their statements, or they must construe the judgment that an action is right as meaning only that this judgment coheres best with the evaluator's other moral beliefs. The thesis that an action can be right according to one framework but not according to another follows from the central idea of truth as determined by coherence within a framework, and it is essential to the coherentist's explanation for interminable lack of agreement. If, then. a coherentist is to hold both that those arguing from different frameworks fail to contradict one another when making apparently divergent moral judgments, but also that those with different beliefs may genuinely disagree on the truth of a particular evaluation, then she must not view those with different beliefs as always arguing from different frameworks.

In Chapter 2 I pointed out that there is no purely objective test for whether apparent disagreements represent different moral frameworks. This depends on whether the disputants are willing to argue rationally on the issue in question. If they are, then the ground rules for such arguments require that they reason from a data base consisting of those particular evaluations and principles generalized from them which they share. This union of their respective moral beliefs constitutes the single framework in terms of which the argument is to proceed and the issue is to be settled. The answer to the issue in question most coherent with the rest of this framework is the true resolution of their dispute.

If we consider this reduced, shared framework as that which determines the truth of claims in dispute between two parties, then in such contexts the meaning of their statements ascribing rightness and wrongness will be determined, not by the totality of their moral beliefs – the full frameworks with which particular true beliefs must ordinarily cohere – but rather by this reduced core. In the contexts of such disagreements, they therefore can share referents for their moral terms (or, if terms that fail to refer to real properties lack referents, they can at least address the same issues and use the same criterion of coherence for the truth of their claims). The coherentist may admit that meanings of statements ascribing rightness and wrongness do vary with background moral assumptions. 'Right' always can be analyzed in terms of obligation or permissibility, and all these notions can be analyzed in terms of moral reasons or coherence with the evaluations of an assumed framework. But the truth of ascriptions of rightness varies with the framework assumed. Each such ascription assumes some set of standards on which it depends, and these sets may not always be the same even for the same speakers. There is nevertheless a central core of features that allows us to identify certain reasons as moral reasons. Moral reasons, for example, can oppose those of narrow self-interest, and moral standards can be invoked in settling conflicts among the interests of different individuals.

If one has the intuition that the meaning of moral judgments never varies with context, then the realist may appear to retain an advantage here in maintaining that these judgments always refer to the same properties. First, however, as we saw above, a coherentist can preserve meaning invariance by reducing the meanings of moral judgments to claims concerning coherence itself. Second, if one is wary of a fast distinction between meaning and belief and is willing to admit that people with very different moral beliefs may not mean the same thing by calling a particular action or policy right, then one will see the coherentist as doing well enough in allowing for genuine disagreements and rational debates even among those with quite different views generally.

When I condemn a practice of those with alien standards, I ordinarily do so from the point of view of my own moral framework or that of my group, at least unless or until I attempt to engage the aliens in debate. In terms of my own framework I can say that what they do is wrong and that they ought not to do it, although I may have to admit that they may lack moral reasons of their own for desisting. If I do engage them in debate, then, as noted above, we are both obliged to reason from whatever core of shared beliefs and principles may exist. In the context of this debate, I will argue that this core does provide them with reasons to desist. If the standards governing our respective practices differ sharply enough, there may be too little core to make debate feasible, and in such cases I may retreat to the relativist explanation and oppose them only in action, if at all. If the practice in question is particularly abhorrent, however, then there may be another common ground from which it can be condemned. We can evaluate it in terms of assumptions that are common to any set of beliefs or standards that could be counted a moral system. If the rules it violates are those required for any rational settlement of conflicts of interests, if it fails to cohere with the agents' own fundamental values, if the values it expresses render the society that embraces them fragile or incompatible with others it is likely to encounter, or if the practice is based on clear factual error, then it can be condemned from a more universal point of view.

Thus the coherentist can allow for genuine disagreements even among those with widely different moral views. She can provide a plausible account of how such disputes can be rationally resolved, while recognizing also that some apparent disagreements cannot be resolved and must rather be explained away. The emotivist, on the other hand, cannot account for rational resolution of moral disagreement once the disputants agree on the non-moral facts, as they might. The realist, who allows for genuine disagreements over the truth of moral claims, has no plausible explanation for seemingly irresolvable differences and can at best agree with the coherentist as to how real disagreements are to be resolved.

Disagreement, even if seemingly endless, in itself provides no argument against a realist view of a particular domain. The reality in question might be too complex, or our powers of apprehending it too weak, for us to converge on the truth. Philosophically, it is always a question of which view provides the best explanations for the degrees and types of agreements and disagreements that exist. The problem in ethics is that the usual sorts of realist explanations for moral disputes do not seem to work in the case of fundamental differences in values and priorities among them that affect ascriptions of rightness and wrongness.

The realist will attempt to explain away some apparent moral disputes by holding that identical principles (induced to capture the presence of goodness and rightness) are being applied in different conditions. We have granted that real virtues for the Romans, for example, abilities to excel in combat, might not be virtues for us in our different circumstances. Moral goodness might consist in different dispositions operating in very different contexts. Other apparent moral disagreements will reduce to different perceptions of the non-moral facts. One person might favor preferential hiring for minorities and another oppose it because they disagree on the effects of the policy on productivity, social harmony, and the attitudes of those hired and those not.

When it comes to these genuine moral disagreements that will occur despite common perceptions of the non-moral facts, the realist must hold always that one of the parties is mistaken. He must explain why one would be mistaken in such circumstances. Mistake might result from ignorance, misperception of facts, or error in reasoning. Ignorance might result from incomplete evidence or from the fact that the reality in question is complex or obscure, beyond our powers of apprehension. The problem, to reiterate, is that none of these possible explanations appears appropriate to an understanding of fundamental conflicts in value orientations that result in different judgments concerning rightness.

If one framework emphasizes collective welfare and another individual rights, if one emphasizes loyalty and another impartiality, if one values acquisitiveness and another asceticism, then apparently contradictory ascriptions of rightness and wrongness do not necessarily reduce to disagreements over non-moral facts (adherents might agree on facts of actual psychology, but some might approve and others disapprove). Nor can apparent disputes between such orientations be dismissed as due to the application of common standards to different circumstances (instead, different standards are applied to the same circumstances). Nor, finally must there appear to be ignorance or error on the part of either party to such disagreements. What new evidence could be relevant to the dispute between a collectivist and an individualist? Perhaps an extreme adherent of either ethic might ignore some fact of human psychology that could be better established by further research; but we need not imagine that disagreement results from such extremism. What error in reasoning could underlie disputes between fully coherent frameworks, if moral reasoning is aimed precisely at achieving coherence within a framework? Neither a collectivist nor an individualist need have made any error in reasoning in arriving at her position, if in the end the principles of each fully capture the particular judgments each is diposed to make.

The realist might reply finally that moral convergence or agreement would be more readily attained if we could find or form a society that allows for the greatest possible individual freedom and fulfilment with the least possible interpersonal conflict. The key, she might hold, lies in discovering which social arrangements must conduce to such flourishing, and perhaps prior to that, discovering the ingredients of this flowering of human capacities and contentment. These are difficult and deep matters, and we might hope that practical and social scientific experiment and research might aid in the quest. I do not wish to deny that social progress can sometimes result from increased knowledge of psychology or from the discovery of better forms of social interaction. But the problem with this appeal to present ignorance as an explanation for fundamental moral disagreements is that these disagreements extend to the conceptions of both individual fulfilment and social flourishing. Unless those conceptions are fixed, there can be no measure of progress toward realizing them. That they are centrally in dispute and likely to remain so indefinitely in the absence of social mind control indicates that fundamental conflicts cannot be resolved in the way pictured here by the realist.

I conclude that realism provides no plausible explanation for fundamental conflicts between moral frameworks. This problem appears to be as serious as it was for the older intuitionist, who could invoke only a faulty faculty of intuition in the face of moral dispute. Regarding other disagreements that are resolvable, the coherentist appears to say all that should be said as to their manner of resolution. It is true that sometimes we try to convince an opponent in a moral argument by simply trying to get her to examine the phenomena in dispute more closely. But, as Hume pointed out, this seems to be a matter of attempting to reach agreement on the non-moral facts before arriving at a proper moral judgment. We have seen the problems in trying to identify moral properties either with the non-moral bases for these judgments or with the relation between these bases and evaluative responses. We have seen also that moral reasoning in quest of resolutions of conflicts often occurs after agreements on the non-moral facts have been reached. Here it is not a matter of further empirical inquiry, but of attempting to achieve coherence with an assumed background of evaluation by reasoning from analogies and disanalogies to settled cases. The conclusiveness of such analogical reasoning (as opposed to the probabilistic character of induction by analogy in the empirical realm) indicates once more that we do not infer beyond recognition of ordinary non-moral properties to the presence of real moral properties.

I shall have more to say about supposed moral properties in this chapter and about the nature of moral reasoning in the next.

F. Explanations

In the previous section we examined explanations for moral disagreements and noted that coherentism provides the best explanation for fundamental conflicts between coherent frameworks. The realist, however, may claim superiority in his moral explanations for other phenomena, including actions, practices and policies, political movements and their successes and failures, and finally moral beliefs themselves. We do often couch explanations in moral terms: agent A did action x because it was the right thing to do; government G was widely opposed because its policies were wrong; and the opposition was successful in gaining support because it was right to oppose the government. Only the realist can interpret these as straightforward causal explanations. For him the properties of rightness and wrongness causally influence motivations and actions, hence explain them in the usual way.

When he explains perceptual beliefs or recognitions of the presence of these properties, he takes himself to refer to the properties themselves. He then explains actions in terms of these recognitions. Thus, for him there are direct causal chains of a common sort between moral properties and actions that take account of them. According to the version of realism that I have endorsed as most plausible, an action's or object's being such as to elicit rational approval is also its being such as to prompt actions of various sorts.

The emotivist, by contrast, cannot appeal directly to rightness or wrongness in offering explanations. For her there are no moral properties at all, so there is no question of such properties causing anything. 'Agent *A* did action *x* because it was the right thing to do' can only be shorthand for 'Agent *A* did action *x* because he judged it to be the right thing to do'. Although moral judgments can have effects on motivations and actions – indeed, they must have these effects according to emotivism – moral properties cannot. If an agent can do something not simply because he believes it to be right, but because it is right, then emotivism, in being unable to offer such explanations, is seriously incomplete.

Coherentism occupies a middle position in this area.[15] A coherentist can say not only with an emotivist that agent *A* did action *x* because he believed it to be right, but also that he believed it to be right because it was right, and hence that he did it because it was right. In asserting the latter two claims, the coherentist is saying that the fact that a moral belief (a belief about moral reasons) cohered with the agent's other moral beliefs, or with beliefs of groups with which the agent identified, caused the agent to accept the moral belief, which in turn helped to cause his action. In saying that an action is right, however, the coherentist asserts only that a belief to that effect coheres better with an assumed background framework of evaluations that does the belief's negation. There is no property of rightness that can itself have causal effects. The causation is mediated by a framework of assumed moral beliefs, and in this sense the explanations that cite it are indirect. In the realist's explanatory accounts too, the causal relation between moral property and action is mediated by the agent's belief. But the realist speaks only of the belief that this property is present, which belief is caused by the property itself (or by thoughts about the property that attach to it by causal chains). In the coherentist's account there is no property of rightness that is instantiated in actions, only systems of moral beliefs that make particular assertions about rightness true.

When a coherentist says that an agent did something because it was right, he assumes as background the moral framework of the agent, although, as the evaluator who offers this explanation, he normally shares this framework. The claim that an action or policy was opposed because it was wrong is analyzed in the same way; likewise for certain variations on these paradigm moral explanations. 'Injustice caused the revolution', for example, refers to the fact that the government's policies violated values expressed in judgments about distributions of social benefits and burdens, judgments that are explicit or implicit in the moral framework shared by the revolutionaries and the evaluator who offers the explanation. There can be more complex cases, however, that generate difficulties and require variations on the type of explanatory account that can be offered.

Consider: 'Hitler's depravity caused the holocaust'; 'We can't rely on Jane because she's a bad person'; or 'The soldier fled because he was a coward'. In offering these explanations, coherentists invoke only their own set of beliefs with which the judgments in question cohere, not the moral frameworks of the agents evaluated. But then the causal claims in these explanations become mysterious. The agent's recognition of the coherence of a judgment with the evaluator's moral framework was not a cause of anything in any of these examples. For one thing, there was no such recognition; for another, recognition of a negative judgment by another person normally would not motivate the action to which the judgment refers.

Coherentists must instead refer in these explanations to the dispositional character traits that they judge to be morally bad. They hold these traits (but not their badness) to have caused the actions or policies in question (or to explain why Jane cannot be relied on in that example). The traits themselves, cowardice or overall depravity, consist in certain behavioral dispositions together with evaluations of them. These components may be difficult to separate conceptually, but this difficulty does not refute the claim that only the psychological dispositions, not the evaluations of them, causally explain the actions in question. Once again, these properties may be typed by evaluative responses that are relative to frameworks, but instances may be identified with the non-moral bases of these evaluations. Only the bases play causal roles in the examples cited.

A coherentist may also offer mixed explanations, as when she says, 'He kept his promise because he is a good person, and he saw that keeping the promise was the right thing to do'. In this case she implies that the person with dispositions that she judges to be good does what is right according to the moral framework that she shares with him, that he does so because the judgment that this action is right coheres with the moral beliefs that constitute this framework, and that persons with such dispositions normally are motivated to act on their moral beliefs in this way.

When she appeals to immoral dispositions in offering explanations for actions, the coherentist denies that any strictly moral property of these dispositions causes the actions. The realist may want to disagree and claim an advantage on this score. If he analyzes moral properties as relations (in the way I judged to be most plausible), however, then his explanations that appeal to immoral dispositions will differ little from the coherentist's. Such dispositions must still consist in the agent's being such (where this 'such' is filled in by specific psychological tendencies) as to elicit rational disapproval. The realist must admit that only the psychological tendencies, and not the disapprovals they elicit, function as causes. Remember that realism of this sort will identify tokens or instantiations of moral properties with the non-moral bases that elicit evaluations according to which the properties are typed. Only the tokens or instantiations have causal effects. Hence explanations that appeal to traits such as depravity or cowardice must be analyzed in much the same way by realism and coherentism, at least if the former is to be plausible on other grounds.

For the type of moral explanation considered earlier, for example, 'Agent A did action x because it was the right thing to do', a relational realist can hold that the rightness itself, the fact that the action was such as to elicit rational approval, causally influenced the agent. The action was caused both by the agent's recognition of the nature of the action and by the fact that he was rational. These same causal factors can be recognized by a coherentist, however, who will think of rationality primarily as the ability to recognize and act on the recognition of coherence within a system of beliefs. The difference lies in the prominence of the appeal to assumed moral frameworks or systems of beliefs in the coherentist's account, and this may not be much of a difference at all. First, the realist too may well see coherence within a system of beliefs as a mark of rationality. Second, his ability to do without explicit reference to assumed frameworks of beliefs in his moral explanations rests on his assuming consistent non-moral bases for moral properties. We have seen that fundamental disagreements may block such reductions.

The latter problem aside, both realists and coherentists can allow that agents sometimes do things because they are the right things to do, and both can allow that subjects sometimes believe certain actions to be right because they are right. That moral beliefs are sometimes best explained by their truth is necessary if there is to be moral knowledge. It is doubtful that emotivism can provide a notion of moral truth with enough bite to allow for moral knowledge (hence the label 'non-cognitivism'). Emotivists can allow statements such as 'It is true that action x was the right thing to do', if they interpret the appeal to truth as mere stylistic emphasis. Given their view of the exclusive function of moral judgments, interpreting the truth of such judgments in a disquotational way (the assertion that it is true that x literally means the same as the assertion that x) does not allow appeal to truth to explain anything. According to our analysis of knowledge, a belief counts as knowledge when its being held is best explained by its truth or by the fact to which it refers. The truth of moral judgments in this disquotational sense cannot explain their being held, if they are interpreted emotivistically. For emotivists, the facts that prompt moral approvals and disapprovals do not explain why evaluators approve or disapprove. The explanations for their reactions appeal to their moral training or socialization. Thus emotivists who interpret truth in this explanatorily idle way do not allow for moral knowledge. Perhaps statements such as 'A knows that x is the right thing to do' can be analyzed in a disquotational way also, but then moral knowledge could not be a legitimate aim of moral reasoning, as it is.

We require a stronger notion of moral truth, not only to allow for moral knowledge as a goal of inquiry, but also to account for certain inferences and alleged implications between moral statements that guide moral reasoning. Consider the following hypothetical statement: 'If lying to medical patients about their conditions is wrong, then so is withholding information from them'. One who asserts this statement does not necessarily endorse the antecedent, but instead asserts an implication between the antecedent and consequent. Simon Blackburn provides an account of such statements within an emotivist meta-ethical framework. According to him, an emotivist who asserts a hypothetical statement such as that above is approving of a moral sensibility that approves of the consequent whenever it approves of the antecedent.[16] Such statements express second-order attitudes toward first-order moral attitudes. The notion of moral truth can be analyzed similarly in terms of second-order approvals of first-order approvals or moral judgments themselves. Perhaps the second-order approvals in terms of which truth is to be analyzed might be directed toward those evaluations that are envisaged to survive progressive alterations in moral sensibilities.

This emotivist analysis of moral implication and truth, required for explanations of moral reasoning, does not allow for a distinction to which I appealed earlier (section B of this chapter). We want to be able to distinguish in general between epistemic justification and truth on the one hand, and moral or prudential justification on the other.[17] My holding a certain belief, for example, a belief in an afterlife, might have good consequences for me. It might make me both happier and more courageous. But these consequences are entirely distinct from the question of epistemic justification for the belief, which depends instead on my evidence for its truth. In the moral domain, too, we can distinguish between the consequences, including the moral consequences, of holding a belief or principle and the epistemic justification for, or truth of, the belief or principle. Some utilitarians admit that it may be better if ordinary people do not believe the principle of utility. It may be better if they act on simplified rules rather than trying to figure the utilities in each case, and they may be more likely to act on such rules if they do not believe the principle of utility. But the principle of utility might still be true, and we might have evidence for thinking it true. It might be true in the realist sense, if maximization of total preference satisfaction constitutes the sole non-moral basis for moral evaluations; or it might be true in the coherentist sense, if the principle of utility captures the most coherent set of moral judgments of some group of evaluators. For the coherentist, both the judgment that one morally ought to believe a given principle and the judgment that one epistemically ought to believe it depend for their truth on an assumed framework of moral judgments, but they depend on this framework in different ways. One morally ought to believe a principle if believing it is morally best according to moral criteria implicit in one's other beliefs. One epistemically ought to believe it if it entails some beliefs in that framework and is counter-exemplified by none.

Thus, both the realist and the coherentist can distinguish between the truth of moral judgments and the moral consequences

165

of accepting them. The sophisticated emotivist position now under consideration cannot draw the latter distinction and so again lacks the resources to capture both our moral discourse and our discourse about ethics. For this emotivist, one still approves of certain moral judgments themselves only on moral grounds. Judging that such a judgment is true is once more approving of it or making a (second-order) moral judgment.

Hence, realism and coherentism share an advantage over emotivism in the explanations they offer for moral beliefs and their justifications. Realism may finally seek to distinguish itself from coherentism by its explanations for the acquisitions of certain moral beliefs, or for progressions of moral beliefs that seem to make progress toward knowledge or truth. Just as some philosophers of science hold that historical convergence of scientific communities on more complete theories that explain the successes of their predecessors indicates (is itself explained by) closer approximation of these theories to truth about real unobservables, so moral realists may want to explain moral progress as a mark of better recognition of real properties of rightness and goodness. Of course, just as lack of agreement in a domain does not refute realism for that domain (if the realist can explain the disagreements), so agreement or convergence does not in itself require a realist explanation. In science, for example, we might explain progress in terms of the goal of providing models which capture broader ranges of observable phenomena, without interpreting these models realistically.[18] The question in meta-ethics again is whether the realist provides better explanations for seeming moral progress.

This progress may be measured on an individual or social level. Realists will point first to cases in which individuals take themselves to correct prior moral beliefs, when this correction seems not to be a matter of making the beliefs cohere better with others previously held, but instead seems to express a recognition of moral truth independent of prior beliefs. Consider the following three examples: (1) A professed utilitarian becomes convinced, after watching *Roots* on television, that slavery is wrong no matter how the utilities balance out in given historical contexts;[19] (2) An ardent and loyal Nazi assigned to a position in a concentration camp is morally outraged by the atrocities committed against Jews there;[20] (3) An informed and reflective proponent of abortion upon demand changes her mind when seeing for the first time an aborted five-month fetus. In each of these examples a new moral perception gives rise to a belief that appears to oppose the subject's prior moral set. If these beliefs cannot be explained in terms of prior moral training and beliefs, then it seems more plausible to posit the causal influence of a real moral property (of wrongness) in explaining them. Can a coherentist offer plausible alternative explanations? I believe that these cases differ significantly among themselves and that the coherentist should offer a different explanation in each case.

In the example of the avowed utilitarian, it is not clear that the new moral perception really does oppose his most coherent prior set of moral beliefs. Prior beliefs and attitudes may exist, not as conscious formulations, but as dispositions to respond and react in various ways. In making this claim, however, we must be careful not to beg questions or trivialize the ascriptions of prior moral beliefs in these contexts. Earlier I criticized the ascription of unconscious motivation (by the internalist) as a means of saving a thesis in the absence of evidence for such motivation. If we think of beliefs only as dispositions to respond, then we run the risk of ascribing a prior belief for each new way of responding on the part of the subject, and this ascription trivializes the explanation for an apparently new belief. In the utilitarian's case we have his first person avowal that the principle of utility completely expressed his prior moral attitudes as evidence that the new belief represents a genuine conversion.

It seems very unlikely to me, nevertheless, that this completely general principle fully captures the moral sensibility of any mature, sensitive, and reflective evaluator. My evidence from reflection on concrete social issues is that the moral beliefs of typical groups in our society and of their individual members are far too complex and diverse to be captured by a single principle of this sort. In the example given, it seems far more plausible, despite first person claims to the contrary, to think that the subject was more firmly wedded to his conviction that the type of degradation and oppression that he witnessed in the film are wrong than he was to his general normative principle. His reaction itself can be taken as evidence of this priority, given that the first person testimony on the other side is often unreliable as a guide to the origins of beliefs and attitudes, especially emotionally charged moral attitudes. We may commonly wish for simple and fully general principles to guide our moral lives, but we find that often these do not work to capture convictions in concrete contexts.

In the case of the Nazi, let us assume that he was sufficiently trained or indoctrinated to accept the Nazi moral framework in full. (I assume also only for the sake of argument that we can call the Nazi creed a moral framework. In reality it shares only certain features of such frameworks, such as the demand to sacrifice self-interest in conceivable contexts.) His witnessing atrocities in the concentration camp can nevertheless reveal that his prior moral convictions were based in large part on gross factual errors and misrepresentations. He was led to believe, for example, that Jews are not really persons, that they don't have feelings like those of Aryans, and so on. These beliefs are easily falsified for all but the most blind and fanatic adherent to the Nazi creed. Their falsification then calls into question the set of moral beliefs based on them. Thus, once more we need not assume that the Nazi perceives a real property of wrongness independent of all moral beliefs in order to explain his conversion; he need only recognize obvious errors in non-moral beliefs.

In this case, however (and perhaps in the case of slavery too), we may be tempted to accept the claim to perceive real wrongness because the actions in question may violate norms that must be endorsed by any framework we could recognize as genuinely moral. If there are such universal wrongs, then their existence supports the realist's claim that there are moral properties independent of particular sets of moral beliefs. But the existence of such wrongs does not settle the issue, since the realist cannot restrict his ascriptions of the property of wrongness to cases in which it is universally ascribed by systems recognizable as moral. This restriction would rob moral discourse of its normal use. Without such restriction, the problem of providing a coherent account of moral properties leads us to seek alternative explanations for cases such as that of the Nazi and the utilitarian. I have provided such explanations from the coherentist's point of view.

A different response is available for the remaining example of the pro-abortionist. A negative response to the sight of an aborted fetus, if it occurs despite reasoned and consistent convictions about morally relevant differences between fetuses and infants, should not be sufficient to overthrow the prior set of beliefs on this issue. It should not do so if it can be explained on other, perhaps non-moral, grounds, and if the judgment that abortions are permissible is itself based on convictions about morally relevant differences that continue to generalize to other cases. The emotional reaction to the fetus may be based on morally irrelevant similarities in physical appearance between the fetus and an infant. In general, physical appearance is not a morally significant trait; it normally should not make a difference in appropriate treatment. But psychological differences between fetuses and infants – differences in desires, beliefs, and so on – do generally call for different ways of treating sentient beings. Thus, experiences that genuinely oppose a set of settled convictions that are based on generalized analogies and differences may not in themselves weigh sufficiently to overthrow the prior set, as they would if they were genuine observations of real moral properties. (I shall expand on these requirements for coherence in the next chapter.)

The coherentist, then, has several responses when faced with new experiences and moral beliefs that appear to oppose subjects' prior sets of moral beliefs. The apparent opposition may be spurious or superficial; it may reveal incoherence or non-moral error in the prior set; or it may be resolved so as to maintain the most coherent overall moral framework. This resolution might retain the new belief by modifying other prior ones, if the new belief cannot be explained away as in the abortion example. Generally, those minimal changes required for restoring coherence will be made. The real question is whether the demand for and existence of coherence within sets of moral beliefs is itself causally explained by the influence of real moral properties. In the case of coherence or agreements within sets of empirical, perceptual experiences, for example, there is no doubt that, over time, these are best explained by appeal to the causal influence of independent physical objects. The requirement to maintain coherence within sets of moral judgments is different, amounting in large part to a demand to base differences in moral judgments upon non-moral differences that one is willing to generalize as morally relevant. A coherentist can explain this demand in terms of the need to act consistently, to base one's actions on coherent attitudes, to co-ordinate them with the actions of others and with the norms of the groups within which one interacts. This need, and the fact that the moral beliefs of individuals originate from these group norms, explain both the demand for and existence of coherence within sets of moral beliefs, absent the causal influence of moral properties independent of those norms and beliefs.

As noted earlier, the realist may also appeal to progress on the social level and to historical convergence in moral judgments across societies as marks of movement toward moral truth in the realist sense. In this century we have seen the emergence of more inclusive political and social structures and the near universal recognition (on paper) of certain fundamental human rights. Elitist political structures and the suppression of these rights create pressure for change or revolution. The realist will claim that not simply the belief that such social oppression is wrong, but the fact of its wrongness, creates the potential for such pressure and makes it more likely, other things being equal, that the movement for change will eventually succeed.[21] The potential for change may be there even before oppressed groups recognize their condition or explicitly form beliefs about its wrongness. The realist equates this potential with the presence of wrongness itself. Outside groups can perceive this wrongness as well, and they will then be more ready to sympathize and offer aid to the oppressed.

However, the potential for both internal resistance and outside sympathy and aid in such contexts can be predicted and explained by the non-realist, too. She can certainly predict that oppression will create the potential for resistance among those whose self-interest is at stake, and also that they will be more ready to perceive wrongness when their self-interest is ignored. Outside groups will sympathize if they share the judgment of wrongness (and enough of the moral framework of the potential revolutionaries to imply that judgment). The relativist-coherentist will predict that such support will not often be universal, that groups and nations with different moral frameworks and political ideologies will perceive oppression differently and tend to support different factions within countries under the threat of civil war. Indeed, this prediction is accurate, even discounting motivations of strategic and pragmatic politics. Its accuracy indicates once more the absence of a coherent non-moral base for evaluations across groups with fundamentally different moral views.

I shall now return to this central contention in closing this chapter. In light of it, and given the fact that both individual and social changes in moral views can be explained without positing real moral properties, the realist no more adds to the depth of these explanations than the theist adds depth to the atheist's explanations for physical transformations. In any case, additional depth in explanations should not be welcome when it raises more intractable questions than it answers.

G. *Moral Properties and Inference to the Best Explanation*

In summarizing the advantages and disadvantages of inferring to real moral properties for purposes of explanation, I want first to expand upon the comparison to the case for physical and scientific realism. As noted above in the discussion of convergence, moral realists may want to emphasize the analogies. Certainly the differences between empirical and moral claims, and between the types of justification for them, were exaggerated in the heyday of positivism. We have seen that the notion of moral truth is not only respectable, but required to account for moral reasoning. On the empirical side of the comparison, philosophers have attacked the notion of theory-free observation in science and, more generally, the claim that empirical knowledge rests on a foundation of perceptual experience free from contamination by the subject's beliefs.

In science, agreement in those observational judgments that involve ascriptions of real physical properties such as mass may depend upon agreement in background theory. In this sense observations are 'theory-laden'. In justifying claims to knowledge of physical reality generally, epistemologists must begin with beliefs (not theory-free experiences), perhaps beliefs about perceptual appearances, with which answers to challenges to ordinary empirical claims normally terminate. Unconceptualized perceptual experiences themselves can play no role in justifying claims to empirical knowledge. When we include in the overall epistemological project the justification of those epistemic principles that function in ordinary justifications, it becomes clear that our justificatory criteria must be ultimately coherentist in a broad sense. Just as we cannot begin the process of justification at some stage prior to the formation of beliefs, so we cannot do without assumed

171

epistemic principles at every stage. These principles themselves can be justified only relative to each other and the overall system of empirical beliefs that results from their use.

Despite these admissions and concessions to the anti-positivist thrust of contemporary empirical epistemology, I have argued at length elsewhere that a modified foundationalist theory can be defended and leads directly to the justification of physical and scientific realism by means of inference to the best explanation.[22] The same principle provides an account of empirical foundations themselves. Although the ascription of real physical properties depends on background theory, there remains a class of predicates assigned to properties that are naturally salient within appearances, predicates whose use in describing appearances is not a function of physical theory. Beliefs ascribing such properties to appearances are self-explanatory (the best explanation for my belief that something in my visual field appears red is that something does appear red). Interpersonal agreements in judgments that apply these predicates to appearances in similar conditions are best explained by appeal to physical objects and the causal theory of perception, which explains perceptual illusions and disagreements as well. Interactions among physical objects and their effects on our perceptual systems are in turn best explained by appeal to unobservables. Scientific realism is justified, not as an explanation for success or convergence in science, as was suggested above, but rather in terms of the depth of explanations it affords for those very phenomena that science itself explains.

If explanatory depth is included among the criteria for coherent belief systems (when it does not result in loss of coherence of other sorts), then a coherentist criterion of justification in the empirical realm leads to acceptance of realism for physical objects and processes, both observable and unobservable. Once we justify belief in independent physical objects and processes on these grounds, we must be realists about their properties. The notion of real objects without real properties is empty or incoherent. We then must allow that our empirical beliefs can be true only by corresponding to the presence of these properties.[23]

This briefest sketch of an outline for a defense of empirical realism is intended only to indicate some contrasts with the case for moral realism. First, the moral realist does not infer to independent moral objects in order to explain appearances or experiences, only to moral properties inhering in persons or actions. Thus there is no question of real moral objects having to possess real moral properties. Second, there is no substantial, independent class of moral data stable in itself and causally explicable only as perceptions of real properties. The realist posits moral properties to explain non-moral phenomena such as actions as well as moral beliefs. The latter do not seem to be explained by their truth alone, as are certain beliefs about perceptual appearances. Instead, each evaluator's ethical socialization will help to explain his set of moral judgments. There may be broad agreement on certain judgments, such as that causing gratuitous pain is wrong. But disagreement runs all the way up and down, from the most general judgments (such as what constitutes gratuitous or unjustified causing of pain) to the most particular and observational. Those few observational contexts that might prompt nearly universal moral evaluations are far too narrow to ground deeper agreement on the nature of moral properties.

The problem of disagreement in ethics might be conceived as an instance of the broader problem of underdetermination of theory by evidence. 'Underdetermination' refers to the fact that several incompatible theories or sets of beliefs, implying different assessments of the presence of contested properties in controversial cases, are equally compatible with the evidence. Radical underdetermination, or equal plausibility of incompatible theories in light of all conceivable evidence, leads only to skepticism when combined with a realist ontology for any domain. But in the empirical domain, where there is such broad agreement about observables, radical underdetermination is highly contestable.

If we accept as justificatory all the inductive criteria used in theory evaluation – simplicity, scope, fruitfulness, depth of explanations, and so on – then it is doubtful that empirical theories will remain tied on all these grounds when all relevant evidence is available. Theoretically, one might imagine that two theories might score well on different criteria, so as to balance out in a tie. But in practice it seems clear, once all relevant evidence is in, how to order the priorities and pick the theory that seems more likely to be true. Examples of overall ties among theories of any complexity are lacking in both real science and the antirealist philosophical literature. Furthermore, it seems plausible, given the success of our inductive criteria in generating theories that allow us to predict observations, and given the independence of the physical world to which our inductive practices must adapt, that these criteria can be linked to the goal of (correspondence) truth they are supposed to serve.[24] Attributing an aim of accurate representation (as well as prediction) to science does not land us inevitably in skepticism, and, even if it did, this outcome would warrant anti-realism for scientific theory, not realism for ethics.

In ethics, there appear to be many incompatible normative systems that are internally coherent, that meet all relevant inductive criteria, and that are not only consistent with all observational data, but equally plausible (to different rational evaluators) given the data. Several examples were provided above: collectivist versus individualist frameworks, egalitarian versus libertarian, loyalist versus impartial, and so on. Not only do our non-question-begging inductive criteria for theory choice give us no reason to prefer one such framework over another, but normative standards themselves do not appear to serve an aim of accurate representation. If we do take them to represent real properties of rightness and wrongness, then radical underdetermination leads, as noted, to skepticism. I have also pointed out, however, that disagreements of this sort do not seem to reflect ignorance on the part of either party. The same practices may elicit opposed evaluative responses from observers who are not only rational, but fully informed.

I have held that a historically prominent sort of realist account, which holds that an action's being right consists in its being such as to elicit rational approval or will (volition), is the most plausible available to the realist. We may briefly review the considerations in its favor. First, in providing his analysis, the realist must avoid identifying moral properties in such a way as to require a special faculty for apprehending them. This faculty would be mysterious, and its target properties would bloat the realist's metaphysics. Second, moral properties, if we are to have knowledge of them, must enter causal relations. Third, since we cannot morally judge situations differently if they share all non-moral properties, moral properties, if they exist, must supervene on non-moral properties. These initial considerations indicate that moral properties must be identified with ordinary non-moral properties, perhaps relations involving the causing of certain psychological states such as satisfaction or pain.

On the other hand, there can be no simple identification of types of moral properties, for example, rightness, with first order relations of this sort. If moral properties were reduced without remainder to empirical properties that cause actions and beliefs, then it would be mysterious why we have a separate category of the moral. No such reduction is intuitively plausible. Neither all actions that cause satisfaction, nor even all those that cause a net balance of satisfaction over dissatisfaction or pain, are considered right by most evaluators in our society. Furthermore, normal evaluators issue moral judgments in order to advise others how to act, and they reason morally in order to decide how to act themselves. This connection between moral judgment and motivation and action requires that moral properties be connected to the psychological states of evaluators themselves, and not simply to the states of those affected by actions. The connection, however, is contingent, and so we cannot tie moral properties conceptually to all evaluators, only to normal or rational evaluators.

These considerations combine to show that the best bet for the realist is to identify moral properties as types by their evaluative functions, allowing us to identify their instantiations with those non-moral properties that prompt rational evaluations. Moral properties, if they exist, are second-order relations. This account explains why we have a separate category of the moral, since moral properties are typed uniquely, according to the evaluative responses they elicit. It also explains how moral properties cause responses, since their instantiations or tokens are identified with ordinary (first-order relational) non-moral properties. Finally, the analysis explains why we cannot make different moral judgments about situations that share all non-moral properties. The coherentist may take the finality of arguments from analogy and difference (analogies and differences in non-moral properties) to show that in ethics we do not infer to real moral properties at all. But the relational realist can reply that this form of reasoning shows only that we do not infer beyond all non-moral properties to the presence of moral properties. We need not do so if we identify instances (instantiations) of moral properties with their non-moral bases. Arguments by analogy will be conclusive if the analogies noted are precisely those among properties that determine the real moral properties of the situations being compared.

175

This reply assumes, however, that sameness in non-moral properties does determine that moral properties must be shared, and this assumption points up again the intractable problem for the relational realist. She wants, after the manner of the anomalous monist or functionalist in the philosophy of mind,[25] to allow both for distinct moral types of properties and for identification of instances with properties typed differently. In each case there must be one such identification for a moral property; but the way that such properties are to be typed – according to responses of rational evaluators – prevents that identification from being made. One rational evaluator will approve what another disapproves.

The realist can remain skeptical or agnostic at the frontier of inquiry; but moral disagreement among fully rational and informed evaluators is not limited to the frontier. She can narrow her position to the claim that realist truth values exist for moral assertions only in contexts of broad agreement. Unresolvable disagreements would then imply lack of determinate truth values for moral judgments, and these disputes would call for political, not moral, solutions. Two objections appear fatal to this position, however. First, moral terms do not seem so radically ambiguous as to be used sometimes to asssert realist truth conditions and sometimes not. Terms referring to real properties can be vague, especially if they sort a continuum of properties of the same kind. Then we expect borderline cases, vagueness, or indeterminate truth values. But rightness and wrongness do not appear to shade into one another as redness and orangeness do. The problem with the moral properties is not indistinctness at the boundaries, but lack of any agreement on the vicinity of the boundaries. Second, restricting truth to contexts of universal or near universal agreements, or to resolvable disputes, robs moral assertions of their point in contexts in which they may have great import. It may be important whether one's judgments cohere with one's own moral framework or with the norms of one's group, when those judgments are unalterably opposed by those with alien values.

The only remaining alternative for the realist is to relativize her own position. She can hold that each internally coherent moral framework fixes reference to some real property with which rightness is identified for adherents to that framework. Such properties remain independent of beliefs regarding their instantiations in particular situations, although the meaning and reference of 'right' for each group of users will depend on their set of moral beliefs. The problem with this final realist ploy is that appeal to such properties fails to add any depth to the coherentist's moral explanations. As noted in somewhat different terms in the chapter on Hume, for every action that we consider right, there is some feature of the action that prompts our moral belief. However, if such features vary radically with individuals and groups of evaluators, then appeal to them cannot explain the truth of their beliefs. Hence, such appeal cannot enter significantly into an account of moral knowledge. The only real constraint on moral reasoning and criterion of moral truth will be coherence within sets of evaluators' beliefs. The task for the moral epistemologist will be to provide an account of such coherence. This account will not require the excess baggage of real moral properties.

H. Conclusion

The realist impulse in ethics derives from several sources. First, there is the intuition that moral obligations are imposed from without, independently of the subject's desires and beliefs. Second, there is the conviction that we seek truth in moral reasoning and sometimes achieve moral knowledge. Our moral beliefs can progress and we can correct them. It is natural to interpret this progress as constrained by reality and as achieving closer approximation to truth. Third, when we morally disagree with others (despite agreeing with them about the non-moral facts), we can sometimes reason with them. When we cannot, we still want to say that they are wrong, and in saying that we want not to be merely expressing our feelings. We want our moral principles to be more than a mere summary of our particular intuitions, convictions, or attitudes. We want a deeper justification for them than that. Our motivation to be moral is not only contingent, but vulnerable; it might seem to depend on our belief in moral facts independent of our moral beliefs. The latter beliefs are best viewed as fallible, but as representing a reality to which we must conform.

Many of these claims and aims can be met by a sophisticated coherentist meta-ethic, although not by emotivism. A coherentist can recognize an external source for moral obligations in the norms of those groups in which individuals interact. He can provide an account of moral truth and knowledge beyond apprehension of non-moral facts and can allow an explanatory function for the recognition of moral truth. He can recognize the fallibility of his own moral beliefs (although not of an ideal moral framework), and can hope for progress in achieving greater coherence among broader sets of social norms. He recognizes genuine moral disagreement and provides an account of how it can be resolved. Finally, unlike the realist, he can recognize the genuine contrast between ethics and science, the radical underdetermination of moral beliefs by observational facts that expresses itself in fundamental and irresolvable moral disagreements.

When views representing different moral frameworks or the frameworks of different groups within a broader society clash, we can hope that rational resolution in relation to the union of these frameworks is possible. We can also hope that any political settlement of the dispute will reflect this rational moral resolution. When, however, disputes are not resolvable, because neither side is willing to suspend the beliefs that separate them, when in addition the frameworks from which the opposing judgments derive are neither incoherent nor obviously based on factual error, then liberals at least ought to be wary of using political force to resolve them.[26] The coherentist account in itself does not have this normative implication, and normative implications in any case do not provide tests for meta-ethical theories. But, as I pointed out in the discussion of paternalism, it counts in favor of the coherentist view that it allows for distinctions utilized by normative moral theories.

In light of the fact of irresolvable disagreement in ethics, of radical underdetermination of moral theory by experience and criteria of justification, we must view moral knowledge as different from empirical knowledge. We must settle for a justification of moral norms in terms of their vital social and psychological functions. Our motivation to obey them must derive from common sources: self-interest and our feelings for others. We must hope that these other-regarding feelings are reinforced by moral norms themselves, so that all can fare better than they would under the whip of self-interest alone.

My positive claims on behalf of coherentism remain to be fleshed out in the final chapter.

CHAPTER V

Coherence, Moral Reasoning, and Knowledge

We can best understand the nature of moral reasoning and knowledge in terms of contrasts and analogies with other sorts of reasoning and knowledge. The most important contrast is with empirical knowledge, and I shall argue that legal reasoning provides the most helpful analogy.

A. The Contrast with Empirical Knowledge and Reasoning

One has empirical knowledge when one's belief in some empirical fact is best explained (in part) by appeal to that fact. A belief of this sort normally predicates some real property of some object, and the epistemically relevant explanation can be provided when this property stands in a causal relation to the belief. The normal way to acquire the simpler and more direct forms of empirical knowledge is to position oneself so as to establish this causal relation. Simple disputes over empirical matters can often be settled in the same way. If we disagree about whether someone is in the next room, we do not consult our other beliefs to check further for coherence, but instead seek to establish a direct perceptual connection with the object of our dispute. Other beliefs play a minimal role in the resolution of such conflicts.

When it comes to theoretical matters or disputes about unobservable facts, where we cannot establish direct causal connections between our beliefs and the facts in question, we try to reason or infer to the best causal explanations for our data. Reasoning to causal explanations is justified by the coherence of each inferential step with others and with other beliefs. Explanations and explanatory theories are judged by certain coherentist criteria – particular

179

explanations, by their analogies to other (confirmed) explanations in similar contexts; theories, by their breadth (the number of explanatory or probabilistic connections among theorems and reports of data), simplicity, fruitfulness (usefulness for establishing new explanatory connections), and so on. Such criteria refer to connections among theorems and observation reports that render them not only consistent, but jointly supportive.

Satisfaction of these coherentist criteria should indicate correspondence to the unobservable and observable facts described by these explanations and theories, since their construction involves causal inferences that explain most deeply only if the entities and properties to which they refer are real. If we infer on grounds of coherence (depth of explanation) to real entities and properties, then the resulting judgments can be true only if the entities exist and instantiate the properties, that is, only if the judgments correspond to these facts that are independent of these and other beliefs. (Since I am not concerned to justify empirical beliefs here, but only to point to contrasts between such justification and that for moral beliefs, I assume the soundness of the principle of inference to the best explanation.)

The complete justification for empirical theories terminates with beliefs about appearances that are best explained by their truth alone, and not by appeal to other beliefs with which they must cohere. The best explanation for my belief that I am appeared to redly is simply that I am so appeared to. The truth of this belief does not require that I be able to form reliable beliefs about my real environment, only that I apply the predicate 'red' consistently to my experience. The best explanation for my having a belief about such an appearance is that I can apply such a predicate consistently, that I have a true belief.[1]

Having established properties of appearances in this way, the empirical epistemologist justifies belief in real objects and their properties by similar inferences to best explanations for appearances. These inferences lead quickly to the unobservables of scientific theories, when we form second-order beliefs about the way we form perceptual beliefs, or when we try to explain interactions among real physical objects themselves. The theories remain vulnerable to disconfirmation by more immediately justified observation judgments, when predictions of ways things will appear derived from the theories prove inconsistent with later beliefs about appearances.

Even single observations, if repeatable, can call whole scientific theories into question. Especially beliefs about appearances couched in relatively non-theoretical terms will not be revised to accord with pre-existent theories with which they conflict, although the theories may not be overthrown until alternative explanatory accounts become available. The same phenomenon is found in non-scientific explanatory contexts. A detective's initial theory of a crime will give way to a single resistant observed fact, no matter how fervently he may have previously believed that theory. No similar phenomenon exists in the moral sphere, however. There, in the face of conflicting judgments, the goal is always to make those minimal changes anywhere in the system (including apparently observational judgments) that will restore coherence to the whole.

In contrast to empirical foundations, all moral beliefs are justified only in terms of coherence with other beliefs. Such coherence seems to exhaust our concept of moral truth as well, or at least our knowledge of what makes moral beliefs true. There is no class of beliefs about moral appearances shared by virtually all observers in similar circumstances and causally explained only by appeal to real moral properties. When moral disputes arise in any context, observational or otherwise, it may not help to position the disputants in direct causal relations to the objects of disagreement. Nor do the reasoning patterns that could resolve the disputes appear to represent inferences to the best causal explanations. Instead, other moral beliefs are always relevant in providing analogies and disanalogies in terms of which disputes can be settled and moral knowledge attained.

Moral knowledge is typically knowledge that one morally ought (or ought not) to do something. One morally ought to do something when one has overriding moral reasons to do it. Knowledge of moral oughts and reasons is similar to knowledge of prudential oughts and reasons, except that the latter is still a kind of empirical (psychological) knowledge. An agent has a prudential reason to perform some action when it is rational for the agent to desire an end to which the action is an efficient means. It is rational to desire an end that is an object of one's informed and coherent set of first and higher order desires. Desires are informed when the agent is knowledgeable of their origins and of the characters and effects of their objects. Desires are coherent when jointly satisfiable, and more so when the satisfation of some facilitates the satisfaction of others. The coherence of rational desires does not necessarily depend on the coherence of beliefs about them, which is one reason why prudential knowledge is a kind of empirical knowledge. The truth of a judgment that one prudentially ought to do something does not depend on other beliefs about prudential oughts, but instead on whether the desire that prompts it in fact coheres with other desires.

An agent has a moral reason to do an action, not when the action tends to satisfy a rational desire, but when the action is required by the informed and coherent norms of some group with which the agent identifies, norms that settle conflicts among individuals' desires and interests. Alternatively, a moral reason is a factor that would make a difference to a rational moral evaluator who shares the agent's moral framework. Norms and moral beliefs are informed if not dependent on factual errors, for example, errors about the consequences of the actions to which they refer. Moral norms that require and prohibit various actions are coherent if, and only if, correlative moral beliefs are coherent (in the relevant sense).

Coherence among empirical beliefs requires that it be possible for the beliefs to be all true and that the truth of some make the truth of others more probable. Coherence among moral norms or beliefs requires that relevantly similar actions not be both prohibited and permitted, that actions judged differently have some generally morally relevant differences between them. If grounds for judging differently are not generalized in this way so as to make a (prima facie) difference wherever they are found, then it will be impossible to articulate a set of non-contradictory aims that the moral system protects and furthers. An incoherent moral system will further given aims in one context but not in another, when there is no rationale for distinguishing the contexts in question. Furthermore, in such a system there will be no explanation why a factor counts as morally relevant in one context when it does not in another. Hence explanatory coherence will be lacking as well.

One has moral knowledge when the truth of one's moral belief helps to explain its being held. But in this domain the truth of one's belief that one has a moral reason to perform an action depends on the coherence of the norms that provide the reasons, or, equivalently, on the coherence of moral beliefs of rational evaluators who endorse those norms. Hence, such knowledge is not independent of sets of moral beliefs with which it must cohere. Empirical knowledge, by contrast, can be established through causal relations between beliefs and facts, sometimes largely independently of other beliefs.

In the case of empirical beliefs, I pointed out that coherence is itself an indication of correspondence to independent fact, at least when a coherent set of beliefs can be anchored to the world by a set of foundational beliefs about appearances. Here explanatory depth is gained by inferring beyond the appearances to real properties to which ordinary perceptual beliefs correspond. (The latter beliefs are not ordinarily acquired via such inferences, but the epistemologist can justify physical realism in this way). In the moral domain, I argued, we do not gain explanatory depth (a criterion of coherence) by inferring to real moral properties. Instead we land in contradiction, an obvious form of incoherence. Moral reasoning, after one has become informed of the non-moral facts, aims only at coherence among beliefs, not at causal inferences intended to establish correspondence with unobserved facts. When one's informed moral beliefs are fully coherent, then one believes as a fully rational evaluator. When one holds moral beliefs in part because they are so informed and coherent, then one has moral knowledge.

In both the empirical and moral domains, coherence is a criterion of justification. Only in the moral realm does it determine truth. The main objection to coherence as a sole criterion of justification is the apparent circularity of such justification. Sets of moral or empirical beliefs, it seems, if developed as coherent extensions of smaller initial sets, will be only as worthy as those beliefs from which reasoning begins. Coherence in itself cannot be sufficient for justification in either domain, it can be argued. In the empirical domain, a fully coherent set of beliefs might never connect to the independent world purportedly represented by them, and incompatible but internally coherent sets might lay equal claim to justification or truth. In the moral realm, if one begins with only a set of convictions derived from parental, religious, or educational authorities, and if these represent only the dominant prejudices of the age, then extension and revision on grounds of coherence alone can add little in the way of justification and nothing to merit the label 'truth'.

The proper answer to this objection to coherence as the criterion of justification in either realm characteristically differs depending on which realm we are talking about (just as coherence itself differs in some of its requirements). Coherence among empirical beliefs, whose purpose is to represent independent reality, is not sufficient to indicate truth. The possibility of incompatible sets of equally coherent beliefs demonstrates that insufficiency, since only one such set can contain only true beliefs. There must be some indication within this set that it connects to the world in a way such as to represent it accurately. That indication can consist in grounding to foundational beliefs about appearances. Given such grounding, connection to the real world via causal inference is secured, and the possibility of incompatible, equally coherent sets of empirical beliefs becomes more remote.

If the purpose of a set of beliefs is not to represent a single reality, however, then foundational beliefs are not needed to secure the requisite connection. Moral beliefs primarily function to guide and co-ordinate actions, not to represent real properties. Coherence in the relevant sense is necessary and sufficient for this purpose, if it is sufficiently broad. By this I mean that moral norms and beliefs must cohere not only with each other, but with social aims and norms of individual psychology. Such broader coherence negates the objection that coherent moral frameworks may reflect only those idiosyncratic biases with which a moral reasoner might begin.

If, in contrast to empirical reasoning and the prominence of causal explanatory inferences there, moral reasoning aims primarily at internal coherence (of controversial judgments with analogous settled convictions), and secondarily at external coherence between moral frameworks and extra-moral norms, then our task here is to clarify further the demands of these types of coherence. An initially helpful model is that of legal reasoning. We may consider next the analogies and disanalogies to this relatively familiar and voluminously recorded institutionalized form of justification for decision-making.

B. The Analogy to Legal Reasoning and Knowledge

Before noting those structural analogies between legal and moral reasoning that should be helpful for clarifying the form of the latter, we may point out once more some prominent disanalogies between the two domains. Perhaps the most prominent is the principle of precedent or *stare decisis* in law, requiring judges to conform their decisions to earlier decisions by certain other courts. A great portion of writing in jurisprudence is concerned with the extent and interpretation of this requirement to defer to existent legal sources. It is sometimes held that the justification for this requirement lies mainly in the formal principle of justice, the demand to treat like cases alike. This principle simply states (in an overly simple way) the requirement for coherence among moral judgments. But its use in this direct justification for the principle of legal precedent can be challenged by asking why a prior decision that is considered substantively unjust or legally mistaken should be repeated. Can a judge consider herself to be minimizing injustice by repeating a decision that she considers unjust?

The answer to this challenge to the legal principle itself lies not in repeating the direct appeal to justice or morality, but instead in pointing out certain institutional aims and features of the legal system. That system exists in part to secure the protection of individual moral rights, but also in part to help create and maintain social stability, a social environment in which stable expectations can be formed, useful ventures risked, and interactions conducted in an orderly way. Stability of expectations requires consistency and predictability of legal decisions, both more easily achieved when judges adhere to earlier decisions. Without predictability, legal advice would be more costly and less valuable, and social transactions would be more risky.

Other institutional considerations are the moral fallibility of individual judges and their relative isolation from electorates. Given fallible judgment, it is better that authority for decisions be divided, and that individual judges defer to their predecessors, especially when a common law rule has been derived from a whole line of cases. Furthermore, it is better that radical changes in the law be initiated by legislators who arc answerable to voters. Judges have more limited investigative resources, must make immediate decisions as cases come before them, and would have to apply those decisions *ex post facto* if they represented radical departures from prior law. Given the way that judges must interpret precedents (to be elaborated briefly below), the principle of *stare decisis* allows for a proper blend of moral input and institutional constraint.

No similar interpersonal constraint operates in the moral sphere. One is not generally required to conform one's moral judgments to those of others, not even to recent judgments of others on exactly the same topics in relevantly similar circumstances, and not even (as philosophers may lament) if those others have been trained in the making of such judgments and in the reasoning that precedes it. The justification for this contrast consists both in the absence of those reasons that warrant the principle in law and the positive value of individual autonomy in moral judgment.

Outside of institutional settings, a person's actions and judgments on morally controversial matters do not as often affect strangers in ways that require them to be predictable in the absence of knowledge of that person's own values and ethical orientation. If a person is reasonably consistent in his own actions, then that pattern allows those who know him to rely on certain reactions in morally charged circumstances. That degree of predictability in private actions and judgments normally suffices for purposes of social stability (in the absence of legal requirements). In fact, diversity in judgment and action, disastrous among officials of the courts, here often constitutes a constructive input to the social system. Moral innovation, often healthy, derives from the nonconformity of individuals' judgments, without there being any division of authority similar to that between innovative legislators and more institutionally conservative judges.

Second, fallibility in moral judgment does not enter into division of moral authority as it does in the law. While moral, as legal, judgments are fallible, and in similar ways, there are no moral experts who stand to ordinary people as higher courts stand to lower. Higher courts exert strong local constraints on lower, in that a standing appellate ruling on a case will bind a lower court judge in a later, similar case whatever his opinion of that ruling and its relation to the rest of the law. The notion of legal expertise has clearer application than that of moral expertise, even though moral reasoning requires similar skills. The reason for this difference is the existence of an independent body of data, or settled law, established as a matter of institutional history through a set of legislative and judicial actions, that can be mastered by the legal student (and must be by the legal expert). Errors in legal reasoning lead to judgments inconsistent with that independent body of data. In the sphere of morality errors also consist in inconsistencies. However, there is no independent body of data with which an individual's judgments must cohere.

This difference between the two domains, expressed in the lack of an explicit constraint to conform one's moral judgments to those of others, is lessened in practice by the fact that an individual's set of moral beliefs normally will derive from norms of those groups of which he is a member. But the distinction remains real, deriving, as we have seen, from the institutional aim of social stability, from considerations of fallibility and division of authority, from the value of autonomy in individual moral judgments, and from a difference in the respective data bases. Despite this major distinction, the structure of reasoning in the two domains is similar.

Given a legally controversial case, lawyers and judges will appeal to statutory sources or to analogous earlier cases decided at the appellate level. Cases are analogous not according to how many features they have in common (if that notion makes any sense at all), but according to whether they fall under the same principle or purpose of law. A second case should be decided as an earlier one was if the institutionally recognized moral aim served by the earlier decision requires the same ruling in the later case. The antecedent will be true if the second case shares those features that were relevant to the fulfilment of the previously recognized (at least implicitly) aim. Hard cases are those in which some such features of the first case are absent in the second, or in which the second has additional features relevant to some conflicting, legally recognized, moral norm. Whether the principle from the first case will then be limited or extended depends upon the ordering of such principles according to deeper and more general aims of the legal system.

Similar considerations apply to the application of statutory rules to cases not explicitly envisaged in the language of the statutes. A judge can understand the proper range of such rules only if she grasps the legitimate aims served by their operation.

(Jurisprudentialists once more disagree as to whether such aims should be limited to those envisaged by the legislators who enacted the statutes, or whether they should be those which appeal most to the judges applying the rules.) A judge can also reason in the opposite direction, however, from the range of cases to which a rule has been applied in the past, and from what have been considered exceptions or legally relevant differences limiting the rule, to the legitimate moral and institutional aims it is intended to serve.

Achieving consistency among legal decisions consists not simply in applying rules or principles, but in knowing when to apply them, knowing when cases are relevantly similar and different in relation to the ordered moral aims of the institution. Coherence among such institutionally recognized moral aims prevents the legal system from being arbitrary or self-defeating in its operation. The demand for coherence requires a judge to look both backward and forward. Faced with a hard case, she must look to prior sources for analogies and decide the case similarly unless she can find grounds for distinguishing it. If she does consider such grounds as legally relevant differences, then she must look to the future and to the consequences of taking them to make a legal difference generally to the recognized aims of the law. She must think of her decision as creating a rule for future ones, that is, she must universalize it in the Kantian fashion. Such rule-consequentialist thinking is once more not pure; it aims at consistency with previously recognized moral aims of the legal system.

This reasoning by analogy and generalized difference can conclusively, rather than probabilistically, determine the correct decision in a hard case. This conclusive determination distinguishes legal arguments from purely inductive empirical arguments by analogy. Legal arguments, we have seen, are distinguished on the other side from purely moral arguments by the independent, institutionally established data base from which the relevant analogies and disanalogies must be derived. Legal arguments are purely coherentist, and the truth of statments such as 'x is liable' lies in their coherence with other judgments of the same sort, not in correspondence to a reality independent of anyone's recognition of it. The truth of a proposition of law consists in that proposition's being more analogous to those in the previously settled body of law than is its denial. Nevertheless, legal argument is a hybrid between empirical and pure moral argument, in that its data is established through actual institutional acts.

Providing a legal reason for a decision consists in appealing to a precedent or statutory rule. Errors in such reasoning vary according to whether the appeal is made directly to a prior case or to a rule or principle. If the appeal is to the latter, then a judge may err in citing a rule that does not exist within the law, by thinking that the rule applies to the present case when it does not (perhaps because he misunderstands the facts), or by neglecting to cite some conflicting rule that applies more directly to the present case. If the appeal is to an analogous case taken as precedent, he may fail to note relevant disanalogies or may fail to cite a more analogous conflicting case. A judge or lawyer can misapply or fail to cite a relevant rule because he fails to grasp the moral, legal aim served by the rule. Similarly, failure to grasp the value protected or moral purpose served by a previous decision can result in failure to note analogies or disanalogies to the present case.

Moral reasoning, despite a difference in the data base, shares the structure of legal reasoning. As noted earlier, one attempting to reach a moral decision on a controversial issue typically begins from settled principles or cases considered easy and reasons by a process of analogy and difference to the new judgment most coherent with that data base. The process is the same when arguing with an adversary on a moral issue, only the data base becomes the set of shared settled judgments. When one arrives through this process at a new judgment, one must intend it to be consistent with future judgments, intend it to apply to all persons in relevantly similar circumstances (a relativized Kantian requirement).

Thus, for example, if elective surgery, contraception, and infanticide or murder constitute the cases relative to which I am to decide the morality of abortion, then I cannot believe that abortion is relevantly similar to the murder of young children, or that it is more like such murder than it is like contraception or elective surgery, and yet judge that it is morally permissible. Furthermore, I cannot hold that the relevant difference between abortion and infanticide, between fetuses and infants, lies in the way that infants, as opposed to fetuses, visually perceive or breathe, if experiencing or breathing in that way do not constitute universal prima facie justifications for different treatment.

The demand for coherence is the demand to judge similar cases similarly (on the intrapersonal, not interpersonal, level), Cases are similar when the same moral concepts apply, when the same values or aims underlying the application of moral concepts are at stake. These moral concepts, for example 'murder,' 'theft,' 'heroism,' may not be reducible as types to non-moral terms, even within a given framework. Positive or negative evaluations are included in their applications. An ordinary moral reasoner may not be able to state exhaustively the non-moral bases for these moral evaluations either. When it comes to differentiating possibly analogous cases, however, one must be able to state a morally relevant non-moral difference when judging differently, and one must be willing to generalize the differentiating ground so that it makes prima facie differences elsewhere. We may support this distinction by applying it to two sorts of examples. Consider first the concept of murder. All murders may be wrong, but it is not possible to state non-moral properties that are necessary and sufficient for homicides to qualify as murders (they must be morally or legally unjustified). Nevertheless, it is possible to state a non-moral ground that differentiates each case of justified homicide from cases of murder. A different sort of case is that of lying. Here it may be possible to list non-moral conditions sufficient for telling a lie (uttering a falsehood with intent to deceive), but it is not possible to list all exceptions to the rule that lying is wrong. Once again, however, we can differentiate exceptions as they arise.

Earlier I suggested an analogy between the realist's theses of supervenience – that there cannot be a difference in moral properties between two states of affairs without some difference in morally relevant non-moral properties – and the coherentist's requirement for evaluating cases differently. The latter requirement is actually stronger. It requires not only that there be morally relevant differences for all differences in moral judgments, but that evaluators have such justifying reasons and be able to produce them when their judgments are challenged. These reasons need appeal only to those who share the evaluators' moral frameworks, however. Perceived analogies or common principles that apply are reasons for judging cases similarly; perceived morally relevant differences are reasons for distinguishing evaluations. Both sorts of reasons are factors that would move rational evaluators who share moral frameworks.

Errors in moral reasoning parallel those committed by legal reasoners as well. Once more one may appeal to a principle not really accepted (together with all its implications); one may apply the principle wrongly to the case at hand, invalidly deriving an implication from it; one may fail to note relevant disanalogies when citing analogous cases; or one may fail to cite more analogous conflicting cases. All these errors more or less reduce to the failure to find and generalize morally relevant differences between cases. Generally, an unacceptable principle is one that is too broad, one that subsumes cases that are relevantly different within the framework of the evaluator. A moral reasoner usually draws the wrong implication from a principle if he ignores some relevant difference in applying it. Finally, to cite a case taken to be more analogous to the case in question than the one previously cited, when the new case is judged differently from the one previously cited, is to imply that there is some unnoticed relevant difference between the case at issue and the one previously cited.

Thus, we may think of the demand to find and generalize morally relevant differences for every difference in moral evaluation as the central requirement of coherence in ethics. This requirement captures even the giving of positive reasons for moral judgments, since citing a principle or analogous case is challenging one's interlocutor to find a morally relevant difference in terms of which to distinguish the case at issue. A morally relevant factor is one that generally makes a difference in the judgments of rational evaluators who share one's framework. A factor is morally relevant if it is relevant to the aim or value furthered or protected by a norm expressed in a particular judgment.

A skeptic might wonder once more about the strength of the constraint imposed by this central requirement, when we relativize the truth of moral judgments or the demand for coherence to particular frameworks. A similar skepticism arises in law, when judges are accused of finding grounds for distinguishing cases according to their prior moral preferences. It might be reinforced here by the recognition that I have called the constraint a relativized Kantian requirement, and yet earlier held that Kant's own requirement for willing universally is too weak to capture a plausible set of moral obligations. The present constraint may appear weaker than Kant's, since relational properties expressing personal or group loyalties now can constitute morally relevant differences. The fact that someone is my sister or client can make a difference that I generally recognize in my judgments about my obligations. If exceptions to moral principles and disanalogies to cases exist wherever particular evaluators find or posit them, then how does the demand to follow principles, universalize judgments, or generalize differences have any real force?

The requirement to generalize differences taken to be morally relevant will lack force only if the differentiating features are defined so narrowly as to be unlikely to recur, or if they are later taken to be always nullified or overridden by other factors. Differences defined so narrowly, however, will not move rational evaluators in their judgments, even those evaluators who share one's framework or consider themselves members of those groups with which one identifies. Differences that do move them, if generalized, will not always be overridden in other contexts by other factors. As for our rejection of Kant's principle, that criticism was directed toward the principle as a requirement for rational willing. But, as pointed out in that chapter, I can recognize a factor as morally relevant without willing that all act on principles that incorporate it.

Thus, the requirement to generalize morally relevant differences within frameworks has geniune force, just as it does within legal systems. In the next section I shall defend this requirement against possible objections.

C. *Coherence and Generalizing Morally Relevant Differences*

A rational evaluator, I have maintained, takes morally relevant differences to be generally so. This degree of consistency in judgment may seem a minimal and uncontroversial requirement of practical reason, but in fact it can and has been challenged. Particularists or 'situation' ethicists deny that properties which are morally relevant in one context need be even prima facie relevant in other contexts.

Jonathan Dancy, to name one critic of the generalization theses, has supported his criticism by appeal to an analogy with judgments of aesthetic value.² Clearly a particular line of a given shape and color in a painting might be of great aesthetic relevance and value there, but not in the context of some other (perhaps any other) painting. Likewise, a musical phrase in the context of a particular symphony need not have even prima facie aesthetic value when placed in other musical contexts. All the value of such elements and their properties, it might plausibly be claimed, derives from their places in the unique aesthetic wholes of which they are parts.

If moral relevance is like aesthetic relevance in this way, then morally relevant properties may not be all relevant when instantiated in other contexts. The analogy suggests that each moral situation may be a unique blend of properties that have value or relevance only when co-present. Alternatively, properties may be morally relevant only in the absence of defeaters. When the latter are present, they might completely nullify the relevance of properties for which they are defeaters, despite the fact that those properties may have been morally decisive in contexts encountered earlier. Dancy gives the example of a pious and chaste woman whose piety and chastity count toward making her a good person only in the absence of cruelty. Being cruel completely nullifies being pious and chaste in measuring moral goodness according to him. Similarly, he maintains, that an act gives pleasure can contribute to its being right, but not at all if the act is otherwise depraved. Thus, it seems, properties that affect moral goodness or rightness given certain other conditions, or in the absence of defeating conditions, may not generally do so. It would also seem, then, that there cannot be a constraint on moral reasoning to generalize factors taken to distinguish cases.

The defense of our account of coherence in ethics can begin by pointing to revealing disanalogies between moral argument and reasoning and its counterpart in aesthetics. The first noteworthy difference is that there is much less of the latter, much less argument over beauty than over rightness, and very little normative reasoning about the beauty of art objects either (as opposed to philosophical or meta-reasoning about what makes beautiful objects beautiful). This difference in quantity exists in part because the interests of most persons are unaffected by whether purported art is good or bad, while many are affected by immoral actions. Second, it is important how moral disputes are settled, whether they are settled rationally or by force, for example.

Disputes over beauty need not be settled by rational argument. Although aesthetic judgments are evaluations and not simply predications of real empirical properties, when aesthetic disagreements arise, they are typically settled, if at all, not by analogical argument, but simply by pointing to features of the works at issue in their presence. Argument, where it exists, typically assumes a different form than in ethics, where arguments are inferential and constrained by rules.

There would be no rational argument or settlement of disputes in ethics if grounds for distinguishing cases were not generalized. Consider, for example, a pro-abortionist who holds that infanticide is wrong because infants breathe differently from the way fetuses obtain oxygen. Imagine that we point out to her that manner of breathing is generally irrelevant to having a right to life, in that we can certainly conceive of intelligent, benevolent creatures which do not breathe as do humans but yet have rights to life. She simply agrees that manner of breathing is never morally relevant in any other context, but continues to view it as decisive given the unique set of additional properties in fetuses and infants. Surely there is no basis for rational argument here. The pro-abortionist's reason for her judgment is no better than no reason at all, her position the equal of a bald assertion with no justification or defense. She will be unable to articulate a moral aim, for example the protection of creatures that breathe in a certain way, that she seeks consistently to maintain. Instead, her actions in certain contexts will appear to defeat or conflict with her actions in other contexts.

In moral evaluation one responds not to a unique individual action, object, or person, as one might when evaluating a musical performance or a painting or when falling in love, but instead to repeatable properties of persons or actions – their cruelty, benevolence, duplicity, honesty, and so on. If the presence of such properties constitutes genuine reasons for distinguishing cases, if such properties are what sometimes make actions right or wrong, then, in the absence of other morally relevant properties in other contexts, their presence must generally be decisive. Otherwise, it could not be these properties themselves, but rather some broader properties (perhaps combinations of those thought relevant) that were decisive in the original contexts. Nevertheless, we must consider also the particularist's claim about how these properties might combine.

Although the suggestion of an analogy with aesthetics may be misleading, and although citing a property as a reason for a moral judgment when that property is never taken to be morally relevant elsewhere may be useless for argument, it still may appear that there could be total defeaters for morally relevant properties. Perhaps the moral relevance of these properties when combined with others could be like the color-making properties of pigments. A red-making pigment is no longer so at all when combined with others. Dancy suggests that producing pleasure or being pious and chaste are completely nullified as right or good making characteristics when combined with other properties such as cruelty.[3]

Whether we say that certain morally relevant properties are merely overridden or that they are completely cancelled by other properties in other contexts may be unimportant. What is important is that evaluators not focus on unique wholes, that they take properties judged to be morally relevant to make a difference generally. Dancy's examples of complete nullification by defeaters, however, seem plausible only because the properties that he mentions make very little, if any, moral difference generally. Few of us, I imagine would count piety and chastity very heavily when judging whether someone is a good person. Cruelty (and kindness), on the other hand, is of paramount importance. Similarly, producing pleasure, as opposed to causing pain, generally counts little, if any, toward making acts obligatory or even permissible. We are not obligated to give others pleasure (unless on grounds of reciprocity, which is a different morally relevant property), and it is difficult to imagine a single act that is wrong on other grounds, but right because it produces pleasure. Utilitarians have misled us here by conceiving pleasure and pain on the same moral scale, and this misleading conception lends plausibility to Dancy's otherwise unconvincing example.

If moral disputes and the conflicts among interests that underlie them are to be rationally settled, then appeals to ordinary properties as morally relevant must constitute reasons. If such appeals constitute reasons, these reasons must be generalizable. If there is to be a concept of moral truth in the absence of real moral properties, a concept strong enough to fit an (explanationist) account of moral knowledge, then this requirement of coherence seems minimally necessary. But why should such hypotheticals and necessary conditions convince us that there is moral truth and knowledge, and hence generalizable morally relevant differences between morally distinguishable cases? Perhaps instead skepticism is the proper response.

If we were aiming at knowledge of an independent reality, then to point out a requirement of consistency or coherence would not be to argue that this requirement is satisfied. But in ethics we are aiming primarily at ways to settle rationally and peacefully conflicts among the interests of different individuals, so that they can enjoy the benefits of co-operative endeavors. The constraint on moral reasoning at issue is necessary for articulating a coherent set of social and moral aims that together help to achieve that broader purpose. We therefore have the best of reasons for recognizing that constraint, and it is within our power to do so. Not that given societies adopt methods of moral reasoning self-consciously. But the reality of the constraint to generalize morally relevant differences can be explained in terms of the broad purposes of moral systems for which it is necessary.

Normally the fact that beliefs or forms of reasoning satisfy pragmatic desiderata is quite divorced from questions of truth. In this case, however, there are other reasons for calling judgments that meet the constraint in question, that are distinguished only when they refer to generalizable morally relevant differences, true. Truth in this sense is the goal of moral reasoning, reasoning that avoids those errors (mentioned above) which lead to wrong (false) judgments. Reasoning that obeys the generalization constraint allows inferences that can be deemed truth preserving. Consider an earlier example: If it is wrong for doctors to lie to their patients, then it is wrong for them to withhold information as well. This inference is warranted if and only if there is no morally relevant difference between lying to patients and withholding information from them, if the medical context differs relevantly from others in which there is a moral difference between lying and withholding information. To decide whether differences here are morally relevant, we must think about their effects on moral judgments in other contexts as well, and thus we require the generalization constraint.

Truth as the goal of reasoning, as what contrasts with error, and as what is preserved in sound inferences, contrasts also in a natural way with (mere) justification for moral beliefs. An evaluator is justified in believing those judgments that seem to her after careful reflection to cohere with her settled data base. Judgments are true that do cohere in the way specified. We call such judgments true first, to contrast them with mere prejudices, guesses, or judgments that result from errors in reasoning; second, to identify them as results of sound inferences and as premises for further reasoning; and third, to distinguish them from justified beliefs that are not really coherent.

I have shown why a generalization requirement is necessary for moral reasoning, truth, and knowledge, and why moral beliefs that satisfy this demand for coherence deserve the title of truth. I have not yet exhausted the objections of particularists, however. Others who might be so labelled, for example Stuart Hampshire, object not to the claim that morally relevant differences must make some difference generally, but rather to the demand that an evaluator be able to state some such difference in justifying his judging cases differently.[4] Once more the objection is supported by appeal to purported analogies. In some areas of judgment we trust more to intuitive feelings or reactions to situations than to the ability to articulate reasons for one's judgments, and in some areas we even prefer unreflective, immediate reactions that reflect fully internalized norms over reflective, reasoned reactions.

An example of an area of behavior and judgment in the latter category is that of etiquette or manners. Good manners ought to be more or less automatic, fully internalized rather than self-conscious or reflective. There are also cognitive activities that we trust to intuitive judgments without requiring articulation of reasons. These include translating, and once more judging art, food, or wine. In all these domains unreflective judgment may reflect years of training and experience that render one capable of making subtle and complex distinctions not always able to be articulated. Many sorts of perceptual recognitions, identifications, and distinctions depend on subconscious cues of which a subject is not consciously aware, but judgments based on them are no less accurate for lying beyond explicit articulation or justification. If moral judgments too may be based on such intuitive, quasi-perceptual typing of morally charged situations, then, it seems, we should not require explicit justification by appeal to analogies and generalized differences. We should trust more to the judgments themselves than to evaluators' abilities to justify them by rational argument.

The key difference in the case of ethics, however, is that moral argument is often intended to settle conflicts among important interests of different individuals. Intuitive reactions are therefore likely to be emotionally laden and biased. One may be confident of an intuitive reaction to a moral question, but such a reaction may well be based on some morally irrelevant similarity or difference, and it is better to check for genuine coherence. One example mentioned earlier is the typical reaction to the sight of a fetus, based purely on physical appearance, the fact that it looks like a small infant. In general, even aside from this lack of reliability in gut reactions, it is important that disputes be settled by rational argument in terms understandable to all.

The same considerations apply to legal cases. Judges may feel confident of their initial impressions in certain cases. Precisely to counteract the tendency to base judgments solely on such personal impressions, we require that they hear the strongest possible arguments on the other side and then, in legally hard cases that reach appellate courts, that they justify their decisions publicly by demonstrating coherence with established legal standards. We require public justification not only to counteract bias and leave a record for future decisions, but also to satisfy the parties to the disputes that their cases have been settled reasonably and decisively.

In ethics, as opposed to law, we sometimes aim at private decisions rather than public settlement of disputes. Hampshire would maintain that the legal model is inappropriate in these private contexts, that we should once more trust to quasi-perceptual reactions that may reflect subconscious memories of analogies superior in relevance to those we can articulate upon reflection. There are again important disanalogies between perceptual and moral judgments, however, that weaken Hampshire's case. In perceptual contexts in which we are very accurate without being aware of our methods, for example, the context of face recognitions, we appear to be wired to pick up subtle cues that distinguish physical properties. If we are unsure of such a perceptual judgment, often the best way to check it is to place ourselves again in the proper causal relations and allow the cues to operate on our visual systems. In the case of moral judgments, I have argued at length that we are not expressing recognitions of real properties. The only way to check the reliability of intuitive moral judgments is to check the relevant analogies and differences against other settled judgments in order to make sure that one's initial reaction, perhaps in the presence of the object of the judgment, was not based only on morally irrelevant causal factors.

Such checks, the search for articulated reasons for moral judgments, are to be desired because even seemingly private decisions, if genuinely moral, will result in actions that will affect the interests of others. Those others may demand and will deserve an articulation of the reasons why their interests may be sacrificed, reasons that they can understand and perhaps debate. This articulation may not be complete. I have admitted that relevant analogies may be captured only by moral concepts, that they may not be reducible to explicit comparisons of real properties. But relevant differences, reasons for distinguishing cases, must be made explicit if moral judgments are to fulfill their vital social functions.

D. Examples and Experiences

Confirmation for a theory of moral reasoning and knowledge lies in real examples of reasoning about hard social issues and in the knowledge or goal at which such reasoning aims. This is not the place to engage in lengthy discussion of concrete issues. But I can indicate the form that such discussion has taken in the extensive recent philosophical literature.

The abortion issue, mentioned several times above, has provided ample illustration of the type of reasoning that I have described. The constraints are that similar cases must be judged alike, that cases are similar when they fall under the same moral concepts applied according to the aims of the moral system, and that generalized differences must be cited between cases judged differently. The central questions regarding abortion are first, whether it is similar to, or different from, homicide, that is, whether fetuses are relevantly similar to or different from infants, and second, if they are similar, if they do have rights to life, whether rights of women over their own bodies might nevertheless override their fetuses' rights.

To answer the first set of questions, we would inquire into our aim in granting rights to life. What are the characteristics of beings to whom we grant such rights that require us to do so, characteristics that must be possessed at least by children and adult humans? Do fetuses share these characteristics? In what ways, if any, are they relevantly unlike infants or children? To be relevant, these ways must generally make a difference to having rights to life. To answer the second question, we would ask how in general rights to life impinge on other persons. More specifically, we would look for analogies at the moral obligations of parents toward their children, including obligations to keep their children alive. If fetuses are similar in all relevant respects to infants, then it would seem that they are related to the women who carry them as children to their parents. There are differences, however, in regard to personal interactions and perhaps felt responsibilities on the part of the parents, and we would need to determine whether these differences are generally morally relevant for duties to protect the lives of others.

Of course I cannot attempt to answer any of these questions here. My point is only that the philosophical literature on this issue is replete with discussions of them, at least where it has seemed most directly on the mark.[5] Appeals to abstract normative theories or to completely general principles are of little help; appeals to analogous cases or to narrower principles derived directly from them can be very illuminating, indeed decisive if morally relevant differences cannot be found. We decide whether differences are relevant by noting the aims that prior judgments on purportedly analogous cases serve, and then deciding whether the proposed differences can be generalized.

Other issues are handled in the same way. One also prominent in the recent literature is the issue of preferential appointments for members of minority groups and women.[6] Here we once more ask first for the justifying aim of the proposed policy. If, for example, the aim is to compensate for past injustice, then we want to know whether rights to compensation generally override prima facie distributive rights to goods (here rights of the most qualified to jobs). To find this out, we look to simpler cases in whcih compensation is owed. We also want to know who has rights to compensation in the form of preference. Does preferential treatment constitute proper compensation in kind for all members of the relevant groups simply as members of groups previously victimized, or is it owed only to individual direct victims of discriminatory acts and policies? To answer this question, we examine other contexts in which compensation is owed to whole groups. We ask whether those groups share certain features that make them the proper targets of compensatory payments, features such as interaction of members in pursuit of common goals that were unjustly frustrated. If so, we ask whether minority groups typically have these properties and whether preference for some of their members (the most marketable ones) constitutes the kind of compensation typically and properly paid to groups. Once more we appeal at each stage of the argument to possible analogies with our settled moral judgments and then seek to distinguish the case at issue by appealing to generalizable differences.

We use this method of reasoning not only to decide difficult and complex moral issues, but to criticize (much as Hume did) the moral views of others. If, for example, someone judges homo-sexual acts to be all immoral, we can challenge him to state a reason. He might appeal to some purported natural or divine aim for sexual acts, or, more plausibly, to our aims in allowing certain sexual acts and prohibiting others. He might claim, for example, that nature, or God, or we seek to limit sexual acts to those that serve the function of reproduction. Acts are wrong, he could say, that violate the natural, or divine, or human aims for which they are intended. But he will have great difficulty maintaining this view in regard to sexual acts themselves, if he perceives the proper aim there to be reproduction. Passionate kissing between hetero-sexuals no more serves reproduction than do homosexual acts, yet the former is unlikely to be condemned. Thus the target of our imagined criticism is unlikely to be consistent in his evalu-ations, and he can be attacked on that ground.

I shall resist multiplying further examples of moral reasoning that exemplifies the form and constraints I have described as requirements of coherence. Instead, I shall consider a final set of objections to the equation of moral truth with such coherence and of moral knowledge with beliefs best explained by their being true in this sense.

Earlier, I noted an objection to the principle of *stare decisis* in law, namely, that it may perpetuate and extend earlier unjust decisions. The proper reply to the objection there did not appeal directly to moral considerations, but instead to institutional reasons for requiring conservatism toward the settled law on the part of judges. Although there is no interpersonal constraint in ethics requiring that one conform particular judgments to earlier judgments of others on the same issues, the demand for coherence as I have described it might elicit an objection similar to that raised against the legal principle. It might be claimed that this demand produces unwarranted conservatism in moral attitudes, that it requires undue deference toward one's prior moral beliefs, and gives insufficient weight to new experiences as sources of moral change in view and improvement. This charge of unwarranted conservatism may be coupled with a worry voiced earlier about coherence as the criterion of moral truth and knowledge – that coherent extensions of sets of moral beliefs will be only as worthy of endorsement as were the smaller, original sets.

I shall address the latter worry again in the next section. Here it remains to clarify the role of new experience in shaping moral views. In hard cases, such as those social issues discussed above, that role is not often decisive. It is a feature of all non-foundational belief systems (I have argued that moral frameworks lack epistemic foundations) that all beliefs, even those that arise spontaneously and non-inferentially in the presence of their referents, are vulnerable to revision for the sake of coherence. In a case that an evaluator recognizes to be morally difficult, he will have no confident initial beliefs from direct observation. He will then have no alternative but to reflect on principles or analogies within his moral framework in order to arrive at a settled judgment. On the other hand, moral judgments, if they are to serve their aims and guide actions consistently, must be informed. One can become informed of the relevant non-moral properties of the objects of one's evaluations either by description or by acquaintance or observation. It might be thought that direct acquaintance would afford a better indication of what would move a rational evaluator; but that is so only if the observer does not himself react to morally irrelevant factors when observing the object of his evaluation.

Experiences can be more significant in shaping moral beliefs when evaluators make confident judgments on the basis of them, when they do not view the situations they observe as morally difficult cases. Evaluators may on occasion form firm beliefs on the basis of experience even when their judgments seem to them to oppose their prior moral beliefs. I noted in the previous chapter the example of a professed utilitarian becoming unalterably opposed to slavery after seeing a dramatization and so abandoning his utilitarian principle. A new belief of this sort need not be interpreted as resulting from an apprehension of a real moral property in order to motivate changes elsewhere in the system. In the discussion of that example, I denied that a single belief based on experience could in itself require wholesale changes throughout a previously coherent moral framework. But new experiences and beliefs based on them can reveal earlier inconsistencies (the most likely outcome for the professed utilitarian). In addition, they can quickly connect to clusters of new and old beliefs and thereby lead to revisions or abandonments of other beliefs. They can convince the evaluator that differences previously believed to be morally relevant do not generalize, or that cases previously believed to be analogous must be distinguished on grounds of newly-discovered differences.

Beliefs based on new experiences can be either explained away as reactions to morally irrelevant, ungeneralizable differences, or they can be generalized and incorporated into the evaluator's moral framework. The basic rule is that one who reflects on a set of new and old beliefs seen to be incoherent in the ways described makes those minimal changes, takes the path of least resistance for her, required to restore coherence to the set. The demand for coherence in itself favors neither conservatism nor radical shifts in moral beliefs. In law, the interpersonal constraint of precedent is genuinely conservative, but there are good institutional reasons for judicial conservatism. In ethics, the constraint is essentially forward-looking, reducing, as we have seen, to a requirement to generalize morally relevant differences, to be willing to count them as grounds for distinguishing future judgments.

Individuals normally approach morally significant situations with sets of moral beliefs that express norms of groups of which they are members, with which they identify, and from which they absorb their sets of values. The relevant groups normally broaden as an individual matures, ranging from family, to peer groups, to career groups and broader societies. Perhaps the crucial ethical role of experience is as catalyst to this broadening process.

Experiences that reveal the joys and anguishes of members of other groups can lead normally sympathetic persons to expand those other groups with which they are willing to identify. Divided groups loyalties can create tensions and inconsistencies within the moral framework of individuals, but they also expand the reasons for which those individuals are willing to defer to the interests of others. Broad experience of interpersonal interactions can result in divided and widened loyalties, and finally in more extensively coherent moral frameworks, as adjustments are made to accommodate new judgments.

It is also possible, however, that as loyalties expand they tend to weaken, so that not only narrower loyalties, but self-interest, comes to predominate when in conflict. This is not to say that narrower loyalties are generally less worthy of respect. Having granted that different moral frameworks (some based on narrower and some on broader loyalties) may be equally coherent internally, it remains to indicate more fully how we are to justify commitments to some such frameworks rather than others. It may seem that a coherentist faces a final telling objection here. In the next section I shall expand upon the reasons why the objection seems troubling and how it can be answered.

E. Broad Coherence and Commitment to Whole Moral Frameworks

We have seen how particular moral beliefs can be justified in terms of their coherence within sets of evaluations. This answer to the question of local justification, however, immediately raises the deeper question of justification on the global level. Given my values and commitments, or those of the moral communities to which I belong, given those settled judgments and principles that express the kind of person that I am, I will have a straightforward way to resolve moral doubts and disputes (although errors in reasoning always remain possible). But this method only accentuates the question whether anything can justify my overall commitments or my being the moral kind of person that I am.

If moral realism were true, if in addition to truth and falsity for moral judgments there were real moral facts or properties to which those judgments had to correspond to be true, then the issue of global justification and truth might admit of an equally straightforward answer. Commitment to an entire system of moral beliefs or set of values would then differ from assertion of particular moral beliefs only in scope. In both cases the goal would be simply that of getting it right. But this simple sort of additive model is unavailable to the coherentist. The coherence criterion of truth and justification, together with the lack of a set of common foundational beliefs with which others must cohere, raises the problem of global justification in a clear and pressing way, since it implies the possibility of incompatible but internally consistent sets of moral beliefs. Indeed, I have welcomed this implication as the best explanation for interminable moral disagreements. Foundations for empirical beliefs are needed precisely to avoid that possibility, but the need cannot be met in ethics. In the absence of foundations and of real moral facts or properties to which foundations would anchor discourse, it might seem that internal coherence is insufficient to render moral frameworks worthy of commitment and obedience. If any internally coherent set of action guiding beliefs can count as a moral system, and if there are no grounds for judging whole systems except internal coherence, then indeed it would appear that all might be permitted and anything goes.

However, there are constraints on attitudes, principles, and judgments that could be recognized to be moral, constraints imposed first of all by language. For example, to be recognized as moral, discourse must express values that do not reflect merely the short-term self-interest of the agent, values that often oppose such interest and are taken to override it. An attitude recognizable as moral, while it need not consider the interests of all toward whom it is directed on the same scale, must at least consider the interests of some others on a par with its subject's short-term desires. Reasons acknowledged as moral must be viewed as important, if not always as overriding, by some members of the groups whose norms they express. They must not be generally overridden for reasons of pure etiquette or personal convenience, for example, unless etiquette is elevated or transformed into moral reasons (a remark's being insulting may become a moral reason against making it).

Judgments recognizable as moral must have certain features that make them at least prima facie worthy of respect. They must tend to oppose selfish, aggressive, or harmful behavior by appealing to the good of some broader community. As I have been arguing, they must also meet the constraint of internal coherence, which in itself commands our respect. Judgments must be universalized at least within a moral community; morally relevant differences must be generalized, which rules out certain kinds of arbitrariness that disqualify judgments and actions based on them as respectable. These constraints must be observed if one is to speak language recognizable by others as moral, or if one is to partake in institutions governed by moral rules. Nothing necessitates a person's doing either, and there are degrees to which persons do both, although they may have reasons of self-interest – indeed, genetically wired and socially reinforced motivations – for joining groups and partaking in moral institutions.

These formal and linguistic constraints take us but little way toward justifying commitments to particular moral frameworks. A Nazi could perhaps satisfy them by universalizing reasons for action within his own group. There still remain enormous variations among systems that could satisfy these constraints, and this fact continues to press the question of global justification upon the coherentist. He might want to object that the question is artificial and inapplicable to real individuals in societies. It gives the impression of a neat division between adjustments of particular beliefs within moral systems on the one hand, and choices of overall moral frameworks or orientations on the other. In practice, while the former phenomenon is common enough, the latter rarely or never occurs.

We have noted that a person typically absorbs a set of moral beliefs and grows into a set of social roles as part of the normal process of social maturation. Even when roles or careers are consciously chosen, the choices are not usually determined by the moral frameworks connected with, or presupposed by, those roles and institutions of which they are a part. A person's mature commitments, even those of a narrowly moral nature, do not emerge *ex nihilo,* but normally represent modifications, first of a rule-worshipping, childish interpretation of parental restrictions, and later of genuine societal expectations and rules. Not only do people grow into sets of values and norms in this way; many never become conscious of having, let alone of choosing, a particular moral orientation as opposed to alternative ones. Even when individuals make monumental moral choices that alter the courses of their lives or oppose the run of ordinary expectations, they probably more often than not feel their decisions to be necessitated by circumstances, by the demands of true character, or by higher social forces. Such causal explanations represent bad faith according to existentialists, but their ideal of total freedom from such influences seems to express more a pathological alienation from self and society than an authentic human condition.

The coherentist's resistance to the question posed (if in fact he resists) is nevertheless misplaced. Admitting this account of normal moral development does not defuse the issue of global justification. A reflective person can question her commitments and moral orientation even though she does not experience them as conscious and free choices when formed. Contact with alien value systems can raise one's critical self consciousness, and in our age of social fragmentation, mobility, and change, the loss of fixed roles and roots has rendered such experience very common. The ideal of the fully autonomous person who chooses and assumes responsibility for her own value system is part of the liberal as well as existentialist ideology. But while the free-floating, radical freedom of the latter may be a misplaced (psychologically misinformed) ideal, the goal of self-critical reflection is not. Once the morally reflective person recognizes that she has been justifying particular moral views only relative to analogies with others as yet unquestioned, once she relinquishes the idea of a fixed teleology for humans or of an external source, divine or natural, for moral truth, she not only can, but seemingly must raise the deeper question of the justification for commitment to a whole moral framework (and to a particular one as opposed to others).

Arise as it will, it can still be argued that this question can never receive a satisfactory rational answer. The argument might paraphrase from Wittgenstein's comments on his central but elusive notions of language games and forms of life.[7] In the slightly narrower case of value systems, we have already noticed the key analogy. I do not come to have the set of values I do because I am convinced that they are right. Instead, my judgments of right and wrong normally emerge from the background of values to which I am committed. Furthermore, any sincere questioning of particular values would seem to require a point of view that at least temporarily leaves others unquestioned. Even my recognition of possible alternatives seems to be a function of values I now have. Thus, the moral framework to which I am committed, as the broader forms of life or language games in which I engage, provides a context of meaningfulness and criteria of justification. How then can the question of justification for the framework as a whole be met? Certainly an entire system could not be justified (or, if coherent, even called into question) from within that system itself. It seems that I could judge in this global context only from the viewpoint of some other framework; but then, even if the systems are not simply incommensurable, questions will be begged. Why should it affect my view of my own coherent system that it is justified or unjustified from the point of view of some other system? But, barring such external justification, must my own commitments not remain existential or groundless?

Despite the force of these points, the prospects for justification are not so bleak. It is true that if we begin from unworthy moral beliefs, our coherent extensions of them will remain unworthy. But the very force of this point indicates that there are extra-moral standards for assessing moral systems. While we may not single out one best moral system (the non-realist need not try to do so), at least we can differentiate among them not only according to criteria of internal consistency, but also by their coherence with these extra-moral standards, what we might call broad coherence. We may distinguish moral codes in the narrow sense – sets of mainly prohibitive rules and judgments that prevent and resolve conflicts so as to make social living possible – from broader sets of values that guide actions. From the individual's viewpoint, commitment to the former is justified both in terms of the latter and in terms of his commitment to or identification with those social groups which the codes in question govern.

A person often becomes committed to a certain moral code and broader set of values because he wants to be recognized or identified as a member of a particular social group and as a particular kind of person within that group. Normally this is no shallow, self-interested motive to appear other than one really is, to reap the benefits of a moral appearance without acquiring the substance of a moral character. Rather, an individual's genuine identity must be constituted, at least in part, through his identification by others as a certain kind of person and his consequent self-recognition in those terms. The kind of person with which he is identified will be constituted partly by a system of values including moral norms. The need to be identified by others in this way means that the morality to which one becomes committed will be that of some social group, and the need to identify oneself in this way means that one normally will be sincere in endorsing those norms. Even in its incipieint stages moral restraint and commitment develops in this way. Although a child first internalizes particular prohibitions under parental threats without understanding the values they express, the broader context in which this process becomes possible involves her affective attachments to her parents, and the threats involve the withdrawal of their affection.

I have been speaking of a deep psychological need of individuals for identification with or commitment to sets of social norms and values. Economic motives aside, this need provides the individual with the best of reasons to partake in social institutions and to adopt willingly a set of social roles. Having done so, she will then have reasons to act in ways that oppose her self-interest. One may wonder how this could be so if the reasons for being a moral person (relative to some group's morality) are at bottom self-interested. But the question ignores the extent to which those social norms to which an individual becomes committed can reinforce her unselfish motives and suppress her selfish ones.

The set of institutions with whose values and aims individuals can identify serves the function of the older notion of a natural human teleology, although we can no longer recognize a single teleology or an automatic commitment to it. The seriousness with which one takes moral requirements and the degree to which these constitute one's own reasons for acting or refraining are a function of the extent of one's commitment or identification with a community that recognizes such requirements. Conversely, alienation from particular communities is the source of amorality in relation to their members. The position I have defended on moral reasons falls between that which holds that a person must always directly will or accept such reasons in order for them to give him reasons to act, and that which views moral reasons as completely independent of the motives of the agents to whom they apply. A person is provided with moral reasons by the norms of those social groups with which he becomes identified. But that simple account too must be qualified and complicated. A person may be committed to more than one social group, and their norms may not always coincide. He may also occupy a social role while vetoing some of its publicly recognized requirements (although not its most central norms). The extent to which such norms obligate him depends on the expectations of others within the institution, on his own views, and on the ways these have modified through interaction.

The psychological account of moral development provides a general justification from the individual's point of view for commitment to narrower (moral) and broader sets of social norms. Presumably a genetic evolutionary explanation will underlie the psychological account, the former explaining the need for social identity as wired into individuals, selected as a means to prolong survival of kinship groups and ultimately of the species. Of course, on the cultural level, too, such personal commitments allow societies to develop and flourish, a justification of sorts as well. Nevertheless, these general justifications of moral norms in terms of individual psychological needs and the survival of societies does not yet resolve the issue of commitment to particular groups and sets of social norms rather than others. Here again, however, we can judge in terms of external standards, including epistemic standards (moral judgments must be informed), in terms of the relation beween the moral norms in question and the fulfilment of individual psycholoigies, and in terms of their utility for furthering co-operative social aims, preventing socially destructive disorder, and furthering those values they purport to express.

In regard to individual psychology, one may wonder how a person could be committed to a set of norms that does not express her particular psychology, given that personal identity is itself partly constituted by such commitments and that commitment is itself dispositional. The answer lies in the complexity of motivations. Individuals can act in self-destructive ways, and the groups to which they belong can reinforce rather than repress or redirect such tendencies. That social norms depict individual psychology writ large and that healthy personalities require the moral restraints imposed by society were first emphasized by Plato, and in the more contemporary psychoanalytic literature by Erik Erikson.[8] Each person must strike a proper balance between the acceptance of restraint and the exercise of will in interaction with various peer groups and institutions. Each needs to see verification of his identity in his social relations and achievements, both of which normally require some understood moral basis. The moral social order can complement the individuals within it in these ways. On the other hand, certain aspects of group ethics can express the self-aggression and hatred of outsiders typical of the totalitarian personality that is incapable of achieving a balanced integration in relation to family and broader society.

These sorts of claims are of course evaluative, but less relativistically so than straightforward moral evaluations. Our normative notion of health, including even mental health, is at its core less variable and controversial than our moral norms. I am not claiming that norms of mental health can always be distinguished from moral norms. The former often reflect, albeit unwittingly, the latter. Nevertheless, since the notion of mental health is not entirely a moral notion, the justification of a morality as a whole in these terms need be only partly circular. And even in regard to social or moral norms in themselves, the circularity of self-justification is not entirely vacuous. Those sets of values and norms that pass this test can be positively distinguished, since other sets prove in practice to be incoherent or self-defeating.

Moral systems that do not appear in practice to further the values they express may tend to self-correct. Suppose, for example, that a thoroughgoing utilitarianism of the Benthamite sort proves to be worse on its own terms, less productive of aggregate utility, than a moral system that recognizes individual rights and loyalties as constraints on the pursuit of collective welfare. Or suppose that a hedonistic theory of value when followed produces less happiness than one which recognizes and requires the pursuit of other goods. These theories may then be transformed into multi-tiered structures, with the basic level norms justifying higher level exceptions to, or constraints on, their direct application. In theory systems incoherent in this way can be modified and complicated so as to restore practical consistency. But actual action guiding social norms may remain individually or socially self-defeating. An individual who is consciously committed to utilitarianism may through his particular judgments logically commit himself to the more complex version suggested above; but in practice he may oppose individual rights through failure to understand the situation or its implications. The same can be true of actual social norms and the groups that embody and follow them.

On the social level the problem of justification can be hidden behind the process of historical change, but this very same process can also raise these questions of continuing internal coherence for institutions and their fundamental norms. Some systems become incoherent because of changing social conditions and institutional practice. I have argued elsewhere that prominent examples at present include both the American legal institution of fully zealous advocacy, when the bulk of legal practice and the appropriate models to reflect it shifted away from criminal defense to the large corporate sphere, as well as the paternalistic model of medical practice, when the medical establishment shifted away from the personal family doctor to group and specialized practice.[9] We might include here also the common assumption of national boundaries as the outer limits of moral obligations, of the nation as the largest group to which one owes allegiance or commitment. In general the notion of tribal morality that I have endorsed must expand its conception of relevant tribes as technological, economic, and weapons systems expand to unite and mutually threaten smaller tribes and formerly alien cultures within their scopes. This is a yet more crucial example of the way in which group ethics must adapt to changing conditions in order to correct inconsistencies between values and the means to realize them.

In sum, the problem of justifying global commitments does admit of answers in epistemic, psychological, social, and logical terms, although not answers that will single out a particular moral framework as best. We can ask whether a given moral framework or social institution is based on factual error or ignorance, whether it is consistent with the healthy character traits of the individuals within it, whether it contributes to fulfilled lives, whether it fosters favorable social interactions and the stability of the group within which it operates, and whether it furthers those social values that it purportedly exists to realize and protect. We can demand that an individual's commitment to an institution withstand reflection on its actual grounds, that these not be hidden behind false rationalizations that evaporate when the tests just mentioned are applied.

Those institutions that pass these tests, however, will remain varied, since there will always be interaction between individual values and expectations and their cultural embodiment in social and moral frameworks. That there can be incompatible moral frameworks that pass all these tests implies that some choices among them might be groundless or existential; but from the point of view of individuals in historical social contexts, such choices, even when conscious and reflective, need not be seen that way.

F. Conclusion

We may evaluate moral systems or sets of beliefs on grounds of both internal and broad coherence. Internal coherence may be understood by conceiving moral reasoning after the model of legal reasoning. Although in ethics there is no interpersonal requirement to conform particular judgments to those of others, as there is in law, the structure of reasoning in the two domains is similar. One justifies judgments by appealing to analogous cases or, what amounts to the same thing, to principles that summarize analogous judgments. Cases are analogous when their decisions further the same legal or moral aims. The basic constraint is to find morally relevant differences for all differences in judgments and to generalize the morally relevant properties so that they are held to matter to moral judgment elsewhere.

This requirement is not universal among value judgments of all kinds: for example, it is not prevalent in aesthetics. But it is necessary for rational moral argument, and it derives from the broad aim of moral norms and judgments – the rational settlement of interpersonal conflicts so as to foster co-operative behavior within groups or societies. This broad aim requires the articulation of generalizable reasons for moral beliefs.

It also indicates those extra-moral standards that whole frameworks must satisfy if they are to be broadly coherent. They must not be based on factual error or ignorance, or on faulty methods of acquiring and weighing empirical evidence. They must be consistent with norms of individual psychological health and with those social aims for which they exist. They must further those values that they purport to express.

There is no reason to believe that these tests single out one moral framework as best, and good reason deriving from seemingly interminable moral conflict for disbelieving this. But since our aim in moral judgment is not to represent truly a single reality, there need not be a uniquely true moral system. Moral judgments differ from empirical judgments in ways that reflect their different functions. The former lack foundations and they are not explained causally by their relations to real properties. Despite the theories to the contrary of the great figures in the history of ethics, there is no real property of rightness independent of moral beliefs. All accounts of that property land us in contradictions.

The function of moral beliefs is not representational, but action guiding, as emotivists have maintained. Such beliefs may not guide the actions of all, but they govern the actions of those who accept them more successfully when they meet the constraints of coherence that I have described. Judgments that meet all those constraints warrant inferences and are properly described as true. If knowledge is belief best explained in part by its truth, then moral beliefs that are held partly because they meet these constraints merit the title of moral knowledge.

Notes

Introduction

1 Edmund Gettier, 'Is Justified True Belief Knowledge?', *Analysis*, 23 (1963): 121–3.

2 See, for example, Keith Lehrer, *Knowledge* (Oxford: Oxford University Press, 1974) ch. 9.

3 In the latest, most sophisticated variation by Keith Lehrer, a subject must continue to be justified in every set of beliefs that results from the elimination of any of his false beliefs and/or addition of corrections. This continues to make knowledge too dependent on which false beliefs a subject may have. Problem cases include those involving misleading evidence against a subject's justified true belief. Such evidence, even though misleading, may defeat knowledge claims if the subject should have known about it and would have been justified in believing it; otherwise, it may be irrelevant. Even the newer defeasibility accounts, as I understand them, lack the resources to distinguish these cases properly.

4 See, for example, Alvin Goldman, *Epistemology and Cognition* (Cambridge, Mass.: Harvard University Press, 1986) chs 3, 5.

5 Alvin Goldman, 'A Causal Theory of Knowing', *The Journal of Philosophy*, 64 (1967): 357–72.

6 See Alvin Goldman, 'Discrimination and Perceptual Knowledge', *The Journal of Philosophy*, 73 (1976): 777–91.

7 Robert Nozick, *Philosophical Explanations* (Cambridge Mass.: Harvard University Press, 1981) ch. 3.

8 See, for example, Alan Goldman, *Empirical Knowledge* (Berkeley: University of California Press, 1988) ch. 1.

9 Michael Dummett, 'Realism', in *Truth and Other Enigmas* (Cambridge, Mass.: Harvard University Press, 1978).

10 If we want to preserve the notion of truth as correspondence throughout, we can say in the non-realistic case that truth consists in correspondence to the fact of coherence between the belief in question and other beliefs, while in the realistic case it consists in correspondence to other sorts of facts.

215

11 G.E. Moore, *Principia Ethica* (Cambridge: Cambridge University Press, 1903) ch. 1.
12 A.J. Ayer, *Language, Truth and Logic* (New York: Dover, 1936) ch. 6.
13 See, for example, U.T. Place, 'Is Consciousness a Brain Process?' *British Journal of Psychology*, 47 (1956): 44–50.
14 Compare J.L. Mackie, *Ethics: Inventing Right and Wrong* (New York: Penguin, 1971) p. 35.
15 Compare Gilbert Harman, *The Nature of Morality* (New York: Oxford University Press, 1977) p. 29.
16 For a representative collection, see *Readings in the Philosophy of Psychology*, edited by Ned Block (Cambridge, Mass.: Harvard University Press, 1980) vol. 1.
17 See David Lewis, 'An Argument For the Identity Theory', *The Journal of Philosophy*, 63 (1966): 17–25; Donald Davidson, 'Mental Events', in *Essays on Actions and Events* (Oxford: Clarendon Press, 1980).
18 Richard Rorty, 'Mind-Body Identity, Privacy, and Categories', *The Review of Metaphysics*, 19 (1965): 24–54.

I

1 Citations in the text refer to the part, chapter, and pages of Thomas Hobbes, *Leviathan* (New York: Collier, 1962)
2 For the negative view, see David Gauthier, *The Logic of Leviathan* (Oxford, Clarendon Press, 1969) pp. 40–44.
3 This appeal is made explicit in Gauthier's contemporary Hobbesian argument in *Morals by Agreement* (Oxford: Clarendon Press, 1986) pp. 168–70, 177–9.
4 This point is made by Gregory Kavka, *Hobbesian Moral and Political Theory* (Princeton: Princeton University Press, 1986) p. 443.
5 Ibid., p. 206.
6 See Robert Axelrod, 'The Emergence of Cooperation among Egoists', *American Political Science Review*, 75 (1981): 306–18.
7 Kavka, op. cit., pp. 130–31.
8 Gauthier, *Morals by Agreement*, pp. 182–4.
9 For example, by Kavka, op. cit., ch. 9.
10 Gauthier, *Morals by Agreement*, pp. 162, 172.

II

1 Citations in the text of this chapter that begin with T refer to the book, part, chapter, and pages of Hume's *Treatise of Human Nature* (New York: Doubleday, 1961). Those that begin with I refer to the

section, part, and pages of his *Inquiry Concerning the Principles of Morals* (New York: Bobbs-Merrill, 1957).

2 Compare Barry Stroud, *Hume* (London: Routledge & Kegan Paul, 1977) p. 178.

3 John Locke, *Essay Concerning Human Understanding* (New York: Collier, 1965) book II, ch. 8, p. 83.

4 Compare J.L. Mackie, *Hume's Moral Theory* (London: Routledge & Kegan Paul, 1980) pp.72–3.

5 See, for example, R. Burnham, R. Hanes, and C.J. Bartleson, *Color: A Guide to Basic Facts and Concepts* (New York: Wiley, 1963) pp. 56–7.

6 Michael Dummett, 'Realism', in *Truth and Other Enigmas* (Cambridge, Mass.: Harvard University Press, 1978).

III

1 Citations in the text of this chapter refer to the following works of Kant: F = *Fundamental Principles of the Metaphysics of Morals*, translated by T.M. Abbott (Indianapolis: Bobbs-Merrill, 1949); MM, I, MEJ = *The Metaphysics of Morals, Part I, The Metaphysical Elements of Justice*, translated by John Ladd (Indianapolis: Bobbs-Merrill, 1965); CP = *Critique of Practical Reason*, translated by Lewis White Beck (Indianapolis: Bobbs-Merrill, 1956); MM, II, DV = *The Metaphysic of Morals, Part II, The Doctrine of Virtue*, translated by Mary Gregor (Philadelphia: University of Pennsylvania Press, 1964); TP = *On the Old Saw: That may be Right in Theory but It Won't Work in Practice*, translated by E.B. Ashton (Philadelphia: University of Pennsylvania Press, 1974).

2 There is no strictly analytic connection between morality and rationality according to Kant, because the relation is mediated by a third term, freedom.

3 See, for example, Robert P. Wolff, *The Autonomy of Reason* (New York: Harper & Row, 1973) p.221; also H. J. Paton, *The Categorical Imperative* (Chicago: University of Chicago Press, 1948) P.255.

4 Compare Alan Gewirth, *Reason and Morality* (Chicago: University of Chicago Press, 1978) p.105.

5 Stephen Darwall, *Impartial Reason* (Ithaca, New York: Cornell University Press, 1983).

6 *Ibid.*, pp.222–5.

7 Gewirth, op. cit., chs 2, 3.

8 See Bernard Williams, 'Persons, Character, and Morality', in *Moral Luck* (New York: Cambridge University Press, 1981); Michael Stocker, 'The Schizophrenia of Modern Ethical Theories', *The Journal of Philosophy*, 73 (1976): 453–66; Marcia Baron, 'The Alleged Moral Repugnance of Acting from Duty', *The Journal of*

Philosophy, 81 (1984): 197–220; Adrian Piper, 'Moral Theory and Moral Alienation', *The Journal of Philosophy*. 84 (1987): 102–18.

9 See Thomas Hill, 'Darwall on Practical Reason', *Ethics*, 96 (1986): 604–19.

10 This example was provided by Kenton Harris in a graduate seminar at the University of Miami.

11 Compare Onora Nell, *Acting on Principle* (New York: Columbia University Press, 1975) ch. 3.

12 See David Ross, *Kant's Ethical Theory* (Oxford: Clarendon Press, 1954) p. 32.

13 The examples are from Wolff, op. cit., p.90.

14 John Rawls, *A Theory of Justice* (Cambridge Mass.: Harvard University Press, 1971) chs 1, 3.

15 See the critical essays in Parts I and II of *Reading Rawls*, edited by Norman Daniels (New York: Basic Books, 1976).

16 Rawls, op. cit.; Robert Nozick, *Anarchy, State, and Utopia* (New York: Basic Books, 1974) ch. 7.

IV

1 As noted in the Introduction, we can equate truth directly with coherence or, to preserve the form of a uniform semantics, construe truth as correspondence to the property of coherence. In either case, if we equate meaning with truth conditions, we will have to admit that evaluators may not mean exactly what they intend to mean by their moral judgments.

2 While I shall consider sophisticated versions of non-cognitivism that attempt to account for apparent moral fallibility and truth, I shall not emphasize the distinction between emotivism, the claim that moral judgments only express attitudes, and prescriptivism, the claim that they only recommend actions. I take it that moral evaluations normally do both, but that, so far as implications for moral knowledge are concerned, the important feature of both these views is their thesis that such judgments lack ordinary truth values. Thus, just as earlier I made little of the distinction between willing actions and approving them, so here I take the distinction between emotivism and prescriptivism to be unimportant for our purposes.

3 Compare Simon Blackburn, 'Moral Realism', in *Morality and Moral Reasoning*, edited by John Casey (London: Methuen, 1971) pp. 102–3.

4 See Nicholas Sturgeon, 'What difference Does It Make Whether Moral Realism is True?', *Southern Journal of Philosophy*, 24 (suppl) (1986): 115–41, 121–2; David Brink, 'Externalist Moral Realism', *Southern Journal of Philosophy*, 24 (suppl.) (1986): 23–41.

5 See the collection of essays in *Moral Dilemmas*, edited by C. W. Gowans (New York: Oxford University Press, 1987).

6 See, in Gowans, op. cit., his Introduction, p.20; also in that volume, T. C. McConnell, 'Moral Dilemmas and Consistency in Ethics', p. 155; Bernard Williams, 'Ethical Consistency', p. 130.
7 Williams, op. cit.
8 See Thomas Nagel, 'The Fragmentation of Values', in Gowans, op. cit., p. 116.
9 Contrast Nicholas Sturgeon, op. cit., p. 116.
10 Sturgeon argues for moral realism on this ground, op. cit.
11 For expansion on this idea, see Simon Blackburn, *Spreading the Word* (Oxford: Clarendon Press, 1984) pp. 197–202; also his 'Rule-Following and Moral Realism', in *Wittgenstein: To Follow a Rule*, edited by Steven Holtzman and Christopher Leich (London: Routledge & Kegan Paul, 1981) pp. 175–6.
12 Compare David Brink, op. cit., p. 37; T. C. McConnell, op. cit., p. 163.
13 Hilary Putnam, 'Realism and Reason', in *Meaning and the Moral Sciences* (London: Routledge & Kegan Paul); 'Models and Reality', *Journal of Symbolic Logic*, 45 (1980): 464–82.
14 Alan Goldman, *Empirical Knowledge* (Berkeley: University of California Press, 1988) pp. 336–45.
15 Gilbert Harman first posed the issue of moral realism as a debate over the explanation of moral observations and beliefs in *The Nature of Morality* (New York: Oxford University Press, 1977) ch. 1. See also the reply to his anti-realist argument by Nicholas Sturgeon, 'Moral Explanations', in *Morality, Reason and Truth*, edited by David Copp and David Zimmerman (Totowa: Rowman & Allanheld, 1985). Neither philosopher explicitly considers coherentist moral explanations.
16 Simon Blackburn, *Spreading the Word*, pp. 192–5.
17 Nicholas Sturgeon raises this objection to Blackburn in 'What Difference Does It Make Whether Moral Realism is True?', pp. 129–34.
18 See Bas van Fraassen, *The Scientific Image* (Oxford: Clarendon Press, 1980).
19 The example is from Richard Werner, 'Ethical Realism', *Ethics*, 93 (1983): 653–79.
20 The example was provided by Alice Perrin.
21 Compare Peter Railton, 'Moral Realism', *Philosophical Review*, 95 (1986): 163–207, p. 193.
22 Alan Goldman, op. cit., part II.
23 Ibid., part III.
24 Ibid., ch. 13.
25 See Introduction, note 16.
26 Compare Thomas Nagel, 'Moral Conflict and Political Legitimacy', *Philosophy & Public Affairs*, 16 (1987): 215–40.

1 Alan Goldman, *Empirical Knowledge*, pp. 143–52.
2 Jonathan Dancy, 'Ethical Particularism and Morally Relevant Properties', *Mind*, 92 (1983): 530–47, p. 546; see also Dancy, 'On Moral Properties', *Mind*, 90 (1981): 367–85; Robert Gray, 'Ethical Pluralism', *Mind*, 94 (1985): 250–62.
3 Dancy, 'Ethical Particularism and Morally Relevant Properties', op. cit., p. 541.
4 Stuart Hampshire, *Morality and Conflict* (Cambridge Mass: Harvard University Press, 1983) pp. 104–20.
5 See, for example, the collection of essays in *The Problem of Abortion*, edited by Joel Feinberg (Belmont: Wadsworth, 1984).
6 See, for example, *Equality and Preferential Treatment*, edited by Marshall Cohen, Thomas Nagel, and Thomas Scanlon (Princeton: Princeton University Press, 1977).
7 Ludwig Wittgenstein, *Philosophical Investigations*, translated by G. E. M. Anscombe (New York: Macmillan, 1958) part I, nos 100–241.
8 Erik Erikson, *Identity, Youth, and Crisis* (New York: W. W. Norton, 1968).
9 Alan Goldman, *The Moral Foundations of Professional Ethics* (Totowa: Rowman & Littlefield, 1980) chs 3, 4.

Index

221